SUICIDE AND THE LAW

This book investigates the law's approach to suicide in England and Wales. It explores the seismic shift in perceptions of the law's role in respect of suicide from imprisonment as a punishment for attempting suicide, to courts hearing arguments about whether there is not only a right to suicide but also a right to assistance in suicide. This development stands alongside a global recognition of suicide prevention as a public health priority.

In this book, the dual priorities of respect for autonomy and the protection of human life are recognised as equally important and the legal issues surrounding suicide in a range of different contemporary contexts, including suicide in prison and juvenile suicide, are considered. The book also investigates what the relationship between mental health and suicide means for its legal regulation, and evaluates the enduring legal offence of assisted suicide, particularly in the context of the terminally ill.

It is argued that a more refined approach to the topic of voluntary death should be recognised in the law; one that distinguishes more clearly between autonomous decision-making about the end of life, and incapacitated self-caused risks to life that require effective preventative interventions.

Suicide and the Law

Elizabeth Wicks

•HART•
OXFORD • LONDON • NEW YORK • NEW DELHI • SYDNEY

HART PUBLISHING

Bloomsbury Publishing Plc

Kemp House, Chawley Park, Cumnor Hill, Oxford, OX2 9PH, UK

1385 Broadway, New York, NY 10018, USA

29 Earlsfort Terrace, Dublin 2, Ireland

HART PUBLISHING, the Hart/Stag logo, BLOOMSBURY and the Diana logo are trademarks of Bloomsbury Publishing Plc

First published in Great Britain 2023

A catalogue record for this book is available from the British Library.

A catalogue record for this book is available from the Library of Congress.

Library of Congress Control Number: 2022947592

ISBN: HB: 978-1-50993-270-2
ePDF: 978-1-50993-272-6
ePub: 978-1-50993-271-9

Typeset by Compuscript Ltd, Shannon

ACKNOWLEDGEMENTS

I am lucky to work at Leicester Law School with a very supportive group of health lawyers, and I am grateful to all of them for their help and encouragement, especially Clark Hobson, Nataly Papadopoulou and Katherine Wade for reading drafts of material for this book, as well as Tracey Elliott, José Miola and all members of the developing Centre for Rights and Equality in Health Law (CREHL) at Leicester. Of course, the views expressed in this book are my own, as are any mistakes or oversights. I am also lucky to be able to teach on my area of research interest at Leicester and so I have enjoyed, and this book has benefitted from, discussions with students on a Medical Law UG module and a Human Rights and Health Care LLM module, as well as with various PhD students over the years. I'm also grateful to the staff at Hart Publishing for their support throughout the process of writing this book. Parts of chapters three and eight have been adapted from work published in my article in the journal *Medical Law International* in 2020.

This has not been an easy book to write, nor has it been an easy time to do it, so I am especially grateful to my husband Frank for his support, good humour and willingness to debate legal and ethical dilemmas at any time of the day or night. I dedicate this book to my Mum, who has faced some very difficult years with fortitude and compassion and remains my greatest supporter and ally in all that I do.

For anyone personally affected by the issues discussed
in this book, support is always available.
Please reach out to someone.
Call the Samaritans on 116 123 or visit samaritans.org

TABLE OF CONTENTS

1

Suicide: Definitions and Conceptual Approaches

Suicide is a massive problem. It is estimated that more than 700,000 deaths are caused by suicide worldwide each year.[1] In 2019, suicide accounted for 1.3 per cent of all deaths worldwide.[2] For every suicide there are many more people (possibly as many as 20) who attempt suicide every year. Perhaps the most worrying statistic of all is that suicide is the fourth leading cause of death among 15–29-year-olds.[3] The World Health Organization (WHO) recognises suicide prevention as a public health priority and asserts that all suicides are preventable.[4] This book assesses what the law in England and Wales can and should do to meet that objective, but in doing so it also explores whether the goal of prevention is the only appropriate goal for the law or whether a more refined legal approach would better reflect the complex and underexplored topic of suicide in the UK.[5] In this introductory chapter, a brief overview of the different approaches to the topic of suicide will be provided, but first a definition of the meaning of 'suicide' is sought.

I. Defining Suicide

A. Why Define?

The meaning of 'suicide' may at first appear to be unambiguous but, on further reflection, defining the term raises a number of challenging issues which have

[1] World Health Organization, 'Factsheet on Suicide', available at www.who.int/news-room/fact-sheets/detail/suicide.

[2] World Health Organization, 'Suicide Worldwide in 2019: Global Health Estimates' (Geneva, WHO, 2021).

[3] ibid.

[4] World Health Organization, 'Preventing Suicide: A Global Imperative' (Geneva, WHO, 2014).

[5] The goal of suicide prevention has been described as 'normatively weak' because 'what constitutes acceptable self-killing defies coherent description and attempts to do so in law appear to be based less on a sound metaphysical or jurisprudential footing than on shifting intuitions about which lives are worth preserving and which are not': S Callaghan, C Ryan and I Kerridge, 'Risk of Suicide is Insufficient Warrant for Coercive Treatment of Mental Illness' (2013) 36 *International Journal of Law & Psychiatry* 374, 375.

been the subject of extensive debate in the literature. Defining suicide in a way that matches the common usage of the term seems particularly difficult given the inherent moral judgment that still pervades discussions of suicide. How can we distinguish the final acts of Hitler from those of Jesus? Did not both take their own life? And yet only one is commonly regarded as having performed suicide, while the other performs the noblest of actions in his self-sacrifice. Similarly, the actions of Captain Oates walking out into the Arctic blizzard to save others, or religious martyrs who died rather than recant their faith, or any number of soldiers marching to certain death in battle, are not usually classified as suicides.[6] What distinguishes them – or, rather, what makes us *want* to distinguish them – appears to be the noble motive. As Minois points out, we continue to admire such noble deaths while simultaneously condemning 'all the ordinary suicides of unhappy people whose motives do not seem noble enough'.[7] It is the unhappy fact that suicide continues to carry with it negative connotations that creates this urge to 'define away self-killings we believe are justified as something other than suicide'.[8] In doing this, we are not relying upon conceptual differences, but rather seeking to reflect our moral judgements of the death into the term used to describe it. A further, and related, difficulty arises when defining suicide: that of the intention of the person choosing to end her own life. Does all intentional self-killing amount to suicide or only that where the primary intention is to end life? And what of the most common form of suicide, namely those associated with a mental illness: are these really suicide if the person taking life is incapable of forming a rational intention to die?[9] Such issues must be discussed before we can arrive at an agreed meaning for suicide.

However, it might also be queried why we should seek a single definition of suicide given that, as we shall see, suicide is no longer prohibited in English law and yet the label continues to stigmatise in its use. Nonetheless, there are a number of reasons why seeking a basic definition is important at this stage. First, while suicide is not a criminal offence, it is still a term used in the law, most obviously in relation to enduring criminal offences of encouraging or assisting suicide, and suicide pacts. Secondly, a risk of suicide may initiate preventative legal obligations and protective mechanisms. Thirdly, suicide is still used in death statistics, and statistical information about suicide rates may be helpful to inform efforts to tackle this problem. Finally, it will be undeniably useful for a working definition of suicide to be proposed in this first chapter of a book focused on

[6] These and other examples are rife in the literature. See, for example, G Minois, *History of Suicide: Voluntary Death in Western Culture* (Baltimore, John Hopkins, 1999, translated by LG Cochrane) 323; M MacDonald and TR Murphy, *Sleepless Souls: Suicide in Early Modern England* (Oxford, Clarendon Press, 1990) 222; and M Battin, *The Least Worst Death: Essays in Bioethics on the End of Life* (Oxford, Oxford University Press, 1994) 188.

[7] Minois, *History of Suicide* (1999).

[8] M Cholbi, 'Suicide' in Edward N Zalta (ed), *The Stanford Encyclopedia of Philosophy* (Fall 2017 edition), available atplato.stanford.edu/archives/fall2017/entries/suicide.

[9] Battin, *The Least Worst Death* (1994) 188.

suicide and the law. While it is necessary to understand the type of behaviour that is being discussed in subsequent chapters, this will not preclude the development of arguments around the removal of the label of suicide from English law later in the book.

B. Self-caused Death

An obvious starting point for defining suicide – indeed, the phrase most commonly used when seeking to do so – is a 'self-caused death'. The word 'caused' appears in the definitions of suicide by Durkheim ('any cause of death which results directly or indirectly from the positive or negative act of the victim'), Chobli ('self-caused death') and Szasz ('deliberately causing one's own death'), to give just a few prominent examples (their definitions otherwise differ significantly).[10] This gets to the heart of suicide without grappling with the mental state of the causer of death. But it is not a *sufficient* condition for suicide because we may be causally responsible for our own death without it being suicide, for example by pursuing harmful activities or being responsible for an accidental death. To amount to suicide, there needs to also be a mental element in the definition, which will be discussed at length below. However, it is also not certain that causing one's own death is a *necessary* condition of suicide because a scenario such as the infamous 'suicide by cop' arguably does not involve a death caused by the act of the person intending suicide. Nonetheless, some writers have argued that agency is the key consideration and that a self-instigated or self-initiated death may qualify as suicide even if not self-inflicted.[11]

A further point of contention in relation to the causing of death in suicide is whether it needs to be caused by an act or whether an omission will suffice. Durkheim in his influential early work on suicide may have taken the view that 'refusal to take food is as suicidal as self-destruction by a dagger or fire-arm',[12] but the refusal of life-sustaining medical treatment is generally not regarded as suicide in English law. Indeed, there seems to be a strong reluctance to classify it as such. In *Airedale NHS Trust v Bland*, when discussing a refusal of treatment by a competent patient, Lord Goff said:

> [T]here is no question of the patient having committed suicide, nor therefore of the doctor having aided or abetted him in doing so. It is simply that the patient has, as he is entitled to do, declined to consent to treatment which might or would have the effect of prolonging his life.[13]

[10] T Szasz, *Suicide Prohibition: The Shame of Medicine* (Syracuse, Syracuse University Press, 2011) 8.

[11] K Posner et al, 'The Classification of Suicidal Behaviour' in MK Nock, *The Oxford Handbook of Suicide and Self-Injury* (Oxford, Oxford University Press, 2014).

[12] E Durkheim, *Suicide: A Study in Sociology*, 2nd edn (London, Routledge, 2002) 42.

[13] *Airedale NHS Trust v Bland* [1993] 1 All ER 821, 866.

Similarly, in *Secretary of State for the Home Department v Robb*, the court was adamant that the refusal of food during a prison hunger strike was not suicidal in nature.[14] Indeed, Price has noted that jurisdictions throughout the world have almost invariably declined to view refusals of medical treatment as suicide.[15] He points out that there are only two possible explanations for this: either there is no intention to die (which will be discussed below); or a death by omission is not suicide.[16] The latter can be easily disputed, however, as was effectively achieved by Scalia J in the US case of *Cruzan v Director, Missouri Health Department* when he noted that it 'would not make much sense to say that one may not kill oneself by walking into the sea, but may sit on the beach until submerged by the incoming tide'.[17] Price agrees with this argument, concluding that 'even if the treatment refusal is an omission, it is the cause of death where this is the known, inevitable consequence of the patient's decision'.[18] Schramme reaches the same conclusion, arguing that the means of death is not important when the requisite mental state for suicide exists and thus some refusals of treatment do amount to suicide.[19] Furthermore, it is arguable that a refusal of treatment is not really an omission at all, but rather a positive act of refusing. The act/omission distinction has preoccupied medical law and ethics for many years and it is not necessary to seek to resolve the issue here, but merely to point out that, even if the definition of suicide requires an act rather than an omission, refusals of treatment may satisfy that definition, whereas not moving away from an incoming tide may not do so. It is also clear that the key issue in defining suicide will not be the steps taken in causing death, but rather the intention behind those steps.

C. An Intention to Die

That the person causing their own death intends to die is a vital component of a definition of suicide. It is what distinguishes a suicide from an accidental death. The intention of the person causing death is not ever easy to establish, however, not least because that person is, by definition, deceased.[20] In addition, using intention to discriminate between behaviours requires accurate insight into one's motivations for a behaviour during a time of significant distress, which will

[14] *Secretary of State for the Home Department v Robb* [1995] 1 All ER 677.

[15] DPT Price, 'Assisted Suicide and Refusing Medical Treatment: Linguistics, Morals and Legal Contortions' (1997) 4 *Medical Law Review* 270, 272–73.

[16] ibid 273. These issues will be discussed more fully in ch 7 below.

[17] *Cruzan v Director, Missouri Health Department* (1990) 111 L.Ed.2d.224, 249.

[18] Price, 'Assisted Suicide' (1997) 287–88.

[19] T Schramme, 'Rational Suicide, Assisted Suicide, and Indirect legal Paternalism' (2013) 36 *International Journal of Law and Psychiatry* 477, 480.

[20] K Andriessen, 'On "Intention" in the Definition of Suicide' (2006) 36 *Suicide and Life-Threatening Behavior* 533, 534.

not always be possible.[21] Furthermore, it is possible that there may have been multiple intentions, or that the intention evolved during the process, or that there was ambivalence about death, all of which may make establishing a clear intention to die difficult.[22] In this section, five thorny issues in relation to recognising an intention to die in a self-caused death will be discussed.

The first potential difficulty in recognising an intention to die in the context of self-caused death is the possibility that death is imminent anyway. This will be particularly relevant to suicide by the terminally ill where the intention may be to cut short the dying process.[23] This is not a significant obstacle, however, because in a sense we are all dying and, as Brandt has noted, the choice is never one between death at our own hands and immortality, but rather a choice between death now and death at some, possibly short, finite time from now.[24] Brandt terms this a choice between two 'world-courses' – death now or later – but there are also other distinctions between the choices because, in the case of a terminally ill person, for example, the cause of death will differ between the two world-courses.[25] Thus, a terminal illness and an imminent death do not prevent a person intending to die at a sooner time and also by a different cause. Imminence of death, therefore, is not a significant obstacle to establishing an intention to die.

There is a second factor that may complicate the issue of intention in respect of the person choosing to cause their own death due to terminal illness, namely that it is sometimes argued that they have been coerced into that decision by the illness. Similarly, it has been suggested that the death of Socrates was not suicide because he had been sentenced to death and drank the poison that killed him in response to that sentence. Schramme has argued that this was not suicide because Socrates 'lacked the will to die', having no autonomous decision or wish to die but merely obeying the sentence.[26]

This raises the question of whether we intend to do something if we have been coerced into doing it. Cholbi is particularly convincing in his argument that a coerced act is still that very act: 'A person coerced into singing is nevertheless singing'.[27] Reed also takes this view, noting for example that a person who causes their own death due to the coercion of the circumstances of a terminal illness still had a meaningful choice about whether to adopt this course of action or not.[28] Furthermore, there may well be a pertinent distinction between coercion into suicide by persons and coercion by circumstances. Reed has argued that 'coercion

[21] JJ Muehlenkamp, 'Distinguishing Between Suicidal and Nonsuicidal Self-Injury' in MK Nock, *The Oxford Handbook of Suicide and Self-Injury* (Oxford, Oxford University Press, 2014) 24–25.
[22] ibid.
[23] P Reed, 'Is "Aid in Dying" Suicide?' (2019) 40 *Theoretical Medicine and Bioethics* 123, 127.
[24] RB Brandt, 'The Rationality of Suicide' in M Battin and DJ Mayo (eds), *Suicide: The Philosophical Issues* (London, Peter Owen, 1980) 119.
[25] Reed, 'Is "Aid in Dying" Suicide?' (2019) 127–28.
[26] Schramme, 'Rational Suicide' (2013) 478.
[27] Cholbi, 'Suicide' (2017).
[28] Reed (n 23) 130.

is not just anything that comes to a person outside of her control and constrains her choice; it is something that comes to her in that way by another agent'.[29] Cholbi disagrees, however, suggesting that factual circumstances, as well as interference by other people, may be coercive, but it is for this very reason that Cholbi rejects any suggestion that to be regarded as a suicide a self-caused death must be non-coerced. This is because if 'any factor, natural, human, or otherwise, that influences an individual's reasoning so as to make death the most rational option counts as coercion' then almost all self-caused deaths would be coerced and thus not regarded as suicides.[30]

It is worth reiterating the context of this present discussion, less it be misunderstood: we are searching for an appropriate definition of suicide, not reflecting on the role of the law in respect of that action. Thus, while the arguments that being coerced by circumstances or persons into causing one's own death does not prevent it being labelled as a suicide are highly convincing, that does not imply the absence of legal liability for the coercer, nor that such a 'suicide' should be regarded as a lawful one.

A third, and perhaps more significant, issue in establishing an intention to die in respect of a self-caused death is that death may be, and indeed often will be, a means to a desired end rather than an end in itself. Common examples might include a desire to escape pain, relieve suffering or prevent a future loss of autonomy. This is also an important consideration for the types of cases mentioned above, where there is often a reluctance to label them as suicide due to a noble intention, such as Captain Oates walking into a blizzard, knowing or believing that this would cause his death, but intending by his actions to save the lives of his fellow explorers. Did he intend to die, even though he would rather have lived? Does the terminally ill patient who faces a painful and lingering death intend to die when her motivation in taking an overdose is merely to end the pain? Establishing an intention to die in respect of suicide is so difficult because, as Chobli notes, suicide usually does have another aim or justification beyond mere death:

> Suicidal behaviour can have any number of objectives: the relief of physical pain, the relief of psychological anguish, martyrdom in the service of a moral cause, the fulfilment of perceived societal duties (e.g., suttee and seppuku), the avoidance of judicial execution, revenge on others, protection of others' interests or well-being.[31]

In none of these examples is death chosen for its own sake, and so the question arises: was there really an intention to die? Generally, the concept of intention would indeed be satisfied in such cases. For example, most philosophers view intention as applying to both means and end: in order to make an omelette, you must intend to break a few eggs.[32] The patient seeking to escape pain intends to die because death is the only means of achieving her goal.

[29] ibid.
[30] Cholbi (n 8).
[31] ibid.
[32] Reed (n 23) 131.

A fourth point of concern in relation to establishing an intention to die, and one that is closely linked to the previous one, is the issue of double effect. Generally this doctrine seeks to avoid the conclusion that 'an agent intentionally brings about all the consequences of an action that an agent foresees'.[33] It has been applied by the courts in the healthcare context to avoid a finding that a doctor intended to cause death when providing a dose of morphine which it was known would hasten death in addition to relieving pain,[34] but it is a problematic concept and has only been selectively applied. If applied in relation to suicide, this would imply that an intention to avoid pain by taking an overdose of (pain-relieving)[35] drugs would not amount to an intention to die even when death was foreseen to be the inevitable consequence. But arguably this is the same reasoning rejected above about intending means as well as ends. Intention is not about desire or motive. Foresight suffices in the criminal law for an intention[36] and is generally accepted in the literature. Indeed, as Reed points out, the 'objective character of the world' can 'dictate accurate descriptions of what agents intend, especially when it comes to the means'.[37] Thus, a person intending to make an omelette, who denies intending to break any eggs in doing so, can nonetheless be regarded as having an intention to do so. To claim that she only foresees the breaking of eggs but does not intend it would undermine the entire concept of intention.

Intending to die is not the same as wanting to die, and this raises a fifth issue in this discussion and a factor frequently present in relation to suicide: ambivalence about dying. It is well established that many suicidal persons are ambivalent about death.[38] Questions arise, therefore, as to whether they really intend to die and, if they have mixed feelings about dying, whether paternalistic steps should be taken to intervene. Cholbi has argued that the prevalence of ambivalence justifies a separate category of deaths that are neither suicide nor accidental.[39] Cholbi labels such deaths 'neither intentional nor accidental' (NINA) self-killings and suggests that 'unless a person takes precautions to prevent death, whenever a person engages in a behaviour known to be life threatening but does so without intending to die, yet they die none the less, their death is not accidental'. Nonetheless, a degree of ambivalence does not necessarily undermine an intention to die, and may be compatible with a label of suicide itself. As Schramme points out, suicide is always 'a kind of bet on the future'[40] because it is a choice between one certain future (immediate death)

[33] TL Beauchamp and JF Childress, *Principles of Biomedical Ethics*, 8th edn (Oxford, Oxford University Press, 2019) 208.

[34] H Palmer, 'Dr Adams' Trial for Murder' [1957] *Criminal Law Review* 365; *Airedale NHS Trust v Bland* [1993] 1 All ER 821.

[35] One weakness of the double effect doctrine is that it only works in relation to certain drugs, namely those which can also be prescribed for a therapeutic effect. See *R v Cox* (1992) 12 BMLR 38.

[36] *R v Woollin* [1998] 4 All ER 103, 113.

[37] Reed (n 23) 134.

[38] Cholbi (n 8).

[39] M Cholbi, 'Self-manslaughter and the Forensic Classification of Self-inflicted Death' (2007) 33 *Journal of Medical Ethics* 155.

[40] Schramme (n 19) 482.

and one uncertain future (postponed death). The current situation, which might be intolerable to the person contemplating suicide, may not last for ever, or it may become more tolerable, or death may intervene anyway to end it. We do not know what the future holds, any more than we know what, if anything, happens after death. A decision to attempt suicide will always be based on uncertain knowledge, and will also frequently be made in a temporary mental state, for example of depression, which may or may not change in the future. A degree of ambivalence about dying, even amongst those who have decided to choose that over further living, is almost inevitable and does not in itself undermine that decision.

The discussion of intention so far has identified a number of concerns about establishing an intention to die, but none have been accepted as legitimate restrictions on the concept. A self-caused death with an intention to die amounts to suicide. The fact that death was imminent anyway, or was merely a means to an end, or an unwanted consequence, or that the choice to die was coerced by circumstances, or that there is ambivalence about it does not undermine an intention to die. With the simplistic working definition of *a self-caused and intended death*, we can now proceed to consider how suicide has been perceived over time, and how those varying perceptions have grounded starkly different legal approaches to the issue.

II. Different Conceptions of Suicide

Over the centuries, suicide has been discussed in a number of very different terms. An understanding of the different approaches to the topic will help in clarifying the law's relationship with suicide, how it has changed over time, and how it may further evolve in the future. Five differing approaches to suicide will now each be briefly discussed in turn. While they are presented in a broadly chronological order, they have often overlapped in their prominence, and indeed all five views are still articulated by some in the present day.

A. The Moralistic View

Historically, the traditional approach to suicide was a moralistic one, usually based upon religion. It views suicide as a sin or, in its more recent secular perspective, as contrary to nature. It is based upon the principle of the sanctity of life, and views suicide as wrong because it violates our moral duty to honour the inherent value of human life. It is a deontological position as it focuses on whether the action of suicide is right or wrong in itself, rather than focusing on the consequences of it.[41]

[41] Cholbi (n 8).

It is the simplest moral outlook on suicide and has dominated social, political and legal approaches to suicide over many centuries. The legal consequences of the moralistic view of suicide will be explored in chapter two. We will discover that the Christian condemnation of suicide dates from Augustine in the fifth century,[42] and was further strengthened by the writings of Thomas Aquinas in the thirteenth century,[43] and that by the fifteenth and sixteenth centuries, the law in England was both condemning and punishing in extremely harsh terms, the act of suicide.[44] Even when suicide was legalised in the twentieth century, parliamentarians were keen to remind us that suicide is 'a dreadful offence against nature'[45] and 'a mortal sin'.[46] The moralistic view of suicide, which has been so dominant for centuries, leads to an expectation that the law's role in respect of suicide is one of condemnation, prohibition and (traditionally) punishment. Only in the last 100 years or so has there been the development of a number of alternative views of suicide[47] which have in turn led to new roles for the law in this context.

B. The Sociological View

Émile Durkheim's sociological and determinist approach to suicide, evident in his 1897 book,[48] sought to explain the social causes of suicide and, in doing so, introduced a fundamental and influential transformation in thinking about suicide. No longer was it to be viewed as an exercise of individual choice contrary to religion, but instead as a produce of social forces (specifically, in Durkheim's writing, social integration and regulation)[49] over which the individual has no control. If suicide is caused, rather than chosen, the individual is relieved of responsibility for it and therefore condemnation and punishment seem increasingly inappropriate. The law's role under this sociological approach must therefore shift from one of condemnation to one focused on prevention. The criminalisation of suicide becomes inappropriate if society, rather than the individual, is responsible for

[42] Augustine, *The City of God Against the Pagans* (Cambridge, Cambridge University Press, 1998, edited and translated by RW Dyson).

[43] T Aquinas, *Summa Theologica* (New York, Benziger Bros, 1947). For discussion, see A Alavarez, 'The Background' in M Battin and DJ Mayo (eds), *Suicide: The Philosophical Issues* (London, Peter Owen, 1980).

[44] See MacDonald and Murphy, *Sleepless Souls* (1990).

[45] Hansard, HC (series 5) Vol 644, col 838 (14 July 1961) (Eric Fletcher).

[46] ibid 841 (John Hobson). See also ch 3.

[47] This is admittedly an over-simplification as will become apparent in the following chapter. In both antiquity and from the enlightenment, opposing views of suicide have been proposed.

[48] Durkheim, *Suicide* (2002).

[49] More refined approaches have been proposed in recent years, such as that of Marzio Barbagli who relies upon psychiatric, societal and cultural factors to distinguish four types of suicide: M Barbagli, *Farewell to the World: A History of Suicide* (Cambridge, Polity Press, 2015, English edition translated by L Byatt).

suicide, but the law may still have a role to play in seeking to prevent suicide by tackling the social causes of suicide.[50]

C. The Medical Model

At the same time as Durkheim was proposing social causes for suicide, a medical model was also being developed that proposed medical causes for suicide. In hindsight, it is this approach that has had the greatest influence upon the law's role in respect of suicide. The medical model proposes that suicide is caused, not by society nor by individual choice, but by a malfunction or disease of the body. It came to the fore in the late nineteenth century when the Victorian instinct for institutionalisation led to members of the medical profession encountering the suicidal on a regular basis. Initially linked to melancholia, suicide has subsequently been steadfastly connected to mental illness, especially depression. Studies show that at least 90 per cent of those who take their own life suffer from a mental illness[51] and so the connection between suicide and mental illness is strongly substantiated. This connection will be explored fully in chapter four and, as we shall see, it is the assumption that suicide is a symptom rather than a choice that has dominated political and legal thinking on suicide in recent years. As with the sociological view of suicide, the medical view also removes individual responsibility for suicide and thus suggests that the role of the law should not be to condemn, prohibit or punish, but rather to facilitate prevention by means of treatment, including the compulsory imposition of such preventative treatment if necessary.

D. The Rights View

The assumption that suicide is invariably a symptom rather than a choice, perpetuated by the medical model, has led to a *counter-reaction* that suicide can be a rational choice and as such that there is a right to make that choice as part of a broader recognition of a right to autonomy. One specific, but very controversial, line of reasoning rejects the psychiatry movement in its entirety. The anti-psychiatry movement, led by Szasz, takes the view that 'incarceration in a mental hospital is unlawful deprivation of liberty, that mental illnesses are fictitious diseases, and that coercive psychiatry is social control, not medical care'.[52]

[50] There are parallels with the recent approach by Jonathan Herring in which he argues that the state has a responsibility to prevent suicides: J Herring, *The Right to be Protected from Suicide* (Oxford, Hart Publishing, 2022).

[51] See Barbagli, *Farewell to the World* (2015) 10.

[52] T Szasz, *Suicide Prohibition: The Shame of Medicine* (Syracuse, Syracuse University Press, 2011) 96.

In light of this position, it is not surprising that Szasz views suicide as a chosen act rather than a symptom of a disease and laments the 'bureaucratic language' which transforms a person who chooses to take their own life into 'the victim of a fictitious disease. In this idiom, individuals do not choose to kill themselves; they are killed by suicide'.[53] Szasz's approach makes very transparent the significance of the labelling attached to suicide. When labelled as a disease, as the medical model does, it can be treated and prevented; when labelled as a sin or crime, as the moralistic view does, it can be prohibited and punished. But these are not the only options and Szasz's approach to suicide is to view it as a legitimate choice and to argue for a right to freedom from coercive suicide prevention.[54] He notes that although suicide is no longer illegal, it remains 'forbidden' under the control of psychiatry.[55]

The anti-psychiatry movement of Szasz is extreme, but a broader libertarian view proposes that suicide is morally permissible because there is a right to suicide. Historically, this view was supported by Stoics such as Seneca. More recently, in the contemporary human rights age, authors such as Battin have argued for a fundamental right to suicide.[56] Such a right may be developed as either an aspect of a broader right to bodily autonomy[57] or, as Battin proposes, as constitutive of human dignity. The latter basis leads Battin to seek to distinguish between 'violent' suicides, which she describes as 'desperate, aggressive acts, that display both contempt and hatred for oneself and for others as well', and 'non-violent' suicides, which she describes as self-respecting and 'based on a self-ideal: a conception of one's own value and worth, beneath which one is not willing to slip'.[58] This is a difficult distinction to draw and a more common approach (accepted even by Battin) is to seek to distinguish between rational and irrational suicides; the former being regarded as an exercise of autonomy and/or a means of preserving dignity, and the latter accepted as a symptom of mental illness. Thus, the law's approach to suicide would, under this view, need also to distinguish the type of suicide in question and respond accordingly: with respect for a fundamental right or preventative measures as is fitting. Although it is not always explicitly acknowledged, more recent arguments in favour of legalised assisted suicide in certain circumstances, also frequently imply that suicide itself is a right and it is for this reason that assistance in facilitating that right should not be denied on the basis of disability. It is the issue of assisted suicide that has dominated both the literature and the courtrooms in recent decades and yet it seems sensible to query

[53] ibid 5.
[54] ibid 12.
[55] ibid 14.
[56] M Battin, 'Suicide: A Fundamental Human Right?' in M Battin and DJ Mayo (eds), *Suicide: The Philosophical Issues* (London, Peter Owen, 1980).
[57] E Wicks, *The State and the Body: Legal Regulation of Bodily Autonomy* (Oxford, Hart Publishing, 2016).
[58] Battin (n 6) 284.

how we can resolve the assisted suicide debate until we are clear on where society stands on suicide itself.[59]

A rights view of suicide tends to focus upon the right to autonomy and a potential right to suicide, or to die. Other human rights have relevance, however, and in his recent invaluable addition to the scarce literature about the law's role in relation to suicide, Jonathan Herring argues in favour of a right *to be protected from* suicide.[60] He claims that a starting point of whether there is a right to die is mistaken and that the primary human right of relevance to the issue of suicide is instead a right to be protected from it. He bases that controversial right within the established rights to health and life,[61] and also relies upon the argument that suicide is commonly a product of socio-economic inequalities, for which the state must take responsibility.[62] (The latter argument seems to borrow some elements from the sociological approach outlined above.)

In this book, I take a rather different perspective in that I recognise both a right to die and a right to life as equally relevant and important. More precisely, I argue that both a right to make autonomous decisions about the ending of our own lives, and a right to have our lives protected from the threat of suicide are protected in law, and need to be carefully balanced. The real challenge in this context is for the law to determine which of these conflicting rights takes precedence in different scenarios. No two suicide attempts are the same and so a blanket approach from the law will not reflect the complexity and individuality of this issue. Herring is entirely correct to point out that the vast majority of suicides are not careful, autonomous decisions and that preventing suicides can itself be autonomy-enhancing.[63] However, he risks taking the same blanket approach to all intentional self-killings which falls into the same trap as the moralistic view (all suicides are a sin) and the medical model (all suicides are symptoms).

Perhaps ultimately Herring's approach stems from his relational perspective. He argues that 'the idealisation of autonomy and self-sufficiency is based on a fiction. It is in our caring and interdependence that we find value in our lives'.[64] This is an incredibly sweeping statement that leaves no room for those of us who may find some value in other aspects of our lives as well, such as acting independently, making our own choices and being self-sufficient. That some people may find and value their own autonomy, dignity and privacy in such characteristics suggests that there may be some decisions to end life that are not the responsibility of the state or society or community or family but are grounded in the individual.

[59] Szasz makes a good point when he argues that 'it behooves us to debate and resolve the problem of physician-prevented suicide before we legislate about "physician-assisted" suicide': Szasz, *Suicide Prohibition* (2011) 68.

[60] Herring, *The Right to be Protected from Suicide* (2022).

[61] Whether Art 2 ECHR does include a broad right to be protected from suicide is an issue that will be analysed in ch 5.

[62] Herring (n 50) 3.

[63] ibid 223.

[64] ibid 224.

As we shall see, such cases are rare as many suicides are not about an exercise of autonomy. But human rights law is not just about protecting the majority's right to life but also about protecting the minority's right to make autonomous decisions.

E. The Consequentialist View

A final, and perhaps distinct approach to suicide is to focus on the consequences for society of the choice to die. Under this consequentialist view, a suicide may violate moral duties owed to others, either by harming specific others such as family or by harming the community as a whole.[65] One way in which harmful consequences may be felt within broader society from a suicide is that it may precipitate other suicides through so-called 'suicide hot-spots'.[66] In addition, beyond the inevitable emotional harm caused to loved ones from a suicide, having a family member die from suicide is a significant risk factor for further suicides in the family.[67] However, in some situations, there may be positive consequences of a suicide that outweigh its bad consequences, such as relieving suffering or saving others. Indeed, in extreme situations such good consequences may even impose a moral obligation to commit suicide. Thus, for example, suicides perceived as honourable in nature, such as that of Captain Oates walking into the arctic blizzard to save others, might be viewed as positive in moral terms. It is easy to see the dangers of such an approach, however, when applied to the more familiar context of an elderly person choosing to end her life early in order to avoid imposing a burden on others. Such a death might bring some positive consequences for society, but any suggestion that there would be a moral duty to die in such circumstances could be rejected on various grounds such as the sanctity of human life, respect for autonomy or even rule utilitarianism (which would suggest that general adherence to a rule prohibiting suicide produces better overall consequences for society than permitting it in particular circumstances).[68]

Crucially, both the consequentialist view and the right based view of suicide require us to *distinguish* between different types of suicide, and that is essential if we are to avoid the dangerous over-generalisations that all suicides are sins or symptoms, to be punished or prevented. Suicide can occur in a wide variety of different circumstances, motivated by many different factors, representing either a

[65] Cholbi (n 8).

[66] K Wilson, 'The Call for the Abolition of Mental Health Law: The Challenges of Suicide, Accidental Death and the Equal Enjoyment of the Right to Life' (2018) 18 *Human Rights Law Review* 651, 670. For an example of such a 'hot-spot', see the high incidences of suicide by young persons in Bridgend in South Wales during 2007 and 2008: G Raynor and R Savill, 'Bridgend Suicides: A Town Tainted by Death' *The Telegraph*, 23 February 2008, available at www.telegraph.co.uk/news/uknews/1579574/Bridgend-suicides-a-town-tainted-by-death.html.

[67] Wilson (ibid).

[68] Cholbi (n 8).

manifestation of autonomy or an undermining of it; respecting human dignity or violating it; highlighting the subjective nature of the value of life or ignoring the sanctity of all human life. Each suicide is different, and it is this characteristic that presents such a difficult challenge for the law.

III. Conclusion

This introductory chapter has sought to define the meaning of the label 'suicide' and in doing so it has opted for a simplistic definition of *a self-caused and intended death*. It has also briefly introduced some of the different ways in which such deaths have been viewed over time. Society has largely moved on from a moralistic view under which all suicides are sins and must be prohibited to alternative views under which the law's approach to suicide will be less stark. The medical model of suicide sees it as the product of a disease, while the sociogenic model of suicide sees it as the product of social forces.[69] Both share the perception of suicide as something that is caused; as something that happens to the victim. The origins of both understandings of suicide stem from the nineteenth century, but both remain pertinent today. There is undoubtedly also an alternative understanding of suicide: as an autonomous choice. An individual suicide can be explained by one of these understandings or a combination of them. However, the law too often continues to treat suicide as a single unambiguous action and has never sought to regulate it in a more refined manner depending upon its specific cause or nature. In this book, it will be argued that a more refined legal approach is needed; one that responds appropriately to the wide ambit of the label 'suicide'. We will now commence the difficult task of assessing how the law does, and should, respond to suicide.

[69] Battin (n 6) 186–87.

2

The History of the Law against Suicide

This chapter will trace the history of the English law's approach to suicide before its legalisation in the 1960s. It will explore how the law has evolved from condemning suicide, to punishing it, to seeking to prevent it, and will also illustrate how those with the job of enforcing the law on suicide have regularly sought to soften the law's approach. The law's approach to suicide travelled a long road from condemnation to legalisation. Recognition that suicide could be caused, rather than chosen, was a crucial landmark on that journey.

I. Historical Background

The history of the law on suicide is one of judgement and condemnation, dating back centuries although not perhaps as far as might be imagined. For example, given a later Christian rationalisation for the severity of laws against suicide, it is perhaps surprising that there is no condemnation of suicide to be found in the Bible. Despite numerous incidents of the taking of one's own life in both New and Old Testaments, there is no adverse comment upon them. The most infamous of biblical suicides, that of Judas, is, as Alvarez notes, 'recorded perfunctorily; instead of being added to his crimes, it seems a measure of his repentance'.[1] The ancient world also lacked an unambiguous denunciation of suicide. In Rome, although the suicide of slaves and soldiers was prohibited (as theft or desertion respectively), free men were permitted to take their own lives without legal interference in line with stoic philosophy.[2]

On the other hand, Plato and Aristotle were more critical of suicide,[3] and in due course it was Plato rather than the Bible that supported the Christian move to extreme condemnation. This began in the fifth century when Augustine laid the foundations for Christian ethics on suicide. The historical context of the time is significant. Building upon Roman toleration of suicide, Christian martyrs had

[1] A Alvarez, 'The Background' in M Pabst-Battin and D Mayo (eds), *Suicide: The Philosophical Issues* (London, Peter Owen, 1981) 12.

[2] ibid 22.

[3] G Minois, *History of Suicide: Voluntary Death in Western Culture* (Baltimore, John Hopkins, 1999, translated by LG Cochrane) 45–46.

adopted the practice for themselves and this was taken to the extreme with the martyrdom of the Donatists and also with the suicidal response of women raped by the Visigoths who overran Rome in 410.[4] Augustine condemned both groups, alongside suicide more broadly, utilising the sixth commandment of 'thou shalt not kill' and applying it for the first time to killing oneself as well as others. In *The City of God*, Augustine declared that 'no man ought voluntarily to inflict death upon himself, for this is to flee from temporal ills by falling into eternal ones'.[5] Suffering on earth was now seen as a good thing and certainly preferable to seeking to flee from it: 'we might more properly call a soul great if it can bear a life full of calamity and not flee from it'.[6]

Soon after Augustine's death in 430, the Council of Arles in 452 officially condemned suicide and in the following century the Council of Braga in 562 decreed that those who committed suicide died in mortal sin and were thus to be denied religious burial rites. In 693, the Council of Toledo addressed the question of those who had attempted suicide and ordained that they must be excommunicated from the church. In the thirteenth century, the writing of Thomas Aquinas was influential in further strengthening the Christian condemnation of suicide, combining Augustine's interpretation of the sixth commandment with the natural law reasoning of Plato and Aristotle.[7] Therefore, as Pabst Battin has pointed out, the view that suicide is intrinsically and absolutely wrong is specifically associated with post-Augustinian, especially medieval, Christianity and the view is not characteristic of other cultures.[8] For example, some other historical societies have gone beyond toleration of suicide to outright acceptance of it as a noble end, including the Druids, Vikings and some African tribes.[9] Nonetheless, the Christian view of suicide has been the most influential for English law. As Alvarez explains, the concept of suicide as a mortal sin 'spread like a fog across Europe because its strength came from primitive fears, prejudices and superstitions which had survived despite Christianity, Judaism and Hellenism'.[10]

From the sixteenth century onwards, alternative views began to be put forward. Perhaps best summed up by the musings of whether 'to be or not to be' that Shakespeare put into Hamlet's mind,[11] writers including John Donne, Michel de

[4] M Barbagli, *Farewell to the World: A History of Suicide* (Cambridge, Polity Press, 2015, English edition translated by L Byatt) 41.

[5] Augustine, *The City of God Against the Pagans* (Cambridge, Cambridge University Press, 1998, edited and translated by RW Dyson) 39.

[6] ibid 34.

[7] T Aquinas, *Summa Theologica* (New York, Benziger Bros, 1947).

[8] M Pabst Battin, *The Least Worst Death: Essays in Bioethics on the End of Life* (Oxford, Oxford University Press, 1994) 191.

[9] Alvarez, 'The Background' (1981) 15. Other societies view suicide as noble only in certain circumstances, such as the Hindu 'suttee'.

[10] ibid 13.

[11] Hamlet continues by questioning 'Whether 'tis nobler in the mind to suffer the slings and arrows of outrageous fortune, or to take arms against a sea of troubles, and by opposing end them'. His conclusion that 'conscience does make cowards of us all' would seem to meet the intent of post-Augustinian Christian ethics on suicide.

Montaigne and later David Hume contemplated whether there is an obligation to live.[12] Significantly, from today's perspective, such writers not only argued for the lawfulness of suicide but regarded it as an expression of individual autonomy. In the stirring words of Montaigne, 'Living is slavery if the freedom to die is wanting'.[13] Ironically, these sixteenth-century musings coincided with the most vigorous legal responses to suicide.[14] And even when other western countries began to decriminalise suicide in the eighteenth century, including Prussia in 1751, France in 1791 and many of the new US states following the revolution in the 1780s,[15] in England the law continued to condemn and punish suicide.

II. Punishment of Suicide in English Law

The denial of religious burial rites for those who took their own life was first incorporated into English canon law in the Council of Hereford in 673. Two centuries later, the civil sanction of forfeiture was added. By the 1260s, Bracton was able to describe suicide as '*felo de se*' – a felony of self. In 1565, in the famous case of *Hales v Petit*, Dyer LCJ equated suicide with murder.[16] Indeed, suicide was soon regarded as an even worse crime than murder, not only because it was viewed as a public crime against God and the King (in contrast to murder, which was originally seen as a private offence against the victim and her family), but also because there is no possibility of repentance for the sinner before death.[17] As such, the penalties for this particular felony were extreme. As Barbagli describes:

> From the moment that the death was deemed to be suicide, a process commenced that aimed at dehumanizing the mortal remains of the person who had dared to take his or her own life. With inordinate force, this process expressed the horror, repugnance and aversion felt not only by the civic and religious authorities but by the entire population. Regarded as despicable and bestial, the lifeless body of the guilty party provoked contempt, fear and disdain, and was treated with deliberate brutality.[18]

Desecration of the body was as creative as it was abhorrent. Common 'punishments' for the dead body included being dragged through the streets, branding with marks of ignominy, a second symbolic death by hanging or burning of the

[12] See Barbagli, *Farewell to the World* (2015) 76.
[13] Quoted in ibid.
[14] MacDonald and Murphy point out the rigour with which the law against suicide was enforced between 1485 and 1660, distinguishing that period from those both before and after: M MacDonald and TR Murphy, *Sleepless Souls: Suicide in Early Modern England* (Oxford, Clarendon Press, 1990).
[15] Barbagli (n 4) 99; Macdonald and Murphy (ibid) 198.
[16] *Hales v Petit* (1565) 1 Plowd 253, 260.
[17] Barbagli (n 4) 112–14.
[18] ibid 32.

body, and burial at a crossroads with a stake driven into the body.[19] Macdonald and Murphy graphically describe a typical process in the Tudor ages:

> [T]heir bodies were interred profanely, with a macabre ceremony prescribed by popular custom. The night following the inquest, officials of the parish, the church wardens and their helpers, carried the corpse to a crossroads and threw it naked into a pit. A wooden stake was hammered through the body, pinioning it in the grave, and the hole was filled in.[20]

The community's desire to degrade the body of a suicide stemmed from a conviction that suicide was 'supernaturally evil'[21] and seems to have been informed less by Christian belief and more by 'demotic folklore … that dramatized the supernatural ramifications of self-murder'.[22] As Alvarez points out, there had been a long history of degradation of bodies and its application in relation to suicide simply lasted longer than in relation to perceived vampires and witches.[23]

It is the state's appropriation of these practices that introduces legal consequences for suicide. In the thirteenth century, forfeiture of the property of a suicide was introduced ensuring that property reverted to the Crown. This served as a deterrent against suicide, as one's family would be disinherited, but it also conveniently served as a source of wealth for the state.[24] Thus, in Alvarez's words, the 'primitive revenges were duly dignified and made economically profitable to the state by the law'.[25] The purported punishment of a suicide was, of course, fatally flawed: the person who had taken their own life was now beyond the reach of earthly justice or revenge. The punishment, whether in terms of restrictions on burial, desecrating the corpse or the forfeiture of property, had to be endured by the deceased's family and friends. If this seems unjust to modern eyes, it was also increasingly felt to be so in the past. Indeed, it is the misfit of the punishment with the perceived criminal that ultimately started the road towards legal reform.

III. The Insanity Exception

A. The Pivotal Role of Coroner's Juries

It proved to be extremely significant that the legal punishments for suicide were triggered by a verdict of *felo-de-se* at the inquest. In effect, it was the coroner's juries who enforced the crime of suicide. This panel of the deceased's peers held

[19] ibid 32–37.
[20] Macdonald and Murphy, *Sleepless Souls* (1990) 15.
[21] ibid 44.
[22] ibid 76.
[23] Alvarez (n 1) 8.
[24] DE Hoffman and VJ Webb, 'Suicide as Murder at Common Law' (1981) 19 *Criminology* 372, 377.
[25] Alvarez (n 1) 9.

the power to declare the death to be *felo-de-se* and thus a felony, from which the negative consequences discussed above would inevitably follow, or to declare the deceased to be *non compos mentis*. During the sixteenth and early seventeenth centuries, the law against suicide was rigorously enforced with over 95 per cent of the men and women who took their own lives between 1485 and 1660 convicted as *felons de se* and fewer than two per cent excused as persons *non compos mentis*.[26] By the late eighteenth century, however, the numbers reverse so that over 97 per cent of suicides were recorded as *non compos mentis*[27] and a finding of *felo-de-se* became a rarity, reserved for those who might be regarded as marginal members of the local community such as criminals, people in disgrace, servants, paupers or strangers.[28] By the beginning of the nineteenth century, therefore, the idea that anyone who killed themselves must be, at least temporarily, insane had become established by means of the coroner's juries' verdict and the significance of this new perception on the law of suicide was (and arguably continues to be) profound. As we will see, the impetus for legalisation came from an understanding that those who tried to kill themselves needed treatment rather than punishment, new mental health legislation facilitated the removal of criminal detention powers and even today the law encourages preventive measures in relation to suicide on the basis that it is often the result of a mental illness. This crucial linkage between suicide and insanity originally dates from the radical change in approach of the coroner's juries during the late seventeenth and eighteenth centuries (only supported much later by the influence of medicine). As Macdonald and Murphy explain,

> declaring that suicides were mad unavoidably challenged durable popular beliefs about the crime. A non compos mentis verdict was an implicit rejection of religious and folkloric interpretations of suicide that condemned it utterly in favour of medical explanations that excused it.[29]

So why did these juries shift from viewing those who killed themselves as felons to viewing them as innocent but insane? The main impetus for a revised approach seemed to be the local distaste of forfeiture which departed from the normal customs of inheritance. Coroner's juries were drawn from local men and, as Hoffman and Webb point out, 'most common people did not want the severe penalties of suicide law to be visited upon their friends and neighbours'.[30] The local resentment of the forfeiture penalty, the effects of which were felt so strongly by the heirs of the deceased, led to coroner's juries palliating the law by 'colluding with families to frustrate the rights of the crown and lesser lords'.[31]

[26] Macdonald and Murphy (n 14) 16.
[27] ibid 133.
[28] ibid 129.
[29] ibid 124.
[30] Hoffman and Webb, 'Suicide as Murder at Common Law' (1981) 378.
[31] Macdonald and Murphy (n 14) 114.

Thus, the increase in the use of the *non compos mentis* verdict began primarily as a strategy for avoiding forfeiture. As this verdict began to dominate, there was concern that the juries were undermining the rule of law. Blackstone, for example, accused coroner's juries of 'pious perjury'.[32] But there was to be no turning back and, by the late eighteenth century, the failure of juries to enforce the penalties of the law in relation to suicide was widely condoned.[33]

The original linking of suicide with insanity by coroner's juries was undertaken almost entirely independently of the medical profession. At the inquest, it was the non-medical witnesses that provided the justification for a *non compos mentis* verdict. Families and friends of the deceased would describe and interpret the behaviour of the deceased, in full knowledge of both the legal and social consequences of a sane suicide. Often the medical witnesses were not able to comment on the deceased's state of mind, particularly as the Medical Witness Act 1836 ensured that the medical witnesses who appeared at inquests were usually those who practiced closest to where the body was found, rather than where the deceased had lived.[34] Furthermore, by the nineteenth century, some medical professionals who encountered suicide at asylums and inquests began to criticise the almost universal assumption that those who committed suicide were insane.[35] In particular, the impossibility of assessing the sanity of the deceased after the fact led some doctors to argue that the *non compos mentis* verdicts 'were being made on the basis of the act itself rather than strict scrutiny of the mental health of the deceased'.[36] This was undoubtedly true, and was primarily happening for the reason outlined above, namely to avoid unjust penalties being imposed on the family of the deceased. It is worth pointing out, therefore, that the apparent assumption of insanity in relation to those who committed suicide stands in stark contrast to the other use of insanity in the criminal justice system during the nineteenth century: the criminal defence of insanity. In *M'Naghten's Case* in 1843, Lord Tindall CJ required juries to be told that 'every man is to be presumed to be sane, and to possess a sufficient degree of reason to be responsible for his crimes, until the contrary be proved to their satisfaction'.[37] Thus, a person was to be presumed sane for all crimes except that of suicide, where there was undeniably a presumption of insanity.[38]

The influence of the coroner's juries on the law relating to suicide is a rare example of successful popular action that softened the law and changed society's response to suicide. Macdonald and Murphy describe it in the following evocative words: 'The mysterious alchemy of the coroner's inquest transmuted the

[32] W Blackstone, *Commentaries on the Laws of England* (Oxford, Clarendon Press, 1770).

[33] Macdonald and Murphy (n 14) 175.

[34] G Laragy, '"A Peculiar Species of Felony": Suicide, Medicine, and the Law in Victorian Britain and Ireland' (2013) 46 *Journal of Social History* 732, 736.

[35] ibid 733.

[36] ibid 734.

[37] *M'Naghten's Case* (1843) 8 Eng Rep 78.

[38] CL Wright, 'The English Canon Law Relating to Suicide Victims' (2017) *Ecclesiastical Law Journal* 193, 197.

insubstantial stuff of attitudes and beliefs into the tangible matter of collective action.'[39] Even today, the role of the coroner's inquest remains crucial in relation to suicide and at least some coroners appear to be continuing the nineteenth-century juries' sympathetic approaches to grieving families, until recently assisted by the retention of the criminal standard of proof for a verdict of suicide.[40] Tait and Carpenter interviewed a number of coroners who admitted that suicide is under-represented in statistics of causes of death because of a reluctance to return such a verdict in front of grieving relatives. One coroner is quoted as saying, 'I think a lot of coroners – me included – sometimes take a sympathetic view of the family, and perhaps, well, you know – why leave them with the stigma of this, when we can actually make their situation better?'.[41] Thus, even without the shadow cast by the legal punishments of *felo-de-se*, a coroner's verdict of suicide is regarded as carrying such negative implications that those charged with enforcing the law may seek means of evading it.

B. Life Insurance Suicide Exclusion Clauses

It was not only the criminal justice system that was concerned with the connection between suicide and insanity during the nineteenth century. The civil justice system also grappled with the connection but in a very different context and with very different consequences. As discussed above, a suicide would not be regarded as a felony if the deceased was found to be insane, and they almost always were so found. However, even if the forfeiture penalty was avoided by means of a *non compos mentis* verdict by an amenable coroner's jury, there might still be financial implications for the family of the deceased as suicide exclusion clauses were ubiquitous in life assurance contracts and these purported to cover all self-inflicted deaths, regardless of whether a felony or not. In 1843, the case of *Borradaile v Hunter*[42] presented an opportunity for the courts to confront the issue of suicide exclusion clauses. Rev William Borradaile had taken out a life insurance policy in 1828 which included an exclusion if he died 'by his own hands'. Ten years later, he jumped from Vauxhall Bridge into the Thames and was drowned. At the coroner's inquest, the jury predictably refused to return a verdict of *felo de se*. They instead took the view that, despite voluntarily jumping from the bridge with the intention of ending his life, he was not capable of judging

[39] Macdonald and Murphy (n 14) 110.

[40] Until 2020, a finding of suicide at inquest needed to be established beyond reasonable doubt. Only in 2020 did the Supreme Court replace this standard with one of the balance of probabilities: *R(Maughan) v HM Senior Coroner for Oxfordshire* [2020] UKSC 46.

[41] G Tait and B Carpenter, 'The Continuing Implications of the "Crime" of Suicide: a Brief History of the Present' (2016) *International Journal of Law in Context* 210, 218.

[42] *Borradaile v Hunter* (1843) 5 Manning and Granger 639. For a detailed discussion, see D Mendelson and I Freckelton, 'The Interface of the Civil and Criminal Law of Suicide at Common Law (1194–1845)' (2013) 36 *International Journal of Law and Psychiatry* 343, 346–47.

between right and wrong at the time of the act, and they awarded the policy.[43] The insurance company appealed on the basis that the exclusion applied to all self-inflicted death, regardless of insanity. Justices Maule, Erskine and Coltman, while sympathetic to the argument that insanity should be treated as a disease and that sanctions should not generally attach to those who take their own lives as a result of their state of mind, nonetheless found that the exclusion clause in this case was clear and the deceased's voluntary action fell within it.

The case is perhaps better remembered, however, for the strident dissent of Tindal CJ, who rejected the idea that the jury had found the deceased to be insane, holding instead that they had found him lacking in the essential characteristic of felony.[44] This was significant as it suggested that a suicide could be both without felonious intent and without mental illness.[45] Tindal CJ also found the wording of the exclusion clause – 'by his own hands' – to be ambiguous and felt that this should therefore be interpreted favourably to those who did not draft it. If the insurers had intended to exempt non-felonious suicides, they ought to have expressed it clearly in the policy, in his view.[46] The dissenting Chief Justice would have found the death to be covered by the life insurance policy, but for the majority it fell squarely within the exemption clause, indicating that while a *non compos mentis* finding at inquest might remove criminal law penalties such as forfeiture, it did not entitle the deceased's family to benefit from a life insurance policy with a suicide exemption. Thus, while the state of the mind of the deceased was crucial in the criminal law, it was irrelevant to the civil law.

Only two years later, the issue reached the courts again in *Clift v Schwabe*.[47] In this case, the life insurance policy's exclusion clause used the wording of 'commit suicide'. Louis Schwabe died from ingestion of sulphuric acid and was found to be of 'unsound mind' at the time of death. Cresswell J suggested to the jury that the exclusion clause applied only to felonious suicides and thus the jury awarded damages to the plaintiff. Once more, the insurance company appealed to the Court of Exchequer in which the majority held that, giving the exclusion clause its ordinary meaning, any voluntary act of self-destruction was included, requiring only that death was an intentional act of a person knowing the probable consequence.[48] Thus, the exclusion clause would apply even when the deceased was of unsound mind at the time of death, provided the act was intentional and they understood the consequences. The court did, however, assume that exclusion clauses would not apply in the case of suicides where there is no exercise of will, such as where the self-inflicted death results from an accident or delirium.[49]

[43] *Borradaile v Hunter* (ibid) 643.
[44] ibid 669.
[45] Mendelson and Freckelton, 'The Interface of the Civil and Criminal Law' (2013) 347.
[46] *Borradaile v Hunter* (n 42) 669.
[47] *Clift v Schwabe* (1846) 136 ER 175. See Mendelson and Freckleton (n 42) 347–48.
[48] *Clift v Schwabe* (ibid) at 185.
[49] ibid at 187.

As with the previous case, the most interesting aspect of this judgment is the dissent. In *Clift v Schwabe*, Pollock CB dissented, arguing that once a person

> has lost his sense of right and wrong, it matters not what else of the human faculties or capacities remain; he ceases to be a responsible agent; and, in my judgment, can no more commit suicide than he can commit murder.[50]

Thus, Pollock would redefine 'suicide' to mean felonious suicide in much the same way as the criminal law imposes punishment only on those few suicides declared to be felonies. While the majority of the court did not agree with this approach, they did open the door to a more refined understanding of suicide by acknowledging that suicide exclusion clauses would not apply where the death is the result of 'delirium'. Pollock criticises the majority's apparently arbitrary distinction between deaths caused by delirium and deaths caused by insanity:

> [I]f the act be not the act of a sane, responsible creature, but is the result of any delusion or perversion, whether physical, intellectual, or moral, it is not the act of the man; and, to hold otherwise, seems to me a departure from the simplicity of the law, and to be repugnant to sound philosophy.[51]

Again, this dissent seems to mirror the approach of the criminal justice system enforced by the coroner's juries by seeking to remove legal responsibility for a suicide that is the result of mental illness (or any other external influence). While it was not the approach of the majority, it seemed to better reflect the views of nineteenth-century society. Indeed, Anderson claims that the majority judgment in *Clift v Schwabe* was a 'pyrrhic victory' for the insurance companies because it was widely regarded as unfair.[52] Of the 32 insurance companies surveyed in 1885, nine made no mention of suicide in their policies, 17 excluded it only for a limited period after the policy was created and only six excluded it entirely. Furthermore, in practice, unless fraud was suspected, all of the insurance companies would pay in full following a self-inflicted death.[53]

These two mid-nineteenth-century cases highlight the breadth of legal issues raised by a self-inflicted death. They also demonstrate the increasing mismatch between the severe legal consequences of a suicide and society's increasing sympathy for the family of those who commit it. The underlying question in these cases is whether the legal label of 'suicide' should be confined to those cases where the deceased had full mental capacity at the time of death.[54] The answer by the majorities in both cases was that it should not; that suicide is a broader concept under the law and that the families of the deceased should have to face the proper legal consequences for all intentional self-killings, regardless of the state of mind

[50] ibid at 191.
[51] ibid at 192.
[52] O Anderson, *Suicide in Victorian and Edwardian England* (Oxford, Clarendon Press, 1987) 267.
[53] The survey was by Westcott and is cited in Anderson (ibid) 268–69.
[54] Mendelson and Freckleton (n 42) 348.

of the deceased at the time of death. Broader society struggled to accept that approach, however, leading to a very real possibility of dodging the legal financial consequences of a suicide with the help of a coroner's jury's *non compos mentis* verdict and a pragmatic life insurance company. While both society and the law still struggle with this connection between rationality and suicide today, it is from a very different perspective. Today the idea of a rational suicide – suicide as an autonomous choice by an individual – is often overlooked in the law's regulation of it. In the nineteenth century, however, the issue was whether the suicide label should be reserved for just such an act.

IV. The Nineteenth-century Removal of the Penalties for Suicide

The two types of legal penalties for suicide – denial of Christian burial rites and forfeiture of property – were still firmly entrenched in the law at the start of the nineteenth century. The reluctance of coroner's juries to return verdicts of *felo de se*, as discussed in the previous section, significantly reduced the application of these penalties, but for the few suicides still regarded as felonies and not excused by insanity, a ritual burial and denial of usual inheritance practices still applied. Indeed, the ritual burial of the bodies of *felons de se*, including burial at a crossroads with a stake driven through the heart, continued until the 1820s as, for example, in relation to John Williams who had committed suicide while awaiting trial for a series of brutal murders.[55] But the nineteenth century also saw a movement for legal reform which argued that it was the severity of the legal penalties for suicide that had led to its non-enforcement by coroner's juries. The first formal legal change occurred in 1823 when Parliament passed the Right to Burial Act,[56] which prohibited burial on the public highways. The 1823 Act made it illegal for coroners to issue a warrant for burial of *felo de se* on a public highway, requiring instead that the bodies were interred in private ground or in a churchyard. The Act did not go so far, however, as to require a Christian burial for those who had committed the crime of suicide; the bodies were buried at night with no Christian rites performed.

Later in the century, the law concerning burial was relaxed once more. The Burial Law Amendment Act 1880 eased the restrictions on religious rites for the burial of the bodies of those who had committed suicide. It permitted a religious service in a churchyard or graveyard by someone other than an officiating minister of the Church of England. It also permitted clergymen to use prayers from the

[55] Macdonald and Murphy (n 14) 138–39.

[56] 'An Act to alter and amend the law relating to the internment of the remains of any person found felo de se' (4 Geo 4).

Book of Common Prayer and extracts from the Holy Scripture.[57] Just two years later, the Internments (Felo de se) Act 1882 made it lawful for the burial to be performed during the daytime, rather than at night. These changes to the legislative consequences of suicide were still somewhat theoretical, given that the *Book of Common Prayer 1662* prohibited the use of the Burial Service for 'all who laid violent hands upon themselves'. Although this restriction provided no exception for those of unsound mind, it appears that most clergymen during the latter half of the nineteenth century, were prepared to accept a *non compos mentis* verdict as exonerating the deceased from responsibility for their sinful actions and would be prepared to read the Burial Service at the burial.[58] What happened in practice, however, depended on the interpretation of the ecclesiastical law by the individual priest concerned.[59]

The nineteenth century also saw the removal of the penalty of forfeiture from the law for all crimes under the Abolition of Forfeiture Act 1870. It was a move that fitted with other reforms to inheritance law of that period. In the words of Hoffman and Webb, it was 'merely another aspect of feudal land law subjected to the legislative scalpel of bourgeoise reformers'.[60] Interestingly, the 1870 Act specifically mentions *felo de se* and seems to distinguish it from other felonies. It declares that 'No confession, verdict, inquest, conviction or judgment of or for any treason or felony or felo de se shall cause any attainder or corruption of blood, or any forfeiture or escheat'. This wording led to a subsequent argument (by a man sentenced to six months' imprisonment with hard labour for attempted suicide) in the 1914 case of *R v Mann (John William)*[61] that suicide was therefore not a felony, but this argument was rejected by the Court of Appeal. Thus, by the end of the nineteenth century, while suicide remained a criminal offence (and would remain so throughout the first half of the twentieth century), there were no longer any legal penalties for either the body or the property of the deceased. It is a point of irony, however, that just as the punishments for suicide were being removed in the nineteenth century, the offence of attempted suicide was first being developed.

V. The Development of the Offence of Attempted Suicide

It is perhaps surprising how late the offence of attempted suicide developed. For much of the lengthy period when suicide was punished so severely, a failed

[57] Wright, 'The English Canon Law' (2017) 199–200.

[58] Anderson, *Suicide in Victorian and Edwardian England* (1987) 281.

[59] Wright (n 38) 200. Wright suggests that this remained true into the twenty-first century with many priests ignoring a canon law that denied burial rites to a sane suicide on the basis that it was 'outdated and pastorally insensitive' (203).

[60] Hoffman and Webb (n 24) 380.

[61] *R v Mann (John William)* [1914] 2 KB 107.

attempt was not subject to any legal penalty. That changed, however, during the second half of the nineteenth century. The first judicial confirmation that an offence of attempted suicide existed came in *R v Doody* in 1854.[62] Anderson argues convincingly, however, that it was the creation of the new police forces which made it practicable to treat attempted suicide as an offence. Thus, within metropolitan areas, an offence began to be developed in the 1830s, but was not applied in the provinces for another 50 years.[63] The significance of the police in relation to attempted suicide is that without them, there was no one likely to seek to charge the offence. From the establishment of the Metropolitan Police in the Metropolitan Police Act 1829, the police sought to establish public order on the streets of London. They took into custody the drunk and disorderly, prostitutes, vagrants, beggars and also those persons who had attempted suicide.[64] The latter were invariably charged. Anderson notes that during the 1840s, 1,807 individuals were charged with attempted suicide.[65] She also reflects on how this legal intervention in relation to attempted suicide was really not about suicide itself. It was, Anderson says,

> less in order to punish or prevent attempts at suicide for their own sake, than as part of a general effort to enforce higher standards of public order, decency, and safety in the towns and cities of an expanding society.[66]

By 1878, there was no doubt remaining that attempting suicide was a serious criminal offence. When a Royal Commission of that year was charged with drafting a criminal code, it proposed the offence of attempted suicide be punishable by two years' imprisonment with hard labour.[67] Furthermore, the number of persons charged with attempted suicide steadily increased through the late nineteenth and early twentieth centuries. By the 1870s, there was an average of 800 persons charged with the offence in England and Wales each year; by the 1890s, that had risen to over 1,000 per year; and by 1910–13, there were over 2,000 charged each year.[68]

However, being charged with the offence did not inevitably lead to being tried for it. Even by the early years of the twentieth century, only about 10 per cent of attempted suicide cases that came before the metropolitan magistrates were sent for trial,[69] although the percentages were higher (but overall numbers much lower) in rural areas.[70] Until 1925, the offence of attempted suicide was triable on

[62] *R v Doody* (1854) 6 Cox CC 463.
[63] Anderson (n 52) 282–83.
[64] ibid 283–84.
[65] ibid 284.
[66] ibid 289–90.
[67] S Moore, *The Decriminalisation of Suicide* (PhD thesis, LSE, 2000) 43, available at etheses.lse.ac.uk/1573/1/U136493.pdf.
[68] Anderson (n 52) 286–88.
[69] ibid 291.
[70] ibid 292.

indictment only so, rather than being tried for the offence of attempted suicide, many persons initially arrested for this were instead dealt with under other summary-only charges, such as being drunk and disorderly or the vagrancy laws. Even more were simply discharged. Anderson reveals that three out of four persons taken into custody by the Metropolitan Police for attempting suicide between 1909 and 1913 were discharged.[71] It is significant, however, that even if the end result is a discharge, this would only follow a period in custody. This is because magistrates would typically remand in custody those brought before them on a charge of attempted suicide in order to obtain reports from the prison chaplain and prison surgeon.[72] This served a number of purposes: it acted as a safety measure to ensure there was no immediate further suicide attempt; it ensured that each case was dealt with on its individual circumstances rather than as a blanket approach to suicide; and it encouraged a focus on preventing suicide and protecting those who had attempted it, rather than mere punishment of a criminal offence. As Anderson explains:

> It was not through the process of trial, conviction, and sentencing that the machinery of the law usually worked to prevent suicide, but through the night at the police station, through the examining magistrate's reproof, caution, and practical assistance, and through the individual attention given by the chaplain and medical officer of the local prison used for remand.[73]

In this manner, the offence of attempted suicide operated in a similar way to the much older offence of suicide: the strict letter of the law was palliated by a pragmatic approach by those tasked with enforcing it.

This included the police force. Until the creation of the Crown Prosecution Service (CPS) in 1986, it was the police who decided whether or not to prosecute, and there was a significant discrepancy between the number of attempted suicides known to the police and those prosecuted. Between 1900 and legalisation in 1961, only one attempt out of every nine or 10 of which the police had knowledge were proceeded against.[74] This was not coincidental; the first guidance given to the Metropolitan Police concerning suicide in 'General Orders' in 1916 made clear that persons brought to the station having attempted suicide were not to be charged with the offence if there was someone willing to be responsible for them, and provided there were no special circumstances (such as the commission of another crime, a previous attempt at suicide, insanity or continued threats of future attempts).[75] (The parallel to the later policy on assisted suicide, which remains a criminal offence but is rarely prosecuted, is clear.)

[71] ibid 294.
[72] ibid 295.
[73] ibid 308.
[74] Moore, *The Decriminalisation of Suicide* (2000) 78.
[75] ibid. Similar instructions were issued by the Home Office to provincial police forces in 1921: ibid 79.

By 1915–24, the number of prosecutions of attempted suicide in the Assize and Quarter Sessions had fallen to under 100 per year.[76] However, there then followed a significant development in relation to the prosecution of attempted suicide. The Criminal Justice Act 1925 brought adult attempted suicide within summary jurisdiction for the first time. While this could be viewed as an official downplaying of the offence, its immediate impact was an increase in prosecutions. These rose to 376 in 1926, and then to just over 700 by 1929, continuing at roughly that rate until eventual decriminalisation in 1961.[77] Almost all who were prosecuted for attempted suicide were convicted. The increased prosecutions after 1925 seems to indicate that the offence was usually not deemed suitable for trial before a circuit judge, but was more comfortably seen as a minor offence to be tried before magistrates. In addition, a summary trial before magistrates facilitated a prompt dealing with a person now increasingly viewed as in need of treatment rather than punishment.

Instructions on how to dispose of those prosecuted for attempted suicide were provided in *The Magistrate* in 1946. It advised that such persons should always be remanded in custody for a report by the prison doctor as to their mental health. If the report revealed that the prisoner was of unsound mind, then the police would usually offer no evidence and ask for a discharge in order that they could be dealt with under the Lunacy Acts. If, on the other hand, the report revealed that the prisoner was mentally sound, and provided there was no previous attempt nor reason to anticipate a future attempt (in which case, she should be committed to trial), the magistrates were advised to deal with the case summarily with punishment 'seldom imposed'. A supervision order might in some circumstances be appropriate, but the usual outcome was a probation order, rather than imprisonment.[78] Under the Probation of Offenders Act 1907, magistrates could only issue a probation order 'without proceeding to conviction', but following the Criminal Justice Act 1948, a convicted offender could be placed under the supervision of a probation officer. This soon became the most common disposal of those convicted of attempting suicide. In the period 1952–56, 63 per cent were given probation, 28 per cent a conditional or absolute discharge or bind over, and only 6.7 per cent were given sentences of imprisonment.[79] It should be noted, however, that this still amounted to nearly 200 persons imprisoned during this post-war period for attempting to take their own lives and, furthermore, that even those who avoided custodial sentences would have spent time in prison while on remand. The focus of the law and its enforcement might have shifted from punishment to prevention,

[76] ibid 81.
[77] ibid.
[78] ibid 82–83.
[79] ibid 84.

but attempting suicide remained a criminal offence. The seriousness of that offence was the subject of some debate.

In the 1955 case of *R v French (Edward)*,[80] a man who had pleaded guilty to attempted suicide was given two years' imprisonment by the Recorder, who stated that 'Self-murder is one of the most serious crimes on our calendar. An attempt threat, therefore, is a very serious crime'. The recorder noted that the evidence from the defendant had established that it was a serious and sane attempt on his life and thus could not be taken lightly. On appeal against the sentence, Goddard LCJ suggested that the Recorder's views were outdated:

> No doubt attempted suicide has always been regarded as an offence, but to say that it is to be regarded as a very serious crime indeed shows an entire lack of proportion. It is not a very serious crime in point of law. Whether it is regarded as a sin or not is not a matter for the court.[81]

The two-year sentence was regarded as 'absurd'. It was, however, recognised by the Court of Appeal that a short custodial sentence was often given for the offence in order to 'protect the man against himself' and thus a sentence of one month was substituted for the two years. The Court of Appeal's approach perfectly reflects the law's evolved relationship with suicide by the mid-twentieth century: regardless of religious views of it as a sin, suicide was not in law a very serious crime and although it remained an offence to attempt suicide, this was primarily for the purpose of providing assistance to those in need of support. While it might be thought (and indeed very soon would be accepted by Parliament) that a felony was not the most flexible mechanism for providing this social support, the history of its enforcement, especially since the beginning of the nineteenth century, had revealed a surprising degree of manoeuvrability in its operation.

In the late nineteenth and early twentieth centuries, the focus of the law's role in respect of suicide had shifted from punishment to prevention. Indeed, it is this shift that first encouraged the use of the offence of attempted suicide to arrest and detain those who had attempted to take their own lives. Identifying those at risk enabled medical attention to be given to them. A number of factors came together in the Victorian era to revolutionise the law's approach to suicide: the assumption that anyone who attempted suicide must be insane; the Victorian faith in institutions, especially the insane asylum; and a concerted move by the medical profession to bring suicide within their own jurisdiction. Given the enduring legacy of this medicalisation of suicide, these factors will now be considered in more detail.

[80] *R v French (Edward)* (1955) 39 Cr App R 192.
[81] ibid.

VI. A Medical or Social Problem: Treatment not Punishment

Nineteenth-century positivism encouraged a new view of suicide. It was no longer seen as a moral choice, but rather as something that must have been caused. Sociologists, including the influential Durkheim,[82] argued that suicide was caused by society, but to the medical profession, suicide was caused by a malfunction or disease of the body. Both new explanations removed responsibility from the person who attempted or achieved suicide. The days of suicide as a felony were therefore numbered.

The involvement of the medical profession in the issue of suicide began later than might be expected. As mentioned above, the first crucial link between suicide and insanity was invariably made without professional medical input and was instead a layman juries' effort to palliate the severe legal penalties for suicide visited upon surviving family. In an 1840 book called *The Anatomy of Suicide*, Forbes Winslow advocated that postmortems be performed on the bodies of those who had died from suicide in order to identify the organic cause.[83] As the nineteenth century progressed, the Victorian trend of institutionalising those perceived as deviants led to many of those who survived a suicide attempt being placed in lunatic asylums, requiring medical certification and thus forcing doctors into close proximity with those who had attempted suicide. Anderson notes that by the 1880s, doctors were certifying around 4,000 persons each year as having suicidal propensities and in need of confinement.[84] Indeed, the reception orders accompanying medical certificates of insanity required when having a person committed to an asylum appear to contain the first use of the word 'suicidal', which was not a familiar concept until the nineteenth century.[85] Jansson explains, however, that the meaning of the label 'suicidal' given to people upon admission to an asylum was ambiguous and could encompass a wide range of actions.[86] Jansson cites the patient books from Brookwood Lunatic Asylum from 1868–72 in which,

> suicidal melancholics ranged from those who has reportedly tried to throw themselves out of windows or cut their throat, to those who would not eat, to those who were reported to be 'despondent', those who claimed to have committed a great sin and must be punished, and those who expressed a fear of being killed.[87]

Furthermore, the admission form to commit someone to an asylum could be filled in by many different persons, such as family or friends for the private patients

[82] E Durkheim, *Suicide: A Study in Sociology*, 2nd edn (London, Routledge, 2002).
[83] Moore (n 67) 49.
[84] Anderson (n 52) 387.
[85] A Jansson, 'From Suicide to Diagnostics: Medical Certificates, Melancholia, and "Suicidal Propensities" in Victorian Psychiatry' (2013) 46 *Journal of Social History* 716, 717.
[86] ibid 719.
[87] ibid 723.

or a workhouse official or magistrate for the pauper patients, and a 'yes' answer to the question of whether the patient had suicidal propensities might be used merely to ensure a bed was available.[88] After admission to the asylum, the Lunacy Acts required a diagnosis to be made within a week and thus doctors undertaking this task would be doing so in light of whether suicidal propensities had been identified.

It was also in this asylum context that the connection between suicide and melancholia was first formed. In the early nineteenth century, suicide was viewed as merely a possible outcome of melancholia, but by the beginning of the twentieth century, there was an established psychiatric view that a majority of melancholics were suicidal.[89] By this time, being 'suicidal' was such a defining symptom of melancholia that suicidal propensities might be suspected even when they were not observable to the doctor.[90] Thus, the medical takeover of suicide and the suicidal during the nineteenth century is more significant for the new perception that suicide is caused by factors that can be observed and potentially treated, than for any systematic or reliable approach for actually doing so. It was now medical men, rather than either priests or lawyers, who had primary responsibility for dealing with those at risk of suicide, and who were regarded as most effective at preventing suicide. Prevention rather than condemnation was now the focus of society's response to suicide, and while a medical cause was pushed by the medical profession, other nineteenth-century thinkers sought to find the causes, and thus the remedy, in society itself.

The emergence of a notion of 'society' in the late eighteenth century meant that suicide came to be seen as 'evidence of not only individual, but also social pathology'.[91] It was no longer an individual sin but rather an important indicator of the health and wellbeing of the population.[92] Émile Durkheim in the very influential 1897 book *Le Suicide* sought to explain the causes of suicide. Durkheim ascribed all variations in the frequency of suicide to two causes: social integration and regulation. Social integration refers to the number and strength of the ties binding an individual to groups, and Durkheim argued that the suicide rate increases when such ties are either scarce or excessive. Similarly, if society is either too weakly regulated or over-regulated, then the suicide rate will also increase. In recent years Durkheim's theory has been criticised, both for the veracity of the data on which he relied,[93] and for his model of purely sociological

[88] ibid 719–20.
[89] ibid 718.
[90] ibid 722.
[91] A Bähr, 'Between "Self-Murder" and "Suicide": The Modern Etymology of Self-Killing' (2013) 46 *Journal of Social History* 620, 628.
[92] Tait and Carpenter, 'The Continuing Implications of the "Crime" of Suicide' (2016) 213.
[93] MT Brancaccio, EJ Engstrom and D Lederer, 'The Politics of Suicide: Historical Perspectives on Suicidology before Durkheim. An Introduction' (2013) 46 *Journal of Social History* 607, 608.

factors for suicide which excludes more nuanced cultural interpretations.[94] There is no room in Durkheim's nineteenth-century sociological explanation of suicide for any focus on the intentions of the individual attempting suicide, nor the way in which they do so, the significance that the individual and others attribute to the act of suicide, or the rites celebrated before and after the act.[95] In his recent impressive attempt to rectify these omissions, Marzio Barbagli relies upon psychiatric, societal and cultural factors to distinguish four types of suicide. While this more refined approach shines a light on the different reasons for suicide and its ambiguous position as, at different times, both choice and (medical or social) symptom, it does not detract from the historical significance of Durkheim's quest to find the social causes of suicide.

In removing the responsibility from the person who attempts or commits suicide, the sociogenic model of suicide joined with the medical model to transform understandings of suicide in the late nineteenth and early twentieth century, without which decriminalisation could never have occurred. As Moore argues:

> So steady was the promotion of the idea that suicide was caused, and so unwavering its advocates, that by the 1950s, the conception of self-killing as a symptom of a pathology – either of the individual or society – had assured virtually the status of a cliché, and the scene was set for it to be formally removed from criminal justice jurisdiction.[96]

This determinist approach removed responsibility from the perpetuator, rendering the criminalisation of suicide inappropriate, but also importantly reconfirmed state responsibility to take steps to prevent suicide.[97] Such steps could have related to social measures to counter Durkheim's focus on the social causes of suicide, but it was in fact the medical model of mental illness that was pursued. Those at risk of suicide would be 'treated'. The switch from punishing a sin to treating a disorder was complete. When decriminalisation finally came before Parliament, in the form of the Suicide Bill, Moore notes that 'not a single speaker dissented from the idea that the appropriate response to attempted suicide was treatment'.[98]

Changes in the perceived role of the criminal justice system also played their part in decriminalisation of suicide. In the late 1950s, in the context of rising crime and a growing prison population, Rab Butler's White Paper on 'Penal Practice in a Changing Society' included a commitment to 'deal with that part

[94] See Barbagli (n 4).
[95] ibid 8.
[96] Moore (n 67) 51.
[97] ibid 68–72.
[98] ibid 72. See further ch 3 below.

of the prison population which could be and should be avoided by adequate alternatives'.[99] The medical model of suicide provided a clear alternative. Although not many persons were given prison sentences for attempted suicide, most who were charged with it were, as noted above, remanded in custody. Thus, a medical model which would provide treatment to a person who had attempted suicide outwith the criminal justice system was a promising means of reducing the prison population. The Mental Health Act 1959 finally made such a treatment-centred approach a viable option by providing civil powers of detention. As will be discussed further in the following chapter, the decriminalisation of suicide ironically represented a tightening of control over those who attempted suicide but, as with its contemporary, the legalisation of abortion, it replaced a criminal justice jurisdiction with a medical jurisdiction. It was soon to be doctors, rather than the police, who would bear primary responsibility for preventing suicide.

The way in which the law has dealt with attempted suicide nicely illustrates its approach to suicide more generally, with a clear evolution from punishment to prevention (to be followed by tolerance and, potentially, right). Until the eighteenth century, there were some severe legal punishments following a suicide, but it was only in the nineteenth century that failed attempts to commit suicide might be met with arrests and detention. Once acknowledged as a crime, there was increasing legal pressure to prevent suicide. Later, as we shall see, the twentieth century saw a move towards, and perhaps beyond, the legal tolerance of suicide.

VII. Conclusion

The law which once sought to condemn and punish suicide, by the mid-twentieth century sought only to prevent it. The long connection between suicide and insanity, first used crudely and pragmatically by coroner's juries to protect the reputation and property of the families of the deceased, and later commandeered by the medical profession to establish jurisdiction over attempted suicide, eventually provided the excuse for decriminalisation. If attempting suicide is a symptom of a mental illness, then not only should there be no criminal liability for it, but also the illness could be treated and thus suicide prevented. Unfortunately, this assumption that all those who attempt suicide are mentally ill is just as much a convenient label as the earlier assumption that they were all sinners before God.

[99] 'Penal Practice in a Changing Society: Aspects of Future Development (England and Wales)' (1958) Cmnd 645.

The law's operation during the nineteenth and early twentieth centuries was pragmatically softened by those charged with enforcing it. From coroner's juries returning findings of *non compos mentis* for almost all who took their own lives, to the new police forces arresting the suicidal but not prosecuting them, to magistrates avoiding sentences of imprisonment after the obligatory period in remand to facilitate both spiritual and medical assistance, the felony of suicide and attempted suicide had ceased to be a reflection of society's approach to these issues long before 1961. What the coroner's juries, police, priests and magistrates recognised, long before the parliamentarians, is that there are many different types of suicide and the criminal law is too blunt an instrument to deal with them all.

3

The Legalisation of Suicide

This chapter explores the most significant step in the evolution of the law's role in respect of suicide: that of its decriminalisation in the Suicide Act 1961. We will begin by looking at the impetus for legalisation, before tracing the Act's surprisingly low-key passage through Parliament. Further legislative change came in 2009 when the wording of the enduring offence of assisted suicide was amended; policy change came from the Director of Public Prosecutions in 2010; and increasingly the courts have had to grapple with how to interpret an offence that criminalises the assistance of a perfectly lawful action. Today there remain challenging questions about whether suicide is a right, whether assistance can ever lawfully be provided and in what circumstances there might be a legal duty to prevent suicide. We will see therefore that decriminalising suicide and its attempt has done little to resolve the underlying debate about whether suicide should be condemned or respected; prevented or assisted; understood or treated.

I. Impetus for Legalisation

As discussed in the previous chapter, by the mid-twentieth century, it was widely accepted that the law's primary role in relation to suicide was prevention rather than punishment and that the medical treatment of those who attempted suicide was a more effective means of prevention than a custodial sentence. Before suicide, and its attempt, could realistically be legalised, however, there were a handful of concerns that would have to be overcome. These concerns were medical, religious, legal and political in nature. First, from a medical viewpoint, there would need to be an alternative legal mechanism for providing *treatment* to those who attempted suicide; secondly, the *religious* perception of suicide as a mortal sin which required criminal prohibition would need to be side-stepped; thirdly, there would need to be a solution found to the *legal* difficulty that those who pressured the vulnerable to commit suicide should still be guilty of an offence; and finally, from a *political perspective*, a lack of objection to legalisation would need to be transformed into a positive desire to legalise, with all that entails in terms of finding parliamentary time and governmental support. This section investigates how each of those concerns were overcome in the late 1950s to clear the way for the legalisation of suicide.

A. The Treatment Concern – The Mental Health Act 1959

The Mental Health Act 1959 (MHA 1959) was highly significant to the legalisation of suicide because it provided alternative powers to detain and/or treat persons who had attempted suicide. Perhaps of greatest relevance is section 136, which provided the police with power to remove someone suspected of mental disorder to a place of safety if she appears to be in immediate need of care or control and it appears necessary to do so in the interests of that person or for the protection of other persons. The person may then be detained for up to 72 hours with the purpose of enabling them to be examined by a doctor and interviewed by a mental welfare officer. This may then lead into the use of the further powers in sections 25–29. Under section 25, a patient may be compulsorily admitted to hospital for observation for a period of 28 days on the basis of written recommendations by two doctors certifying: a) that she is suffering from mental disorder of a nature or degree which warrants the detention of the patient in a hospital under observation; and b) that she ought to be so detained in the interests of her own health or safety or with a view to the protection of other persons.

A longer detention power is included in section 26, under which a patient may be compulsorily admitted to hospital for treatment. This section further requires that the mental disorder from which the patient is suffering be either mental illness or severe subnormality or, for patients under the age of 21 years, psychopathic disorder or subnormality. Under section 27, an application for the admission of a patient for either observation or treatment may be made either by the nearest relative of the patient or by a mental welfare officer. These all concern civil commitment powers, but in addition, under section 60(1) courts were now permitted to impose a compulsory hospital order if two doctors certified mental disorder, either after conviction or 'if the court is satisfied that the accused did the act or made the omission charged, the court may, if it thinks fit, make such an order without convicting him'. These represented extremely broad powers of detention and treatment which might today raise some concerns about the rights of the patient. At the time, however, they were perceived as an enlightened way to tackle mental disorder by means of diverting from the criminal justice arena.

Indeed, perhaps the most significant aspect of the MHA 1959 in the context of suicide is its implementation of the recommendations of the Percy Commission[1] that if a criminal offence is due to mental illness, it should not be punished but rather the underlying illness treated and thus the offender should be placed within medical jurisdiction. Obviously such an approach would suggest that if a suicide attempt is caused by mental illness, the criminal justice system is not the appropriate forum in which to deal with it. Given that a link had previously

[1] Royal Commission on the Law Relating to Mental Illness and Mental Deficiency (Percy Commission) Report (Cmnd 169, 1957).

been established between mental illness and suicide (as discussed in the previous chapter), it was clear that the criminalisation of attempted suicide would be increasingly difficult to justify for two reasons: because alternative powers now existed for compulsory intervention; and because the criminalisation of a symptom of a mental illness was now regarded as inappropriate. However, as with the legalisation of abortion later in the 1960s, decriminalisation of attempted suicide was to be less a relinquishing of control over the issue and more a transfer of control from the police, courts and prisons to doctors, social workers and hospitals. For many, this was reassuring and facilitated the passage of the Suicide Act 1961, but it also meant that any autonomy issues surrounding competent choices to die were ignored at this crucial stage.

B. The Religious Objection – The Church of England's 'Ought Suicide to be a Crime?' Report

In October 1959, the Church of England issued an information booklet with the startling title 'Ought Suicide to be a Crime?' to which the answer within the booklet was a surprising no. Given the church's views on suicide as a mortal sin, and its role in the criminal sanctioning of suicide through history, this appears to be a radical change in approach and one that was subsequently, and not surprisingly, relied upon in parliamentary debates on the 1961 Bill to demonstrate that the Church of England had no enduring objection to the legalisation of suicide. However, the significance given to the booklet overstated its providence and conclusions. The booklet was drafted by a committee of only four members, and they did not seek the views of anyone else when drafting the booklet.[2] Although the committee reached general agreement that the law should be changed, it did not reach agreement on whether suicide remained culpable, nor on whether what is a sin should necessarily be a crime. Indeed, the committee side-stepped the difficult question of whether suicide itself should be a crime by focusing instead on whether *attempted* suicide should be a crime. In other words, it concentrated on the practical difficulties of prosecuting attempted suicide, without resolving the more challenging theoretical question of whether suicide itself should necessarily be a crime because it is perceived to be a sin.[3] Thus, the introduction to the booklet states, 'in the present century we have come to feel that the would-be

[2] S Moore, *The Decriminalisation of Suicide* (PhD thesis, LSE, 2000) 136, available at etheses.lse.ac.uk/1573/1/U136493.pdf). The committee comprised John Christie, Principle of Jesus College Oxford; Dr Doris Odlum, consulting psychiatrist for psychological medicine at Elizabeth Garret Anderson Hospital (and already a prominent legalisation advocate); Rupert Cross, Fellow and Tutor in Law at Magdalen College Oxford; and Canon LT Ramsey, Professor of Philosophy of the Christian Religion at Oxford.

[3] ibid 135.

suicide stood more in need of medical or spiritual help than of conviction in a law court' and yet continued to declare that 'suicide is an act which surely demands some kind of moral judgment from us; we cannot treat it merely as a mental aberration'.[4] The link between suicide and mental health was clear in the booklet. It stated that 'there are not many suicides which can nowadays be regarded as wholly voluntary and deliberate'.[5] Thus, the booklet distinguishes between four kinds of suicide; three carrying 'no fault', but the fourth being 'voluntary and selfish' and therefore culpable, albeit not by the criminal law but rather by an alternative burial service to mark its moral guilt.[6]

The booklet was, therefore, limited in its significance. It did not represent the views of more than a small committee of experts from different disciplines and it did not really grapple with the difficult question of whether the 'sin' of suicide should remain criminalised. Nonetheless, its existence soon took on a heightened significance in the legalisation debate. This began by its presentation by the church as an enterprise initiated by the Archbishop of Canterbury, when the evidence suggests that this was not the case.[7] It was then reported in the press as the official Church of England view[8] and subsequently relied upon by the Home Secretary (and architect of the Suicide Bill) Rab Butler to demonstrate that legalisation was 'not likely to be controversial'[9] when proposing this step to the Prime Minister.[10] Church approval for the Suicide Bill was also relied upon during the parliamentary debates, including by Lord Kilmour when introducing the Bill into the House of Lords.[11] Indeed, it acquired an almost mythical status, given a significance far beyond its remit. Lord Silkin (the opposition spokesman), for example, spoke of the influence of the 'very fine pamphlet which has been issued by the Churches'.[12] Thus, not only was the information booklet seen as representing the views of the entire Church of England but now also apparently other churches.

However, it is likely that the booklet did not represent the views of many members of even the Church of England. Moore points out that there is some

[4] Quoted by Moore (ibid 148).

[5] ibid 145.

[6] ibid 146. This conclusion was opposed by Dr Odlum, who rejected any application of 'guilt' to a suicide.

[7] Although later presented as an initiative of the Archbishop of Canterbury, Moore discovered that the idea for the committee was first proposed in March 1958 by the Secretary to the Church of England's Council for Moral Welfare, Rev Dunstan, who wrote to the Archbishop of Canterbury informing him that the Board for Social Responsibility intended to set up a small group to look at the question of whether attempted suicide should remain a crime (Moore, ibid 137). The Archbishop, Geoffrey Fisher, replied acknowledging that he could 'see no grounds on which it is possible to go on treating attempted suicide as a crime', noting that it 'seems to be very definitely more a piece of private morality than, for example, adultery, which is not a crime'. (Letter of 22 March 1958, quoted by Moore, ibid 139–40.)

[8] Moore, ibid 153–54.

[9] ibid 217–18.

[10] The booklet is even appended to the government files on the Suicide Act 1961 at the public records office (ibid 133.)

[11] Hansard, HL (series 5) Vol 229, col 249 (2 March 1961).

[12] ibid, col 254.

evidence during the parliamentary debates on the Suicide Bill that there was a 'religiously based unease about decriminalising a deeply sinful act'.[13] Even Lord Bishop of Carlisle, when speaking on the Suicide Bill in the House of Lords, said he was 'not even satisfied with this report produced by a committee of my own Church, because I feel that there is not strong enough witness borne in it to what I call the sacredness of every human life'.[14] Yet, the existence of the booklet, with its provocative title and apparent high-status support, pre-empted religious debate on the issue and averted religious objection to the Bill. Given the significance of church opposition to other social reforms of the era, including abortion, obscenity, blasphemy and divorce, the lack of objection to the legalisation of suicide was extraordinary and indeed went even further to perceived active support for the Bill. When coupled with the strikingly low-key passage of the Bill through Parliament, the legalisation of suicide can be said to have mysteriously side-stepped moral opposition. Indeed, it is highly likely that in the early 1960s, there remained many people who supported the criminalisation of suicide. The controversial nature of any recent debates on legalisation of assisted suicide, suggest that it remains a highly controversial topic, and yet none of that moral or religious controversy was apparent in 1961 when suicide was legalised. As Moore argues, the only plausible answer for why the Church did not oppose legalisation is that 'most church people did not know it was happening, and would have opposed it if they did'.[15] If such opposition had materialised at the time, it is very unlikely that the Government would have proceeded with legalisation at a time when it was far from a high priority for it.

C. The Political Perspective – Parliamentary Interest in the Issue

On 6 February 1958, backbench Labour MP Kenneth Robinson asked the Home Secretary Rab Butler whether he would introduce legislation to amend the law relating to suicide.[16] Butler responded that he was 'not satisfied that any change in the law is desirable', adding that there was no evidence that 'the alteration of the basic concept would be universally acceptable to public opinion'.[17] While this was not to change within the near future, nonetheless within three years, Butler would be behind the introduction of the Suicide Bill into Parliament. Robinson doggedly pursued the issue, notably asking for the average sentences of those imprisoned during the last five years after conviction for attempted suicide.

[13] Moore, *The Decriminalisation of Suicide* (2000) 166.
[14] Hansard (2 March 1961) col 259.
[15] Moore (n 2) 165.
[16] Hansard, HC (series 5) Vol 581, Oral Answers (6 February 1958).
[17] ibid.

Butler's written reply on 13 February 1958 revealed that 194 people had been imprisoned between 1952 and 1956 for attempting suicide. It is likely that that was a shock to many people, perhaps including Butler himself.[18] Certainly the issue seemed to gather momentum from then on.

On 28 February, an Early Day Motion advocating decriminalisation attracted 150 signatures.[19] Robinson would proceed to ask another dozen questions to Butler on the topic of suicide over the next couple of years but even by November 1958 the principle of decriminalisation appeared to have been conceded by Butler. In response to another question from Robinson, Butler stated:

> Before a change in the law is proposed, it is necessary to ensure that persons who attempt suicide and need care but cannot be given it, or will not accept it, unless they are brought before the courts, can be looked after by other means.[20]

As discussed above, the MHA 1959 would soon provide an elegant and well-timed solution to this dilemma. The point at which Butler was convinced of the need to decriminalise (presumably sometime during 1958) proved to be a crucial turning point in the law on suicide. He had a keen interest in both social reform and mental health.[21] Butler was also in an unusually strong position to influence domestic affairs at this time. Not only was he the Home Secretary, but simultaneously the Leader of the Commons and the Chairman of the Conservative Party. His influence over home office policy, parliamentary timetabling and party unity was unprecedented. It also proved crucial for the legalisation of suicide because it enabled him to skilfully manoeuvre the Suicide Bill through the Government and Parliament, bypassing the usual procedure and any political opposition. His first step was to seek resolution of the legal difficulties presented by decriminalisation.

D. The Legal Issue – The Criminal Law Revision Committee's Report 1960

The Criminal Law Revision Committee (CLRC) was set up by Butler in February 1959 with a remit to review the criminal law. The committee had 15 members, all legally distinguished names, including two Lord Justices, two

[18] Moore claims that 'It is probable that before this it was not widely known that people were being sent to prison for trying to kill themselves' (Moore (n 2) 186).

[19] ibid.

[20] Hansard, HC (series 5) Vol 594, Written Answers (6 November 1958).

[21] Moore points out that Butler served as President of the National Association of Mental Health (later MIND) for many years, and also had personal experience of mental health issues, having suffered two nervous breakdowns in younger life and having had an aunt commit suicide. His first wife had also died a slow death from cancer which might possibly have turned his mind to issues of the voluntary ending of life (Moore (n 2) 183–84.)

High Court judges, the Director of Public Prosecutions Sir Theobald Matthew, and Glanville Williams, whose 1958 book *The Sanctity of Life and the Criminal Law* had eloquently argued for legal reform on suicide as well as grappling with other significant criminal law issues.[22] In some ways, the CLRC was a precursor of the Law Commission, but with one significant difference; unlike the later body, the CLRC could not review matters on its own initiative but had to wait for a matter to be referred by the Home Secretary. In November 1959, the second issue referred to the committee by Butler was suicide law. More specifically, Butler referred the limited issue of what amendments in the criminal law might be required after decriminalisation of suicide in order to retain the criminality of assisting a suicide. This limited referral is significant because, as with the Church of England committee, and however it was later portrayed, the CLRC did not, and was not asked to, grapple with whether or not suicide should be legalised.

The CLRC report was published on 20 October 1960. It stuck to its remit and produced a solution to the need to retain a criminal offence of assisting a suicide, while decriminalising the action (or attempted action) itself. The committee produced what was to become section 2 of the Suicide Act 1961 and the report (unusually) included parliamentary drafting of that clause. Three days before the report was published, Butler chaired a meeting of the Cabinet Home Affairs Committee which agreed that

> the government should introduce a Bill early in the next session on the lines recommended by the CLRC to provide that suicide and attempted suicide shall cease to be offences and that complicity in another person's suicide or attempted suicide shall be punishable by a maximum of 14 years imprisonment.[23]

That same day he wrote to the Lord Chancellor recommending legislation be introduced early in the next session along the lines of the CLRC's report[24] and on the following day he wrote to the Prime Minister, Harold Macmillan, proposing the same.[25] In that latter letter, Butler added that the measure was 'not likely to be controversial' because the Church Assembly Board for Social Responsibility had published a report 'which is broadly in line with what we propose'. He also, in a handwritten addition, pointed out the distinguished nature of the members of the CLRC, writing that the committee 'has no less than four judges and other notables, so the backing is weighty'.[26] By means of this letter to the PM – the first formal proposal for reform of the law on suicide – Butler gives the impression that there is clear support for the decriminalisation of suicide by both the Law and the Church. In reality, it is doubtful that such support existed. As we have seen, the church booklet was the view of only a handful of experts and the CLRC

[22] G Williams, *The Sanctity of Life and the Criminal Law* (London, Faber & Faber, 1958).
[23] Letter to Prime Minister, 18 October 1960, quoted in Moore (n 2) 217–18.
[24] Moore (n 2) 216.
[25] ibid 217–18.
[26] ibid.

never considered the key question of whether or not suicide or attempted suicide should be decriminalised. On the basis of Butler's letter, the Prime Minister agreed and the Suicide Bill was placed on the agenda of a Cabinet Meeting on 25 October 1960.[27] According to Moore, that meeting involved the much more pressing issue of NHS charges, about which there was lengthy debate.[28] Butler then introduced the suicide issue with the comment that 'it has widespread support' and the minutes record that the Home Secretary's submission on a Suicide Bill was 'noted with approval'.[29]

Thus, a Bill which had not followed the usual procedure for governmental approval was soon to be introduced into Parliament. It is worth noting that the legalisation of suicide was not in any of the political parties' manifestos for the October 1959 general election. Nor was it in the list of Bills for the 1960–61 parliamentary session laid before the Future Legislation Committee (notably chaired by Butler) in 1959–60. It only appeared mid-way down the list of Bills 'for handing to private members in the ballot' given to Cabinet in June 1960 (and thus had no chance of becoming law). It was ultimately approved by Cabinet without discussion in October 1960. Moore, who has written a detailed thesis on the decriminalisation of suicide, convincingly argues that Butler 'put the Bill through almost single handedly'. She explains how he

> completely by-passed the traditional, long-settled route for Government legislation and inserted the Suicide Bill into an already crowded Government legislative agenda at the last minute, without discussion or preamble and certainly without any of the long gestation (pressure groups, committees of enquiry, royal commissions, white papers) that usually precedes social reform legislation.[30]

The low-key approach to the issue was to continue throughout the Bill's parliamentary passage. Despite Butler's reassurances, decriminalising this ancient felony was not uncontroversial; indeed, amongst many members of society it is likely that it would have been a highly controversial measure (much as attempts to legalise assisted suicide are today). The lack of opposition to the legal reform appears to be due not so much to widespread agreement with it, but by a lack of awareness of its occurrence.

E. Conclusion

There was, as discussed in the previous chapter, a genuinely revised view of suicide by the mid-twentieth century; one that focused on prevention rather than punishment. The civil detention powers in the MHA 1959 cleared the way

[27] ibid 219–20.
[28] ibid.
[29] ibid.
[30] ibid 169.

for an alternative, but still compulsory, means of helping (and yet also controlling) those who attempted suicide. Nonetheless, the actual immediate impetus for decriminalisation in 1961 revolved around a series of coincidences: the well-timed information booklet from the Church of England that could be used to remove apparently blatant religious opposition to reform; the dogged attempts by a backbencher to put suicide on the political agenda; a Home Secretary, sympathetic to social reform and mental health issues, who had the power and character to introduce the Bill through the backdoor, thus avoiding any public (or political) controversy. Perhaps the most significant aspect of the moves to decriminalise suicide, however, is that the central issue was never openly discussed; never formed part of parliamentary debates; was never the topic of public consultation. The decision that suicide should no longer be a crime was taken somewhere backstage, not in the public arena. Instead, it was the technicalities that were the focus of both pre-legislative scrutiny by the CLRC and parliamentary scrutiny by both Houses of Parliament. Decriminalisation of suicide in 1961 was undoubtedly a positive move but it is shocking that such a significant legal step was taken in such a low-key manner. Arguably, this has allowed conflicts to fester and has created continued ambiguity about the appropriate role of the law in regulating the now-decriminalised suicide.

II. Parliamentary Passage of the Suicide Bill

The Suicide Bill was introduced into Parliament in February 1961 and remained unchanged throughout its parliamentary passage. It is short and concise. The first section simply states that 'The rule of law whereby it is a crime for a person to commit suicide is hereby abrogated'. This is then followed by a somewhat more complex section 2 which states that: 'A person who aids, abets, counsels or procures the suicide of another, or attempt by another to commit suicide shall be liable on conviction on indictment to imprisonment for a term not exceeding fourteen years'. Thus the Bill decriminalises suicide, and by implication attempted suicide, but also creates a new statutory offence of aiding or abetting the suicide or attempted suicide of another. That offence is, of course, a unique one because it criminalises assisting an action that is in itself perfectly lawful.[31] It demonstrates the legal consequences that flowed from suicide being treated as a felony, even though nobody could ever be convicted of that principal offence (because they would by definition be deceased). Suicide as a felony meant that, firstly, attempted suicide, as it amounted to an attempted felony, was a misdemeanour; secondly, killing another while in the course of committing the felony of suicide amounted to murder; and thirdly, an accessory to the felony of suicide was guilty

[31] In D Ormerod and K Laird, *Smith, Hogan and Ormerod's Criminal Law*, 16th edn (Oxford, Oxford University Press, 2021), Ormerod describes the offence as 'an odd one' (668).

of murder as an accessory.[32] Thus, the decriminalisation of the felony of suicide in the Suicide Bill would have implications beyond the deceased themselves. That it also by implication legalised attempted suicide was indeed the main purpose of the Bill.

That it was no longer necessarily murder to kill someone else while attempting to kill oneself seems a just solution, given the merciless outcome of the recent case of *R v Spence (George)*[33] in 1957. In this case, the deceased had been killed in the course of a struggle for a knife which her partner intended to use to stab himself. Glyn-Jones J directed the jury that if the deceased was struck by the knife which was at that moment being using for the purpose of taking the defendant's own life then, as he was engaged in the felony of self-murder, the killing was murder even if he did not intend to kill her. This approach was confirmed on appeal and the death sentence was upheld. Thus, only four years before the legalisation of suicide, a man was sentenced to death for accidentally killing someone who was trying to prevent him killing himself. One consequence of the Suicide Bill was that such unfortunate circumstances would no longer amount to murder, although they would of course still result in criminal liability for manslaughter. More difficult, however, was the consequence of legalisation of suicide for accessories to that death. Since there would no longer be any principal offence committed by the suicidal person, there was no crime to aid and abet. This was the specific issue referred by Butler to the CLRC and it was that committee's solution that formed clause 2 of the Bill. It creates a new offence of aiding, abetting, counselling or procuring the suicide (or attempted suicide) of another, and it was to prove the most debated part of the Bill in its hurried parliamentary passage.

A. House of Lords

The Suicide Bill was given its first reading in the House of Lords on 15 February 1961. The choice of introducing the Bill into the Lords rather than the Commons seems to be another aspect of Butler's expert manoeuvring of the Bill through Cabinet and Parliament while attracting minimum attention. As Moore points out, this involved not bringing the Bill before the Future Legislation Committee, slipping it into a Cabinet meeting focused on other things, introducing it into Parliament via the Lords rather than the Commons, and never himself appearing in connection with the Bill.[34] The Bill's second reading debate was held on 2 March 1961. The Bill was introduced by the Lord Chancellor Viscount Kilmuir[35] (although

[32] ibid 667.

[33] *R. v Spence (George)* (1957) 41 Cr App R 80.

[34] Moore (n 2) 182.

[35] Previously the MP David Maxwell-Fyfe, who had been particularly influential in respect of the drafting of the European Convention on Human Rights and served as Home Secretary from 1951 to 1954.

Moore claims that his speech was sent to him from the Home Office, suggesting Butler's influence once more).[36] Lord Kilmuir explained that the Bill was part of the Government's programme of reform to bring the criminal law up to date:

> Wherever and however we may place the motives of those who take their own lives in the scale of human values, I think we can agree that they have little or nothing in common with what we should nowadays generally characterise as criminal intent.[37]

He added that 'it has for some time been widely felt to be inappropriate' that suicide should remain a criminal offence, referring to the familiar arguments that the person who has committed the crime is beyond the reach of punishment, it is not an effective deterrent and only adds to the distress of relatives.[38]

In his opening speech, Lord Kilmuir also emphasised that attempted suicide is 'very often a sign that medical and social help is wanted' and explained that 'the only justification for retaining the offence has been that it has provided a means of bringing before the courts, and perhaps helping, those who have made suicidal attempts'.[39] He continued by referring to the practical problem of whether alternative methods are available for providing such help and referred to the MHA 1959 as providing the solution to that obstacle.[40] In line with the general downplaying of the significance and controversy of the Bill, Lord Kilmuir finished his speech by describing it as 'a limited measure' and one 'supported by religious opinion, the medical profession and magistrates'.[41]

Only five other people spoke in the House of Lords' second reading debate: Lord Silkin (the shadow Lord Chancellor); Baroness Summerskill (the shadow Minister of Health); Baroness Wooton; Lord Denning; and the Lord Bishop of Carlisle. None of them opposed the Bill and the debate lasted less than two hours. Lord Silkin, speaking for the opposition, said that he welcomed the Bill and that 'I think everyone in this House will'.[42] As mentioned above, Lord Bishop of Carlisle expressed some concerns from a religious point of view. While he was willing to support the Bill because he believed it was 'motivated by compassion',[43] he was concerned that clause 2 was not strong enough 'to convey to everyone that to take life, one's own life, is literally a dreadful thing, contrary to natural instinct and contrary to natural law'.[44] However, what Lord Bishop of Carlisle appeared to want added to the Bill was a means of compulsory treatment, which arguably was already provided by the MHA 1959. Lord Denning, not surprisingly, focused on legal issues and noted the illogicality of the clause 2 offence: 'It is aiding and

[36] Moore (n 2) 220.
[37] Hansard, HL (series 5) Vol 229, col 247 (2 March 1961).
[38] ibid.
[39] ibid 248.
[40] ibid 250.
[41] ibid 253.
[42] ibid 257.
[43] ibid 258.
[44] ibid 259.

abetting an offence which is not an offence, if your Lordships see what I mean, and it's quite illogical'.[45] Nonetheless, he conceded that it 'may be necessary'[46] although he also suggested an alternative under which 'suicide is still unlawful, although it is not a crime, and therefore you can aid and abet it'.[47]

The Bill proceeded to Committee Stage on 9 March 1961 when it was taken by a Committee of the Whole House. Lord Silkin proposed the addition of 'attempt to commit' to clause 1 to make clear that it is also no longer an offence to attempt suicide, but Lord Kilmuir pointed out that this is unnecessary because the rule that attempted suicide is a crime depends upon the common law rule that an attempt to commit a felony is itself a crime and thus when that felony is abolished, so too will be the crime of attempted suicide.[48] More significantly, Lord Silkin also proposed a mechanism for compulsory treatment for those who attempt suicide extending beyond the powers in the MHA 1959. Lord Kilmuir resisted this addition, however, on the basis that there would only be a few cases in which a person who has attempted suicide would not receive treatment, either voluntarily or under the MHA 1959, and that it would be impossible to identify those few in advance.[49] Interestingly, Lord Kilmuir also pointed out that the addition of a compulsory treatment clause within the Bill 'would be to take away from attempted suicide the stigma of criminal conduct and replace it by a presumption of mental illness to which, in the eyes of some people, some stigma still attaches'.[50] There was also some discussion during the committee stage about the appropriate sentence for the clause 2 offence. Lord Silkin moved to reduce the maximum sentence from 14 years to seven years, but Lord Kilmuir pointed out that the 14 years is still a reduction from the current position in which the offence would amount to murder and be given a life sentence. The discrepancy between the same maximum sentences for aiding and abetting suicide and surviving a suicide pact was also discussed by the committee but this discrepancy was easily defended by the Government as, due to the Bill's amendments to the Homicide Act 1957, participating in a suicide pact under the 1957 Act would now only apply where the deceased had been killed by another rather than committed suicide. Thus the longer sentence for participating in a suicide pact seemed justified.

The Bill emerged unchanged from the committee stage and the report stage was then held on 16 March 1961. Lord Silkin and Baroness Wootton took this opportunity to again press the point about the maximum sentence being too high and also inconsistent with the sentence for a suicide pact (apparently missing the

[45] ibid 265.

[46] ibid. Although regrettably his reason for this does not read well today: 'you might get the troublesome case where a man was anxious that his wife should commit suicide and might be quite ready to aid and abet'.

[47] ibid 266.

[48] Hansard, HL (series 5) Vol 229, col 537 (9 March 1961).

[49] ibid 542.

[50] ibid 543.

crucial distinction of who kills) but withdrew their motions after Lord Kilmuir repeated his previous explanations. A final proposed amendment (based on a letter to The Times by Glanville Williams) that suicide shall not invalidate a life insurance policy unless the policy expressly states so or the suicide is within two years of the policy was also unsuccessful once Lord Kilmuir emphasised the general rule of insurance law that one should not profit from insurance when bringing about the result oneself, regardless of whether it is a crime.[51]

Thus, the Bill's progress through the House of Lords was unproblematic. It proceeded to the House of Commons unchanged and having faced little scrutiny and no opposition. Any reservations about this landmark Bill related only to the technicalities of clause 2; no one questioned the merits of decriminalising suicide.

B. House of Commons

Charles Fletcher-Cooke, the new Parliamentary-Under-Secretary of State in the Home Office, was given the responsibility of taking the Suicide Bill through the Commons. As pointed out above, the Home Secretary, whatever his role behind the scenes, never appeared publicly linked to the Bill. The second reading debate of the Bill was held on 14 July 1961. It was a Friday afternoon; the debate began at 3.27pm with the House adjourning at 4pm. Fletcher-Cooke introduced the Bill as 'a further stage in our endeavour to bring the provisions of the criminal law into conformity with the needs and outlook of the present day'.[52] He also emphasised the need for treatment to be available to those who attempt suicide and explained that 'it cannot be right to make use of criminal proceedings merely for the purpose of providing medical and social assistance to people in distress if some other and more appropriate method of giving that assistance can be found'.[53] He then proceeded to explain that the Minister of Health was making arrangements to ensure that persons who were taken to hospital having attempted suicide are 'examined so that need for treatment or supervision can be assessed', and he referred to the MHA 1959's 28- day assessment power of detention.[54]

It is interesting that, as in the House of Lords, the Government's approach was to focus on the practical problem of finding alternative means of providing treatment to those who attempt suicide. By implication it is assumed that the only remaining purpose of the crime of attempted suicide is to help those who have attempted suicide. This is a revolutionary change in outlook from the recent past, where it was the nature of suicide as a mortal sin that was thought to require, if not punishment, at least condemnation. Indeed, in Glanville Williams' 1958

[51] Hansard, HL (series 5) Vol 229, col 988 (16 March 1961).
[52] Hansard, HC (series 5) Vol 644, col 833 (14 July 1961).
[53] ibid 834.
[54] ibid 839.

book, he refers to a case from 1950 in which the Chairman of the Rochester Bench sent a woman to Holloway for six months following two attempts to commit suicide, saying 'You have been here before and we gave you every opportunity to go straight'.[55] This does not give the sense of general agreement that the only enduring purpose of the offence of attempted suicide is as a mechanism to provide treatment. The suggestion that a woman (who Williams claims showed 'symptoms of being unbalanced') should be punished for not 'going straight' after her first attempt to take her own life carries with it a judgemental tone, which perhaps may more accurately reflect the enforcement of the offence in the mid-twentieth century than the government's euphemistic treatment focus. But the emphasis on alternative means of providing treatment enabled the Government to side-step the surely more controversial question of whether suicide/attempted suicide merits moral and/or legal condemnation. Despite the lack of opposition to the Bill, there are numerous examples of speakers in the parliamentary debates reminding us of the immorality of suicide, but they do not proceed to consider whether that moral judgment should be backed up by the law.

Fletcher-Cooke ended his introduction to the Bill by noting that he had been 'extremely brief' in the wish that 'this Bill, which I am sure commands almost universal approval, should get to the Statute Book as quickly as possible in this crowded time of the year'.[56] This hurried approach did not go down well with some other Members of Parliament. Leo Abse described it as 'disgraceful' that the Bill should be hurried through within half an hour.[57] Eric Fletcher (the opposition spokesman) also noted that it was 'a little unfortunate that a Bill of this importance – although it is non-controversial, in a party sense – should be brought on at this hour'. Indeed, Fletcher expressly recognised the great significance of the Bill, describing it as of 'great social consequence' because it sought to change what has been the law of England 'for nearly 1,000 years' and because suicide 'has been regarded as the most heinous of felonies'.[58] He also referred to an assumption that 'the community has a responsibility to try to preserve the life of a person who wants to end it', which Parliament had implicitly confirmed as recently as 1957 when passing the Homicide Act, and he hoped that the Suicide Bill did not depart from that assumption.[59] This is a significant point because, if we accept its accuracy, it raises two questions of broader importance: why does the community have this responsibility to interfere with an autonomous decision to die; and how far can society go in preserving life? Is the use of force or compulsory detention required if that proves necessary to save life? These are questions never really answered

[55] Williams, *The Sanctity of Life* (1958) 252.
[56] Hansard (14 July 1961) 835.
[57] ibid.
[58] ibid 836.
[59] ibid 837.

during Parliament's passage of the Suicide Bill and yet the assumption that even legalisation of suicide does not remove this community responsibility to try to prevent suicide still endures and has proven difficult to clarify. We will return to these fundamental questions throughout the book. During the second reading debate, it was certainly clear that some members would not be dissuaded from their moral view that suicide was intrinsically wrong. Fletcher claimed that suicide 'is regarded by the majority of people as a dreadful offence against nature'[60] and John Hobson concurred that it should be publicly realised that suicide 'remains a mortal sin'.[61]

The Government did not achieve its goal of hurrying the second reading debate through in half an hour on a Friday afternoon because Leo Abse controversially talked it out, saying that he did not agree that the Bill should be hurried through the House.[62] In doing so, Abse argued that the Bill 'is stamped with a lot of mock courage' because 'we are courageously declaring in 1961 that a dead man is not a criminal'.[63] The adjournment of the debate raised a real possibility of the Bill lapsing before the end of the parliamentary session. However, it returned to the House on Wednesday 19 July in a late-night slot, with debate commencing at 11.54pm and the question being put at 12.47am. When debate resumed, Abse continued his speech by complaining that the Bill did nothing to reduce the number of suicides, noting that during the 1950s, deaths by suicide exceeded deaths by road accidents.[64] Perhaps the most interesting point made during this debate, however, was by BT Parkin, who argued that anyone who voted to pass clause 1 could be guilty of an offence under clause 2 unless improvements were made in welfare services.[65] Fletcher-Cooke concluded the second reading debate by emphasising that the Government did not wish to encourage suicide, noting that many people regarded it as a mortal sin and agreeing that there was a duty instead to 'stick it out'.[66] The Bill was agreed without division.

The Bill's committee stage was held on 25 July and lasted only 100 minutes. Twenty members were appointed to the committee, but only 15 attended and only seven spoke.[67] The Bill remained unamended. When it returned to the House for the third reading on 28 July 1961, the discussion was again brief and the Bill was again passed without division. It was given Royal Assent on 3 August 1961.

[60] ibid 838.
[61] ibid 841.
[62] ibid 844–45. Moore quotes from Abse's autobiography in which he explained that he supported the Bill but 'would rather lose the Bill than corroborate in the morbid stealth of the government': Moore (n 2) 231.
[63] ibid 844.
[64] Hansard, HC (series 5) Vol 644, col 1409 (19 July 1961).
[65] ibid 1419.
[66] ibid 1426.
[67] Moore (n 2) 232.

Suicide was now lawful. And it was legalised without opposition and almost unnoticed. In the third reading debate, the government minister, Fletcher-Cooke, introduced the Bill by saying it had been 'universally welcomed and yet practically unnoticed, perhaps because it was universally welcomed'.[68] It seems just as likely, however, that the reverse is true: it was universally welcomed because it was unnoticed by those who might not have welcomed it. The opposition spokesman, Fletcher, wondered whether the Bill's passage through parliament 'practically unnoticed' was due to 'the vicissitudes of parliamentary timetable',[69] but in fact it owed much to Home Secretary Butler's adept handling of it.[70] The Bill was given very little parliamentary time (passing through the Commons in less than three hours in total) and the focus of discussion about it was on two issues only: the new statutory offence in clause 2; and the means of providing treatment to those who attempted suicide. The hugely significant legal change of clause 1 – the actual decriminalisation of the ancient felony of suicide – was barely mentioned. Moore quite rightly credits Butler with this political manoeuvring:

> [Butler] used the powerful positivist paradigm prevailing at the time and focused Parliament's attention firmly on the *treatment* of *attempted* suicide. He refused to engage with the profoundly difficult issue of suicide itself, allowing its moral status as a sin to remain unchallenged as long as it could be officially deemed not a crime.[71]

The legalisation of suicide was somewhat anti-climactic in terms of its parliamentary passage. After centuries of harsh condemnation and punishment for those who committed suicide and their families, and latterly for those who attempted suicide, its removal from the range of behaviours criminally prohibited was politically uncontroversial. Perhaps this was in part due to the gradual demolition of potential opposition to it. The MHA 1959 provided a neat answer to queries about how to ensure compulsory treatment to those who had attempted suicide, and the religious objection was side-stepped by reliance on an information booklet of limited scope. Even more significantly, however, the softening of the criminal law by those who enforced it which, as we saw in the previous chapter, had occurred throughout the last couple of centuries by means of coroner's juries, the police and magistrates ensured that suicide was already viewed as a tragedy to be averted rather than an aberration to be punished. Its removal from the criminal law by politicians was overdue. It did not, however, resolve the issue, and indeed the courts would remain troubled by questions relating to those who had taken, or wanted to take, their own lives for the remainder of the twentieth century and into the twenty-first. It is to the courtrooms that we will now adjourn.

[68] Hansard, HC (series 5) Vol 645, col 822 (28 July 1961).
[69] ibid 823.
[70] Moore writes of Butler's 'politically sophisticated guiding hand' (n 2, 237).
[71] ibid 237.

III. Suicide in the Courts after 1961

A. Suicide Pacts

Until 1957, the survivor of a suicide pact would face culpability as an accessory before the fact of (self-)murder, rendering them liable for murder and facing the death penalty.[72] An example of this stringent approach can be seen in the 1944 case of *R v Croft (William James)*.[73] Croft and the deceased, Joan Lewis, had mutually agreeed to commit suicide in a summer house on the night of 15 October 1943. Croft placed a loaded revolver in front of them and Lewis picked it up and discharged it, wounding but not killing herself. Now being in pain, she asked Croft to go for help and he climbed out of a window of the locked summer house intending to get assistance. However, he went only a few paces before the revolver was discharged a second time and Lewis (either intentionally or accidentally) fatally shot herself in the head. Croft was charged with murder and found guilty by a jury. Humphreys J passed a sentence of death. In an appeal against conviction, Croft argued that the survivor of a suicide pact who is not present when the crime is committed cannot be held to be an accessory before the fact. The Court of Criminal Appeal rejected this argument. Lawrence J delivering the judgment of the Court held that

> a mutual agreement to commit suicide amounts to such a counselling, procuring, inducing, advising or abetting as constitutes the survivor an accessory before the fact even if he is not present when the other party to the agreement commits suicide.[74]

Indeed, the distinction between those who aid and abet and accessories before the fact was held to be that those who aid and abet are present when the felony is committed, whilst accessories before the fact are absent. In order to escape liability as an accessory before the fact the defendant would have to establish that they 'expressly countermanded or revoked the advising, counselling, procuring, or abetting which he had previously given'.[75] In this case, the evidence did not support that and thus the appeal was dismissed. It is clear from this case that it did not matter in the eyes of the law that the deceased killed herself; Croft was held to have committed murder as an accessory simply due to the fact that, by entering into a suicide pact with her, he had simultaneously supported her own decision to end her life.

[72] Before 1861 it was not possible to be charged as accessory before the fact of suicide because it was necessary that the principal felon should first have been convicted which, of course, could not occur when the felony was suicide. So until 1861, the charge would be one of aiding and abetting.

[73] *R. v Croft (William James)* [1944] KB 295.

[74] ibid.

[75] ibid.

The position changed prior to the Suicide Act in the Homicide Act 1957, section 4 of which provides a partial defence to murder if there is a suicide pact. 'Suicide pact' is defined in section 4(3) to mean:

> [A] common agreement between two or more persons having for its object the death of all of them, whether or not each is to take his own life, but nothing done by a person who enters into a suicide pact shall be treated as done by him in pursuance of the pact unless it is done while he has the settled intention of dying in pursuance of the pact.

Therefore, the defendant has to prove that they were party to a suicide pact and also that they had a 'settled intention of dying' themselves. The Suicide Act 1961 changes the law in relation to suicide pacts again. The 1957 partial defence is now restricted to situations in which the defendant kills, or is party to a third person killing, the deceased as part of a suicide pact. In a situation, such as in *Croft*, where the deceased kills themselves, the 1961 Act offence of aiding and abetting suicide will be charged.

This distinction caused some consternation during the parliamentary debates on the 1961 Act. In both Houses, concern was expressed that there was inconsistency between the maximum sentences imposed for surviving a suicide pact under the Suicide Act and the 1957 Act. When government ministers explained that the two situations are distinguished by who causes the death, queries were raised about why this should matter. For example, Peter Kirk said 'which one is the active partner in the death seems to be quite immaterial'.[76] The distinction had been created by the CLRC, which took the view that 'there is greater offence in actually striking someone else than in striking oneself'.[77] This certainly is the view of the current law, and fits with the enduring criminalisation of assisting a suicide once suicide itself is lawful. However, arguably that crucial distinction is not sufficiently respected in relation to the law on suicide pacts. While liability under the 1961 Act for someone who enters into a suicide pact and survives seems consistent with the ethos of that Act, arguably the remaining offence of suicide pact manslaughter is not really about 'suicide' at all if the final step is not taken by the deceased. Such deaths are killing with consent which not only differs in principle from suicide, but is also arguably of a substantially different nature, and more serious, than assisting a suicide. While a reduction of liability from murder to manslaughter continues to be appropriate, the label of 'suicide' may be problematic in this context.

One thing that is clear following the Suicide Act 1961 is that the policy of the law remains opposed to suicide pacts and imposes liability upon those who enter into one (if they survive the event). The case of *R v Sweeney (Martin)*[78] in 1986

[76] Hansard, HC (series 5) Vol 644, col 1425 (19 July 1961).
[77] ibid (Fletcher-Cooke).
[78] *R v Sweeney (Martin)* (1986) 8 Cr App R (S) 419.

is illustrative of this. Twenty-five-year-old Sweeney was prone to depression and his 27-year-old wife suffered from advanced muscular dystrophy. They decided to commit suicide together by setting fire to their car while they were both inside it. They swallowed paracetamol and sleeping tablets, and then Sweeney poured petrol over the back seat of the car and set light to it. Both then desperately tried to escape from the car, with only Sweeney succeeding and Lewis unable to do so despite her husband's efforts to help her. Sweeney suffered serious burns to his face, hands and back and was permanently scarred. He pleaded guilty to manslaughter and was sentenced to four years' imprisonment which was then reduced to two years on appeal. The reduction in sentence was partly due to Sweeney's scars, which the Court of Appeal described as 'a constant reminder to him of the appalling thing which he did'.[79] It was also noted that he continued to be depressed and to constitute a suicide risk.[80] Nonetheless, the Court of Appeal was adamant of the law's role here:

> Sensible people will understand of course what brings people in the luckless position of these two to so desperate a state of mind. However, even people like them must be deterred from going to the extreme of terminating life. This is the policy of the law, guided by the public interest. It must therefore be plainly understood that those who contemplate suicide and do not successfully achieve it in a suicide pact will be punished if the other party to the pact dies.[81]

It appears that around three years' imprisonment is now regarded as an appropriate sentence for surviving a suicide pact. For example, in *R v England (Christopher Michael)*[82] a five-year sentence for aiding and abetting suicide was reduced to three years as being more appropriate for a failed suicide pact. In this case, the defendant and the deceased both took a large quantity of pills together, intending to commit suicide. It might be queried why England's actions amount to a crime. If he had taken the pills alone and survived, he would have faced no legal liability since attempted suicide was legalised in 1961. However, doing the same action in the company of another person doing the same not only creates culpability but results in a significant term of imprisonment. Indeed, it could be said that it is the actions of the deceased that have caused the liability for the defendant in these circumstances. In the case of *England*, however, the judge sought to justify the criminal liability by saying that the deceased was entitled to look to the defendant 'for sensible support and proper advice'[83] on the night of her death. This seems to suggest that there is a duty to dissuade a person from attempting suicide, perhaps especially if they are vulnerable, although perhaps more broadly. If true, this has significant consequences for the law's role in relation to suicide; consequences that have not been fully explored.

[79] ibid at 420.
[80] ibid at 421.
[81] ibid.
[82] *R v England (Christopher Michael)* (1990–91) 12 Cr App R (S) 98.
[83] ibid 99.

B. The New Statutory Offence of Assisted Suicide

As mentioned above, section 2 of the Suicide Act 1961 declared that it is an offence, punishable by up to 14 years' imprisonment, to aid, abet, counsel or procure the suicide of another, or attempt by another to commit suicide. The terminology of 'aid, abet, counsel or procure' is a familiar one in the criminal law. Generally, an aider and abetter will be present at the scene of the crime, encouraging its commission, while the counsellor or procurer will directly instigate or encourage the suicide. The section 2 offence encompasses a very wide range of culpability. This was true at its creation and remains the weakness of its current-day counterpart. This fact was recognised by Lord Lane CJ in *R v Hough* when he said that 'In terms of gravity it can vary from the borders of cold-blooded murder down to the shadowy area of mercy killing or common humanity'.[84]

Initially, the most problematic issue to face the courts when interpreting this offence was the question of whether there could be liability when no suicide could be directly linked to the actions of the defendant. Thus, in the 1978 case of *R v McShane (Yolande Tregenna)* a woman convicted of *attempting* to counsel or procure her mother's suicide appealed on the grounds that this was not an offence known to law. The Court of Appeal confirmed the general rule that every attempt to commit an offence is an offence in itself at common law.[85] This applies whether the crime attempted is one created by statute or at common law. Thus, if a defendant attempts to counsel or procure a suicide, that amounts to a criminal offence whether or not the person so counselled attempts suicide. The defence also argued that that the offence of attempting to counsel or procure a suicide is not committed unless the person counselled to commit suicide later forms an intention to do so, but this argument was also rejected by the Court of Appeal. *McShane* suggests, therefore, that counselling or procuring a suicide can be charged even if there is no actual suicide attempt and also even if the person counselled never intends to attempt suicide. This appears to draw the offence broader than might be imagined and puts the focus very much upon the actions of the counsellor rather than on the reactions of the 'victim'. It demonstrates how stringent is the law's protection for the sanctity of life.

A later case casts some doubt upon this approach, however. *Attorney-General v Able and Others*[86] from 1984 is perhaps the leading case on the original section 2 offence. In this case, the defendants were members of the executive committee of the Voluntary Euthanasia Society and had published a booklet entitled 'A guide to self-deliverance' for distribution to members of the society. The expressed aim of the booklet was to overcome the fear of the process of dying, and it set out five different methods of committing suicide. The Society sought to limit sales of the

[84] *R v Hough* [1984] 6 Cr App R (S) 406.
[85] Subsequently the Criminal Attempts Act 1981 put this on a statutory footing.
[86] *Attorney-General v Able and Others* [1984] QB 795.

booklet by charging £6 for each copy and limiting the sales to Society members of three months' standing, aged 25 or over. Nonetheless, within 18 months, 8,300 copies had been sold. The Attorney-General applied for a court declaration that supply of the booklet to a class of persons known to include, or to be likely to include, persons considering or intending to commit suicide constituted an offence or an attempted offence of aiding, abetting, counselling or procuring suicide. Woolf J refused to grant such a declaration. He held that for supply of the booklet to amount to an offence under section 2 it would have to be proved that the supplier, whilst intending the booklet to be used by a person actually contemplating suicide, and with the object of assisting or otherwise encouraging her, supplied the booklet to such a person who then read it and, except in the case of an attempted offence, was assisted or encouraged by reading it to commit or to attempt to commit suicide.

The judge accepted, therefore, that there were circumstances in which supply of the booklet would amount to an offence, but without proof of the necessary intent of those supplying it, it was impossible to say in advance that any particular supply of the booklet would amount to an offence. Instead, it would be for a jury to decide in each case whether the necessary intent had been proved. That intent, to reiterate, would be that the booklet was to be used by someone contemplating suicide and also that that person would be assisted or encouraged by the booklet's contents to attempt suicide (and with that intention, the booklet was distributed to such a person who read it). For the change of attempt, it remains irrelevant whether the person to whom the booklet was distributed was actually assisted or encouraged to attempt suicide.

More recently, in *R v S*,[87] it was again emphasised that there is no requirement that the 'victim' ever intends to attempt suicide in order for there to be liability for attempting to aid, abet, counsel or procure a suicide. In this case, the Court of Appeal viewed such a situation as one of impossibility (such as attempting to pick an empty pocket or attempting to handle goods which have not been stolen[88]) and noted that the House of Lords had previously decided that it is no impediment to the offence of an attempted crime that the actual crime would have been impossible on the facts of the case.[89] Thus, it does not matter that a person who has been aided, abetted, counselled or procured to commit suicide has no intention of doing so, only that (from *Able*) the person doing the aiding or abetting intends that the person they are assisting does attempt suicide.

The section 2 offence carries with it a maximum term of 14 years' imprisonment which, as discussed above, caused some debate within Parliament at the time of the Bill's passage. The courts have tended to be reasonably lenient when imposing sentences for this offence. For example, in *R v Wallis (Keith Duncan)*[90]

[87] *R v S* [2005] EWCA Crim 819.
[88] ibid [40].
[89] *R v Shivpuri* [1987] AC 1.
[90] *R v Wallis (Keith Duncan)* (1983) 5 Cr App R (S) 342.

a 12-month sentence was thought to be appropriate by the judge (and described as lenient by the Court of Appeal) for a man who pleaded guilty to aiding and abetting the suicide of a 17-year-old girl. The defendant, aged 25, had been sharing a flat with the girl who was a drug abuser and there was some evidence that she had made previous attempts to commit suicide. He bought some tablets containing aspirin and codeine, a bottle of expectorant and a bottle of vodka and left these on the girl's dressing table. He stayed with her while she took the tablets, and later went out for more. He declined to call an ambulance until some time later; when the ambulance arrived the girl was dead.[91] When passing sentence, the Commons Serjeant said:

> When all is said and done, on the day of her death this young girl, who was only seventeen and emotionally immature, was in urgent need of help, and you, a grown man of twenty-five, instead of continuing to help provided her with the means of her death and stood by while she took her own life. In my view you bear a heavy responsibility of a reprehensible nature for her death'.

An appeal against sentence was dismissed on the basis that the sentence was at the extreme of leniency in the circumstances. Indeed, there are a number of factors that make this a serious example of the offence: the young age of the deceased; her vulnerability from drug use and previous suicide attempts; and the significance of the assistance provided by the defendant, which was far from minimal. Another lenient sentence was imposed in *R v Workman (David Paul)*.[92] In this case, a sentence of 18 months' imprisonment for aiding and abetting an attempted suicide was held by the Court of Appeal to be clearly lenient, but it was not in the interests of justice to increase it. The AG argued there were aggravating features, including that there was a purported suicide pact but the person assisting had encouraged the suicide while never intending to commit suicide himself. The Court of Appeal agreed that three to four years would have been more appropriate because seeking to persuade a vulnerable person to take their own life is a serious offence.

Longer sentences have been imposed in some other cases, such as *R v McGranaghan (Terence)*[93] in which a sentence of eight years for aiding and abetting the suicide of a cell mate was affirmed by the Court of Appeal. The defendant had persuaded the victim to make the attempt, fashioned a noose from a sheet, assisted the victim to climb on to a cupboard, waited until he thought that the victim was dead before raising the alarm, and then pretended to support him when they were found. It is as akin to murder as an assisted suicide charge could ever be and the Court of Appeal described it as a 'revolting crime'.[94] The Court

[91] Her death was due to codeine poisoning and it appeared that at least some of the codeine came from an earlier self-injection by the girl rather than from the pills provided by the defendant.

[92] *Attorney General's Reference (No 85 of 2006)* [2006] EWCA Crim 2623 (*R v Workman (David Paul)*.

[93] *R v McGranaghan (Terence)* (1987) 9 Cr App R (S) 447.

[94] ibid at 449.

also noted that there was no established pattern of sentencing to guide it as the offence is rare and often occurs in the context of mercy killing, which is far removed from the facts of this case. The Court spoke of the 'unique' facts of this case and that they 'produce a picture of wickedness on the part of McGranaghan which is quite startling'.[95] Indeed, it is cases such as this one that illustrate the veracity of the comments of Lord Lane CJ with which we started this section; the section 2 offence varies from 'the borders of cold blooded murder down to the shadowy area of mercy killing or common humanity'.[96] The courts' grappling with this complex offence was soon to be overtaken by parliamentary intervention.

IV. Changing the Wording of the Offence

The 2009 amendment to the wording of the section 2 offence is extremely significant in the history of the law on suicide, not only because of the potentially substantive changes to the offence, but also because it reaffirmed Parliament's commitment to an offence of assisted suicide at the start of the twenty-first century. It has proven to represent an obstacle for any judicial reinterpretation of the offence because if Parliament had wanted to soften the absolute prohibition on assisting a suicide, it had the opportunity to do so in 2009 and declined to take action.

The impetus for the change in wording came from three directions. Firstly, a Law Commission Report of July 2006 on inchoate liability for assisting and encouraging crime[97] included a detailed review of the position in respect of assisting suicide and concluded that there was 'a strong case for updating the language' of the provision.[98] Secondly, child psychologist Tanya Byron's report 'Safer Children in a Digital World'[99] published in March 2008 identified websites promoting suicide (as well as those promoting self-harm and eating disorders, cyberbullying, and material depicting the commission of crimes) as an area where there was some confusion about the application of the law to online activity. In particular, the report concluded that the way in which offline laws and enforcement mechanisms can and should be applied to online activity needed to be clarified. Finally, the incidents of suicide amongst young persons in Bridgend, South Wales was causing considerable concern at the time. During 2007 and

[95] ibid.

[96] *R v Hough* [1984] 6 Cr App R (S) 406.

[97] Law Commission Report on Inchoate liability for Assisting and Encouraging Crime, Law Com No 300, July 2006.

[98] ibid, Appendix B, para 28. The Report also recommended broader provisions on extra-territorial jurisdiction for the offence.

[99] Byron Review Report, 'Safer Children in a Digital World: The Report of the Byron Review' (March 2008).

2008, there were 26 known suicides by hanging in or from Bridgend county.[100] This raised the topic of suicide to one of national interest at the time that the government accepted the need for reform of the Suicide Act 1961.

On 17 September 2008, Maria Eagle, the Parliamentary Under-Secretary of State for Justice, issued a statement confirming that the Government would be revising the wording of section 2.[101] Eagle began by noting that there has been 'growing concern in recent years about whether current law is adequate to deal with misuse of the internet to promote suicide and suicide methods'. While she insisted that in the Government's view the current law 'is capable of catching the sort of material that is causing concern', she conceded that 'in practice the application of the law, particularly in terms of what constitutes an attempt to commit the section 2 offence is complicated. It is difficult both to understand and to explain'. Thus, she declared the Government's intentions that 'the existing statutory language of section 2 of the Suicide Act should be simplified and modernised in a way that will make it clearer for everyone to understand'.

The opportunity to do so arose in the Government's Coroners and Justice Bill of 2009. This was a wide-ranging Bill covering many politically controversial elements of the criminal justice system, with one minor section amending the 1961 Act. As noted above, the original section 2 offence of aiding, abetting, counselling or procuring suicide could also be charged as an attempt – ie an attempt to aid, abet, counsel or procure a suicide – due originally to a common law rule that an attempt to commit an offence is also an offence and latterly by the Criminal Attempts Act 1981. Section 59 of the Coroners and Justice Act 2009 amends section 2 of the Suicide Act 1961 by incorporating the attempt offence into the 1961 statute. It therefore replaces the two offences of aiding, abetting, counselling or procuring suicide and attempting to do so with a single offence. In addition, the language of the offence is modernised. Thus, the new single offence applies where a person does an act which is capable of encouraging or assisting another person to commit or attempt to commit suicide, and intends their act to so encourage or assist. The replacement of the old-fashioned language of 'aiding, abetting, counselling or procuring' with the more modern terms of 'encouraging or assisting' was not intended to change the substance of the offence but merely make it easier to understand. In addition, while the changes were introduced against the background of concerns about suicide websites, there is nothing in the amendments that limit it to that context.

The Coroners and Justice Bill was introduced into the House of Commons by Jack Straw, the Secretary of State for Justice and Lord Chancellor.[102] In introducing

[100] G Raynor and R Savill, 'Bridgend suicides: a town tainted by death' *The Telegraph*, 23 February 2008, available at www.telegraph.co.uk/news/uknews/1579574/Bridgend-suicides-a-town-tainted-by-death.html.

[101] The Parliamentary Under-Secretary of State for Justice (Maria Eagle), Statement on the Suicide Act, Hansard HC (Series 6) Vol 479, col 142WS (17 September 2008).

[102] Hansard, HC (series 6) Vol 487, col 26 (26 January 2009).

the relevant clauses, he referred to both the Law Commission and the Byron reviews, as well as representations from the MP for Bridgend (Madeleine Moon), the constituency that had recently suffered the tragedy of a series of suicides. Straw made clear that the provision does not substantively change the law, but rather simplifies and modernises the language of section 2 of the Suicide Act 1961 with the purpose, Straw said, of increasing public understanding and offering reassurance that 'the provision applies as much to actions on the internet as to actions offline'.[103]

In responding to Straw's speech, his shadow Dominic Grieve did not mention the suicide provisions at all and indeed these did not form a major part of the debate about the Bill in the House of Commons. A few speakers did express some concern, however. David Howarth, Liberal Democrat MP, noted 'with alarm' that the relevant clauses were not confined to the specific issue of suicide websites but would instead replace the entirety of the present law on encouraging and assisting suicide.[104] This was of concern because Howarth noted that it removes the requirement that the encouragement or assistance must be aimed at a specific person or group.[105] Howarth was also concerned about the distinction between encouraging suicide and assisting suicide. In his view, encouraging suicide is always wrong, but assisting suicide may not always be wrong, depending upon the circumstances because of the need to respect an exercise of autonomy. This is a strong point and arguably the law should distinguish between these two actions on the basis of autonomy (as will be argued later in the book) and could do so while still respecting everyone's right to life. Howarth explains the distinction cogently:

> Encouraging suicide takes place before the person has decided to commit suicide and is entirely reprehensible, whether it is aimed at a specific person or at the world in general. In that sense, what the Government are doing is right, but assisting suicide can, by contrast, occur after the person has autonomously decided to commit suicide. Many hon. Members think that assisting suicide is also wrong, but if it is wrong, it is a different sort of wrong from encouraging suicide. Other hon. Members think that assisting suicide is not necessarily wrong if the right sort of safeguards are in place.[106]

The disagreement about whether assisting a suicide is always wrong was debated by the House of Lords in relation to this Bill (as will be discussed below) and, of course, has been the subject of growing public, political and legal debate ever since. There has not, however, been much focus on this crucial distinction between encouragement and assistance which speaks not only to the stage at which the intervention occurs but also the significance of the involvement in

[103] ibid 35.
[104] ibid 68–69.
[105] ibid.
[106] ibid.

terms of the decision-making process and indeed the motives of the encourager/assister.[107] It is a very relevant distinction that should be the subject of greater analysis.

Other notable contributions on the suicide provisions during the Commons debate included Madeleine Moon, the Labour MP for Bridgend, who argued for psychological autopsies (a method of research that reconstructs the lifestyle and personality traits of the person who committed suicide) to understand why suicide clusters occur,[108] and Brian Iddon, a Labour MP and chair of the Care Not Killing alliance, who described the provisions as 'extremely responsible and reasonable'.[109] Suicide provision was not discussed when the Bill returned to the House for a third reading, nor after the Bill returned from the Lords. An amendment concerning assisted suicide, promoted by Patricia Hewitt, the ex-Secretary of State for Health, was not reached during Committee Stage.[110]

In the House of Lords, the Coroners and Justice Bill was introduced by Lord Bach, the Parliamentary Under Secretary of State at the Ministry of Justice, and he again emphasised that the changes to the law on assisting suicide were intended 'to increase public understanding that the law applies to the internet as it does offline. Our aim is to simplify and update the law in this area and not to change its scope'.[111] Lord Goodhart, however, doubted that the offence would remain of the same scope. He argued that 'the Bill does not merely restate the existing law, but goes beyond it' because it 'extends the crime of encouraging or assisting suicide expressly to cases where the defendant has encouraged the suicide of people not known to him or her'.[112] Lord Goodhart also recognised a potential threat to freedom of speech on this issue and that view was supported by report of the Joint Committee on Human Rights on the Bill, which claimed that: 'the breadth of the offence remains uncertain and has the potential to have a chilling effect on a range of activities involving reference to suicide or the provision of information or support around end of life decision making'.[113] The need to distinguish between those offering emotional support via the Internet and those websites that seek to encourage suicide was an issue raised by a number of other speakers in the debate including the Lord Bishop of Southwell and Nottingham, who expressed

[107] Baroness Warnock was also concerned about such a distinction when speaking about the Bill in the House of Lords. She said that the revised law would 'criminalise in exactly the same way, and to the same degree, these dangerous people who are putting young lives at risk and who are broadcasting their thoughts and encouragement to the world at large as the other group of people who, perhaps with agonies of conscience, assist individuals who they know and love to end their lives when living is no longer tolerable to them': Hansard HL (Series 6) Vol 710, col 1276 (18 May 2009).

[108] Hansard (26 January 2009) 77–78.

[109] ibid 104.

[110] Hewitt's amendment was not called, which raised some objections about management of time (Hansard HC (Series 6) Vol 490, col 52–61 (23 March 2009).

[111] Hansard (18 May 2009) col 1206.

[112] ibid 1266–67.

[113] Human Rights Joint Committee, Eighth Report – Legislative Scrutiny: Coroners and Justice Bill (17 March 2009) 1.165.

his support for the suicide provisions, recognising that although we 'must avoid criminalising people who are merely discussing their feelings', 'it is vital that the law should continue to prohibit irresponsible or unscrupulous actions which would have the effect of encouraging or assisting suicide'.[114]

By far the most significant aspect of the House of Lords' consideration of the suicide provisions, however, was Lord Falconer's proposed amendment. He first broached the topic in the second reading debate:

> I strongly oppose the law being re-enacted without reflecting one significant change. The Director of Public Prosecutions will not prosecute people who, in good faith and with good motives, assist a loved one to go to a clinic in Switzerland or another place where suicide is lawful. He will not prosecute because he rightly believes that it is not in the public interest to prosecute in those circumstances … It is wrong as a matter of principle … that the law should be set to one side by one individual, no matter how important that individual is. This House should not re-enact Section 1 of the Suicide Act, which makes it a crime to assist suicide, unless it properly reflects the way in which the law operates at the moment.[115]

Some speakers, such as Baroness Finlay of Llandaff, argued that the Bill should not be used 'as a Trojan horse'[116] to try to revisit the assisted dying issues raised previously by Lord Joffe (and discussed below). Others agreed with Lord Falconer that the current state of the law was problematic and that the issue of those who assist their relatives to travel to Dignitas in Switzerland to end their lives should be resolved. Baroness Jay of Paddington argued that

> we should use the Bill to lift the threat of criminal prosecution from people who, with the best of intentions, accompany loved ones who are terminally ill abroad so that they can get help to die in countries where assisted suicide is legal.[117]

The current position, under which such assistance is a criminal offence under section 2 of the Suicide Act but is unlikely to be prosecuted, led Baroness Jay to claim that 'the law as it stands is a fudge, and under this Bill will remain a fudge',[118] while Lord Taverne stated that the law 'is in a mess' and needs urgent clarification.[119]

It was no surprise, then, when Lord Falconer brought forward an amendment during committee stage to deal with this issue.[120] This amendment would have created an exception to the absolute prohibition of encouraging or assisting a

[114] Hansard (18 May 2009) col 1220.
[115] ibid 1222.
[116] ibid 1229.
[117] ibid 1234.
[118] ibid 1235.
[119] ibid 1272.
[120] Hansard HL (Series 6) Vol 712, col 595 (7 July 2009). It should be noted that the Lords considered this amendment after the Court of Appeal's judgment in *Purdy* but before the House of Lords judgment.

suicide in circumstances where the act in question is done solely or principally for the purpose of enabling or assisting a person to travel to a country in which assisted dying is lawful. The exception had two important safeguards: firstly, that two registered medical practitioners certify that the person who wishes to die is terminally ill and has capacity; and secondly that the person requesting assistance has made a voluntary declaration, before an independent witness, that she has decided to travel for the purpose of obtaining assistance in dying. Lord Falconer supported this amendment by arguing that 'It should not be a crime if you accompany someone to a country where assisted dying is lawful if the sole purpose of your accompanying them is to assist them in going to the place where assisted dying is lawful'.[121]

In opposing the amendment, Lord Mackay of Clashfern argued that any proposal to reduce the protection offered by the law to human life would involve 'a judgment that a certain kind of life, or a certain span of life, has become unworthy of support from that principle'.[122] Lord Bach, speaking for the Government, concluded that the current Bill 'is not the appropriate vehicle to liberalise the criminal law as it applies to assisted suicide'.[123] The changes in the law brought forward by the Government were said to merely simplify the law and modernise the relevant language, whereas Lord Falconer's amendment 'seeks to make a decisive shift in the law'.[124] Lord Falconer called for a division on his amendment but it was defeated by 194 voted to 141. This reasonably close result indicated some support in Parliament for a limited change in the law.[125] This issue remains unresolved, and will be discussed more fully in chapter eight.

The changes which were agreed by Parliament to section 2 of the Suicide Act in the Coroners and Justice Act 2009 were intended to achieve two aims: to improve public understanding of the law in this area; and to make clear that the law applies to online actions in exactly the same way as it does offline.[126] Although the Government insisted that the substance of the law was not to be changed, the new terminology ensures that actions intended to encourage or assist suicide which are capable of doing so amount to a criminal offence. The position may not have been so clear previously (as in the case of *Able*). Updating of the language is a positive move to make the offence more easily understood by the public, but the use of the 'encouraging or assisting' phrase does risk conflating two very distinct actions: one which may be autonomy-enhancing and one

[121] ibid 597.
[122] ibid 599.
[123] ibid 631.
[124] ibid.
[125] The Lords were far less tolerant when Lord Alderdice brought forward a broader amendment at the Report Stage and the amendment was withdrawn without division (HL 26 October).
[126] Criminal Law Policy Unity, Ministry of Justice, 'Encouraging or Assisting Suicide: Implementation of Section 59 of the Coroners and Justice Act 2009' Circular 2010/03 (28 January 2010), available at webarchive.nationalarchives.gov.uk/20110201140204/http://www.justice.gov.uk/publications/docs/circular-03-2010-assisting-encouraging-suicide.pdf.

which may be autonomy-threatening. Indeed, arguably it is the law's failure to distinguish between those who seek to convince another person to take their own life (perhaps in circumstances such as those in the *McGranaghan* case; discussed above) and those who for reasons of compassion offer essential assistance to enable a person to exercise their own autonomy when otherwise unable to do so (as in the assisted dying cases soon to be discussed) which continues to bring the law into disrepute, as seen most clearly in the 'assisted dying' debate (to be discussed in chapter eight).

V. Legal Duties to Prevent Suicide

Since the legalisation of suicide, the role and significance of human rights within English law has increased considerably. The Human Rights Act 1998, which brought Convention rights into domestic law, includes both a right to autonomy under Article 8 ECHR and also a right to life under Article 2 ECHR. The latter is significant in relation to the law's approach to suicide because it includes a positive obligation on the state and public authorities to take reasonable steps to preserve life, leading to the possibility that there might be a duty to prevent suicide.

The leading authority on positive obligations under the right to life is *Osman v United Kingdom*,[127] in which the European Court of Human Rights outlined the positive obligation imposed upon a state party under Article 2, explaining that this provision 'enjoins the state not only to refrain from the intentional and unlawful taking of life, but also to take appropriate steps to safeguard the lives of those within its jurisdiction'.[128] This positive obligation may extend to the need for preventive operational measures to protect an individual whose life is at risk. In respect of this, the Court established the important principle that state authorities must do all that could reasonably be expected of them to avoid a real and immediate risk to life of which they have or ought to have knowledge.[129] However, the Court recognised that this obligation must be interpreted in a way which does not impose an impossible or disproportionate burden on the authorities.[130] Thus, while the state sometimes has a duty to act to save life, that duty can be outweighed by duties under other rights, such as for example the obligations not to interfere with a person's private life or autonomy. If the threat to life comes from suicide, how is the state to balance a right to autonomy with a duty to save life?

The Strasbourg Court has considered this dilemma in the context of prison suicide and has placed the focus squarely on the question of whether the prison

[127] *Osman v United Kingdom* ECHR 1998-VIII (1998) 29 EHRR 245.
[128] ibid [115].
[129] ibid [116].
[130] ibid.

authorities ought to have known of the suicide risk.[131] Regrettably, neither the concept of autonomy nor mental capacity have featured in these judgments (which will be discussed fully in chapter five). Domestic courts under the Human Rights Act 1998 have also been asked to grapple with the issue of whether there is a duty to prevent suicide in the context of mental health patients. The Supreme Court first recognised a duty to prevent suicide of compulsorily detained mental health patients in *Savage v South Essex NHS Trust*[132] and then subsequently in *Rabone & another v Pennine Care NHS Trust*[133] extended that duty to voluntary mental health patients. These cases raise a number of difficulties, including an apparent disregard of the principle of autonomy in respect of persons detained by, or otherwise under control of, the state in respect of suicide. Lord Rodger did confirm in *Savage* that 'the need to respect the autonomy of prisoners remains'[134] but found that where a real and immediate risk of suicide has been identified, the protection of life must take precedence over autonomy.[135] This was because of the immediacy of the danger to life. Lord Rodger suggests that there 'will be time enough' for other considerations, such as autonomy, when the danger has been averted.[136] This is a problematic approach, however, because if applied to every choice to die, it would imply a priority to life over autonomy that remains unreasoned and unjustified. If an autonomous choice to die is to be owed respect in any circumstances at all (and Article 8 ECHR suggests that it is), then the 'save life first, worry about free choice later' approach cannot be applied in an indiscriminate manner.

In *Rabone*, Lord Dyson recognises that the Strasbourg Court has in recent years expanded the circumstances in which the operational duty is owed to include what may generally be described as 'dangers for which in some way the state is responsible'.[137] A good example of this is the case of *Mammadov v Azerbaijan*[138] in which the applicant's wife committed suicide by pouring a flammable liquid over herself and igniting it. Although not in detention, she committed this act of self-harm in response to a police operation to evict her family from their unofficial dwelling. The Strasbourg Court held that, once the situation became clear, the authorities had an obligation under Article 2 to prevent the threat to

[131] See, for example: *Keenan v United Kingdom* (ECHR 2001-III); *Renolde v France* (App 5608/05, 16 October 2008, ECHR 2008 (extracts)); *Ketreb v France* (App 38447/09, 19 July 2012); *Çoşelav v Turkey* (App 1413/07, 9 October 2012).

[132] *Savage v South Essex NHS Trust* [2008] UKHL 74.

[133] *Rabone and another v Pennine Care NHS Trust* [2012] UKSC 2.

[134] ibid [42].

[135] ibid.

[136] Lord Rodger: 'the immediacy of the danger to life means that, for the time being, there is, in practice, little room for considering other, more general, matters concerning his treatment. There will be time enough for them, if and when the danger to life has been overcome. In the meantime, the authorities' duty is to try to prevent the suicide': ibid.

[137] ibid [16].

[138] *Mammadov v Azerbaijan* (App 4762/05, 17 December 2009).

life from materialising, by any means which were reasonable and feasible in the circumstances.[139] While no violation was found in this case, because the circumstances surrounding the death were disputed and unclear, the existence of a duty to protect a person from self-harm was found to arise in this case in circumstances far removed from detention. Nonetheless, arguably the control requirement was still relevant here given that state agents were directly involved in the creation of the risk to life.

Is there a duty to prevent suicide more broadly? In the Supreme Court judgment in *Nicklinson*,[140] while Lord Sumption claimed that 'In law, the state is not entitled to intervene to prevent a person of full capacity who has arrived at a settled decision to take his own life from doing so',[141] it was noteworthy that a number of the other judges disagreed with him. Baroness Hale, for example, expressed her 'reservations' in light of *Savage* and *Rabone*, and stated her view that a 'policeman is surely entitled to prevent a would-be suicide from jumping off Westminster Bridge'.[142] However, even Baroness Hale seems inconsistent on this issue as in *Rabone* she acknowledges that autonomous individuals 'have a right to take their own lives if that is what they truly want'.[143] Given that in the subsequent case of *Nicklinson* she claimed that a policeman is entitled to step in to prevent a suicide, presumably the apparent disparity between those statements is in order that the policeman can be assured that suicide is indeed what the individual 'truly wants'. This may indeed be a valuable protection for the law to recognise because it would help to ensure that human life is protected unless and until an adult with mental capacity makes an autonomous choice to die. However, such a distinction is not sufficiently explicit in the current law, especially as the law requires us to assume capacity until it is disproven.[144] We might question whether the act of attempting suicide itself disproves the assumption of capacity. Despite legalisation of suicide and its attempt in 1961, even today there remain some significant unanswered questions in relation to the legal rights and obligations surrounding suicide attempts. Subsequent chapters will explore these issues in much more detail.

VI. Conclusion

This chapter has covered a lot of ground from the 1950s to the present day. It has demonstrated that, although the issue has moved on considerably since suicide

[139] Notably, included within the Court's suggested steps that could have been taken was physically preventing the applicant's wife from pursuing life-threatening actions, as well as providing immediate medical assistance (ibid 116).

[140] *R (Nicklinson) v Ministry of Justice; R (AM) v Director of Public Prosecutions* [2014] UKSC 38.

[141] ibid [255].

[142] ibid [324].

[143] ibid [100].

[144] Mental Capacity Act 2005, s 1(2).

itself was a crime, the law remains intimately involved with suicide and suicide attempts, and unanswered questions remain. The chapter started with a recognition that, by the middle of the twentieth century, the primary role of the law in relation to suicide was one of prevention. It is fitting, therefore, that despite the many significant legal developments since that time, one of the most pressing questions today remains whether there is a legal duty to prevent suicide and in what circumstances that applies.

The most important legal development in relation to suicide was obviously its statutory legalisation in 1961. It is surprising that such a ground-breaking move proved to be uncontroversial within Parliament. Subsequent events, however, have clearly illustrated that legalisation only temporarily obscured the enduring moral and ethical conflicts about suicide and the legal issues thereby arising. Both public and parliamentary opinion remains starkly divided on issues such as whether assistance to commit suicide should ever be lawful, or whether there should be a legal duty to take steps to prevent all suicides. Part of the problem seems to be a failure to recognise the wide variety of circumstances that can lead to a desire to end one's life prematurely. Often this will be a tragic and desperate choice, and perhaps not even a 'choice' but a symptomatic response to a mental illness or a reluctant response to external pressure. However, in other circumstances it can be a valuable exercise of autonomy. These are difficult issues, and the law's ambiguity is perhaps understandable. But the ending of human life is a very grave issue and the law's response to it needs to be appropriate and effective. The following chapters will seek to explore the role of the law in relation to suicide in a variety of different contexts in order to seek greater clarity and understanding of how the law does, and should, regulate (what are now lawful) choices to die.

4

Suicide and Mental Health

Suicide has been inextricably linked with issues of mental health since the late seventeenth century, when coroner's juries first sought to avoid detrimental repercussions for the deceased's family by returning verdicts, not of *felo de se*, but instead of *non compos mentis*.[1] During the nineteenth century, the medical profession extended its involvement in the issue of suicide by linking suicidal propensities with melancholia.[2] The closest linkage between suicide and mental health, however, can be seen in the key role played by the Mental Health Act 1959 (MHA 1959) in the legalisation of suicide in the mid-twentieth century.[3] Since that time, it is the laws relating to mental health and mental capacity which have been applied in efforts to prevent suicide. The natural linkage between suicide and mental health legislation is supported by the undeniable fact that a mental illness is a high-risk factor for a suicide attempt. The scope for preventative measures is highlighted by the fact that approximately a quarter of people who die by suicide are in contact with mental health services at the time of their death.[4]

Given the connection between the two issues of suicide and mental health the relationship between them will be central throughout this book. This chapter, however, seeks to explore the suitability of the current mental health and mental capacity laws in England for the task of responding to suicide risk. Both the mental health laws and the mental capacity laws will be discussed, as will the somewhat problematic relationship between them. First, however, it is important to take a step back and consider whether the linking of suicide and mental illness in the law's response to suicide risks being an over-simplification. In other words, are rational suicides possible? This question will pursue us throughout the book and presents a significant challenge to the temptation to equate all suicides with a symptom of mental illness to be treated by the medical profession.

[1] See ch 2 above.
[2] ibid.
[3] See ch 3 above.
[4] 'Reforming the Mental Health Act' White Paper (2021) Part 2, available at www.gov.uk/government/consultations/reforming-the-mental-health-act/reforming-the-mental-health-act.

I. Suicide and Rationality

A central theme in philosophical debates about suicide has always been whether or not it can be rational to take one's own life.[5] Historically, the idea of a rational suicide was readily accepted, for example by the ancient philosophers,[6] but in the modern era it has been disputed by philosophers such as Descartes, Hobbes and Kant, who have argued that self-preservation is the fundamental principle of practical reason, and thus suicide is in principle irrational.[7] This later philosophical view is now supported by the prevailing view in medicine that suicide is typically a symptom of an illness. However, the question of whether a rational suicide is possible has been reopened in recent years due to an increasing focus, especially in the courtrooms, on 'assisted dying' in the context of terminal or debilitating illness. This has highlighted that for persons such as Dianne Pretty or Tony Nicklinson a death might be a rational choice in comparison with a prolonged life of suffering, humiliation and dependency.[8] When such issues are argued against a human rights background, there is the further consideration that recent intensification of suicide prevention measures might represent a paternalistic restriction on individual freedom if a rational, autonomous choice to end one's own life is possible. This shifting focus in the suicide debate is highly significant because if it is accepted that suicide can be rational, even if only on rare occasions, then 'the mere desire to kill oneself cannot by itself be used as a convincing sign of mental illness or justification for involuntary institutionalisation or treatment'.[9] The possibility of a rational suicide means that not all suicidal desires are symptoms to be treated. So, the question that must now be addressed is this: what are the requirements in order for a suicide to be 'rational'?

There are two types of potential conditions for a rational suicide: those relating to the person making the decision; and those relating to the decision itself. The first might be termed 'cognitive conditions' and ensure that a person making such a decision has the mental capacity to do so and that her appraisal of the situation is well-informed and well-considered. The second type of condition might be termed 'interest conditions' and ensure that the contemplated suicide accords with the person's own fundamental interests.[10] In other words, the two vital questions

[5] H Wittwer, 'The Problem of the Possible Rational Suicide and the Ethics of Physician-assisted Suicide' (2013) 36 *International Journal of Law and Psychiatry* 419, 419.

[6] This was true not only of the stoics who argued in favour of suicide in some circumstances, such as Seneca, but also those such as Plato and Aristotle who morally condemned suicide (ibid).

[7] ibid.

[8] Indeed, some writers simply assume that a suicidal desire in the context of a terminal illness is 'obviously' rational and move on to harder questions: RB Brandt, 'The Rationality of Suicide' in M Pabst Battin and DJ Mayo (eds), *Suicide: The Philosophical Issues* (London, Peter Owen, 1980) 123.

[9] D Wood, 'Suicide as Instrument and Expression' in Pabst Battin and Mayo (ibid) 159.

[10] See M Cholbi, 'Suicide' in Edward N Zalta (ed), *The Stanford Encyclopedia of Philosophy* (Fall 2017 edition), available at plato.stanford.edu/archives/fall2017/entries/suicide; M Pabst Battin, *The Least Worst Death: Essays in Bioethics on the End of Life* (Oxford, Oxford University Press, 1994); Wittwer, 'The Problem of the Possible Rational Suicide' (2013).

in relation to rational suicide are whether suicidal persons are capable of making well-considered decisions, and whether suicide itself can ever be well justified.

A. Can a Suicidal Person have Capacity?

The assumption that suicide usually arises from a mental illness is supported by the reality. Empirical studies estimate that between 90 and 95 per cent of those who take their own lives are suffering from a mental disorder.[11] While English law recognises the important distinction between mental disorder and mental capacity, the distinction is cloudier in relation to the suicide of those suffering from mental illnesses such as depression. As Brandt has recognised, when making the vital choice between two future world-courses (death now or death at an uncertain point in the future), a depressed person will be prone to particular errors that may undermine the decision.[12] For example, a depressed person may overlook the best possible alternative to suicide so that the comparison between suicide and a longer life does not compare the same two futures that she would consider if not suffering from depression.[13] In addition, depression seriously affects one's judgement about the probabilities of the gloomier predictions for prolonged life[14] and also reduces the motivational machinery on which we usually rely for determining if we want something.[15] Thus, a decision to end one's life prematurely made by a person suffering depression raises the possibility that it is not a rational, nor indeed autonomous, decision.

All too often, a suicide occurs during a moment of despair and is an impulsive action reflecting a transient and ambivalent desire to die. It is not unreasonable therefore to require, in addition to the usual standard of mental capacity, a period of reflection before we are able to accept a suicide as a rational one. For example, Brandt argues that if one is contemplating suicide during a moment of despair, there should be 'a moment of reassessment of one's goals and values, a reassessment which the individual must realise is very difficult to make objectively, because of the very quality of his depressed frame of mind'.[16] The need for a period of reflection stems from the dire consequences of the decision in question. While trivial decisions might be regarded as rational even if based on transitory desires, a decision with long-term consequences that cannot be reversed, such as suicide, cannot be so regarded.[17] Suicide is distinguishable from most other decisions because, as Wheat puts it, 'one's future self is irrevocably bound'.[18]

[11] Wittwer (n 5) 421.
[12] Brandt, 'The Rationality of Suicide' (1980) 124.
[13] ibid.
[14] ibid.
[15] ibid 126.
[16] ibid 127.
[17] DJ Mayo, 'The Concept of Rational Suicide' (1986) 11 *Journal of Medicine and Philosophy* 143, 147.
[18] K Wheat, 'The Law's Treatment of the Suicidal' (2000) 8 *Medical Law Review* 182, 209.

It is in this context in which a requirement of reflection becomes essential in order for a suicide to be rational. It may be argued that this requirement does not infringe the autonomy of the person contemplating suicide (who we will assume otherwise has mental capacity) because, as Wheat concludes, 'It is no interference with autonomy to be given more time to make a decision after considered reflection, and to be given the opportunity to investigate the possible alleviation of conditions which are making life intolerable'.[19] Thus, in order for a person to act rationally in choosing suicide, she must meet a number of requirements: firstly, she must have the mental capacity to make a decision, requiring that she understands, retains, uses and evaluates the information relevant to her choice;[20] secondly, she must reflect on her decision, ensuring that she does not act impulsively or on transient preferences. If she is depressed, and it is likely (although not inevitable) that she will be depressed while contemplating suicide, the period of reflection should strive to enable a process of evaluation unhindered by the depression. As Brandt puts it, our preferences of today should not be given special weight over those of the future, and thus one should try to imagine what one's future attitudes to life and death might be.[21] As Mayo notes, this is an extremely difficult requirement because it expects a person suffering from depression to project themselves beyond their present depressed state of mind and take into account the preferences of a future less depressed version of themselves.[22] It is a lot to ask, certainly, but only in doing so can we be confident that a decision to take one's own life has been rationally made.

An important concern remains, however, and it is one that we will see reflected in different contexts throughout this book. The concern is of a catch-22 nature: if a person wants to end her own life, then that choice is likely coloured by depression which it is impossible to set aside, and therefore she is not *capable* of making the decision to die; if a person does not wish to end their own life, then she can be regarded as capable and rational and enjoying a theoretical right to decide to die – up until the point when she makes that decision and is therefore *not* capable or rational. Only if we can evade this catch-22 and are satisfied that the person choosing to die has done so rationally, can we then turn to the question of whether or not the choice itself is rational.

B. Can Suicide Ever be a Rational Choice?

There have been a number of arguments over the years that have sought to disprove the possibility of a rational suicide. One such argument focuses on the

[19] ibid 208.
[20] These specific requirements are drawn from the Mental Capacity Act 2005 which will be considered below.
[21] Brandt (n 8) 121.
[22] Mayo, 'The Concept of Rational Suicide' (1986) 148.

inconceivability of death. It states that as no living person can know what it is like to be dead, there can be no rational choice between life and death. A rational choice, under this argument, requires knowledge of the alternatives, and therefore suicide can never be a rational choice.[23] However, there are major difficulties, or as Mayo puts it 'several things terribly wrong',[24] with this line of argument. Firstly, it would mean that a choice not to undertake suicide is also unavoidably irrational because the alternative of death remains unknown.[25] Secondly, while death may be unexplainable, it is not necessarily unknowable because if we have good reason to believe that death is annihilation, then we know all we need to know about it as an alternative to prolonged life.[26] Thirdly, as Wittwer explains, we cannot meaningfully ask what it is like to be dead:

> Since the ability to experience states has been irrevocably lost by the time of death (at the latest), there is nothing it is like to be dead. The appearance of logical opaqueness only arises when we assume on the one hand that the human body can no longer experience or perceive anything after death, and at the same time insist that we must be able to know what it is like to be dead'.[27]

For these reasons, the argument that suicide can never be rational because death is unknowable is not a convincing one.

An alternative argument states that suicide can never be rational because it is self-contradictory in nature. This argument proposes that suicide as an act of freedom makes further acts of freedom impossible and so must be self-contradictory in nature.[28] Wittwer, however, points out that suicide would be a final act of freedom and that a corpse neither has freedom nor the lack of it.[29] Other arguments, such as that life is always worth living and thus death can never be a rational choice, are increasingly seen as misconceived. While life is usually a good, this is not always the case,[30] and although life always has a value in and of itself, it is a relative value that may be outweighed by other considerations that are regarded as more important to the individual concerned.[31] We can all think of reasons why the premature ending of life might be linked to our (rational) fundamental interests: to escape unbearable pain and suffering; to regain control over the options available to us; to avoid torture; or to save a loved one. This is not to suggest that suicide would be the only rational option in those circumstances, nor that it is a recommended or even approved option, but merely that it would not be an inherently irrational choice

[23] P Devine, 'On Choosing Death' in M Pabst Battin and DJ Mayo (eds), *Suicide: The Philosophical Issues* (London, Peter Owen, 1980)139.
[24] Mayo (n 17) 150.
[25] ibid 151.
[26] ibid.
[27] Wittwer (n 5) 423.
[28] ibid 425.
[29] ibid 425–26.
[30] Mayo (n 17) 145.
[31] See E Wicks, *The Right to Life and Conflicting Interests* (Oxford, Oxford University Press, 2010).

in such circumstances. Mayo has explained that 'to claim a suicide is rational is to claim that the agent had good reasons for ending his life, [and] that doing so made good sense in the circumstances'.[32] This does not require that other persons agree with, or approve of, the choice to die; nor does it require that death be the objectively best solution. It requires only that a choice to die makes sense from the perspective of the person contemplating it and, significantly, their fundamental interests.

An instrumental approach to rationality regards an agent as acting rationally if she chooses the best option available to her to achieve her own goals.[33] Thus, a person seeking to avoid a further loss of autonomy as they grow older may act rationally in choosing to end her life before this occurs. However, as Pilpel and Amsel point out, usually in philosophy rationality has a more robust, substantivist sense which requires that the agent's goals and desires are themselves rational.[34] While the above example of seeking to avoid a loss of autonomy would satisfy such a requirement, a desire to die because one does not want to age might achieve the agent's goal, but the goal in itself is not rational. This robust version of rationality is extremely challenging, requiring an agent who is rational, autonomous and not depressed making a serious, life-determining decision from an objective, rational point of view.[35] Even then, when Pilpel and Amsel sought to provide an example of a woman meeting all of these requirements, they still concluded that choosing suicide was 'a very odd, if not absurd, decision'[36] and one which 'seems deeply wrong'.[37] Arguably, however, such a choice to die is not 'wrong', nor is it 'absurd'.[38] The deaths of Tony Nicklinson and Captain Oates, to give just two starkly different examples, do not seem 'wrong' in a moral sense to this author, and that is largely because they appear to meet the requirements of robust rationality. We may wish that Nicklinson had chosen to live on, but still acknowledge that his choice not to do so was a choice made by a person with the capacity to make that choice and accorded with his rational and consistent fundamental interests.

C. Implications for Suicide Prevention and the Law

What does this mean for the law's approach to suicide? Although the full implications will be teased out throughout this and subsequent chapters, it may be

[32] Mayo (n 17) 144.
[33] A Pilpel and L Amsel, 'What is Wrong with Rational Suicide' (2011) 39 *Philosphia* 111, 116.
[34] ibid.
[35] ibid 120.
[36] ibid.
[37] ibid 115.
[38] Pilpel and Amsel do not interrogate their assumption that the suicide they have described is 'wrong' although they do acknowledge that not everyone will agree with them (as apparently one of their reviewers did not do so): ibid 121.

highlighted here that if we accept that a rational suicide is possible, even though rare, then we cannot simply treat suicide as a symptom of a mental illness to be treated in all circumstances. Furthermore, it may be that we should not regard all suicides as wrongs to be prevented. A rational suicide is more accurately classified as an exercise of autonomy and therefore something to be respected rather than prevented. However, even a 'right to suicide' (should there be such a thing) does not mean that no one can intervene to try to save the life under threat. Rather, it would mean that there should be no legal duty to prevent the suicide, and that the law must respect the choice to die. Neither of those factors preclude the human need to try to help. As Wood argues,

> if we suppose that some people's desire for suicide can be changed by sunshine and fresh air, by relaxation therapy, dietary supplements, or a chance to talk, whether or not one labels them mentally ill, it is madness to leave such people to their own suicidal devices.[39]

We should all try to make life more bearable and worthwhile for someone contemplating ending it, and we should take what steps we can to encourage a change of mind, provided that we stop short of overbearing the will of the person making the decision. Trying to change someone's mind is entirely compatible with respecting an autonomous choice to die;[40] and respecting a choice to die is entirely compatible with respect for the sanctity of life.

The moral obligations in respect of a person contemplating suicide may be somewhat complex and entirely dependent on the circumstances. As Brandt notes, our moral obligation in this context 'is an instance of general obligation to render aid to those in serious distress, at least when this can be done at no great cost to one's self'.[41] Such obligations may be greater in respect of those with whom we have a relationship, but Brandt argues that it is obvious 'that anyone in this kind of distress has a moral claim on the time of anyone who knows the situation'.[42] This is not the end of the issue, however, because the moral obligation identified here is not necessarily to take steps to *prevent* the suicide, but rather may be to *assist* in it. Brandt argues that, while there should be an assumption that suicide is not the right choice in respect of the welfare of the person contemplating it, and therefore the moral obligation would be to intervene and prevent it, if a 'clearly sane person, after careful reflection over a period of time' decides to end her life, the obligation to prevent it ceases.[43] Furthermore, if it is clear that she 'is right' in her

[39] Wood, 'Suicide as Instrument and Expression' (1980) 159.

[40] Wilson notes that Mill's classical liberal theory permits attempts to warn, advise, persuade and reason with persons, provided they are not forced into changing their mind: K Wilson, 'The Call for the Abolition of Mental Health Law: The Challenges of Suicide, Accidental Death and the Equal Enjoyment of the Right to Life' (2018) 18 *Human Rights Law Review* 651, 685.

[41] Brandt (n 8) 129.

[42] ibid 129–30.

[43] ibid 130.

decision and 'needs help in executing the decision', then there is a moral obligation to help her in doing so.[44] Therefore, according to this line of argument, the obligations in respect of suicide may be either to prevent or to assist, depending on the rationality of the suicide.

Although Brandt's argument related only to moral obligations, it is proposed here that there may be much to learn from it in the context of the role of the law as well. Provided that it works alongside a presumption in favour of protecting the sanctity of life when the details of the situation are unknown, it seems to be the type of refined approach that could permit both moral and legal duties in relation to suicide to reflect the complexity of suicide itself. It would be consistent with both the rights-based view of suicide and the consequentialist, or relationist, view of suicide which both demand distinguishing between different types of suicide, but would move away from moralistic views that condemn all suicides, as well as the medical model which classifies all suicides as symptoms of mental illness.[45] That latter view is not sustainable in the context of the possibility of a rational suicide, and such a possibility seems undeniable. This working hypothesis – that the law should adopt a refined and variable approach to suicide, under which it will in some circumstances impose a duty to prevent suicide; at other times, a duty to respect it; and even in some circumstances, a duty to assist it – will be tested in different contexts throughout this book. For the remainder of this chapter, the focus will be on the current legal framework of suicide prevention in the context of both mental health and mental capacity laws permitting compulsory interventions to prevent suicide.

II. Current Legal Framework: The Use of Mental Capacity and Mental Health Laws to Prevent Suicide

Since suicide was decriminalised in 1961, the law's main focus in relation to suicide has been one of prevention through the use of compulsory civil powers. Both the mental health and the mental capacity laws have a role to play in seeking to achieve this. This section will investigate the content of these laws and its application to the issue of suicide prevention.[46] It will also interrogate the overwhelming focus on prevention and question whether the current law is sufficiently

[44] ibid.

[45] See ch 1 for an overview of these different perspectives of suicide.

[46] At the time of writing the mental health laws are due to be reformed. The 'Reforming the Mental Health Act' White Paper of 2021 (www.gov.uk/government/consultations/reforming-the-mental-health-act/reforming-the-mental-health-act) which builds on the recommendations made by Sir Simon Wessely's Independent Review of the Mental Health Act in 2018 (www.gov.uk/government/publications/modernising-the-mental-health-act-final-report-from-the-independent-review) will be referred to where relevant in the following sections.

nuanced to identify when a risk of suicide is a rational choice rather than either a symptom of a mental illness or an indicator of a lack of mental capacity.

A. Overview of Mental Health Laws for Preventing Risk of Suicide

As discussed in chapter three, the new availability of compulsory civil detention powers in the MHA 1959 were a crucial element in the decriminalisation of suicide in 1961. Crucially, these new powers included a police power to remove someone suspected of mental disorder to a place of safety if she appeared to be in immediate need of care or control and it appeared necessary to do so in the interests of that person or to protect others.[47] This enabled a person thought to be at risk of suicide to be detained for up to 72 hours so that she could be examined by a doctor and interviewed by a mental welfare officer. It was the first example of a compulsory intervention which could be used to prevent suicide, without subjecting the person involved to the risk of criminal proceedings. Longer detention powers were also provided for by the 1959 Act, including compulsory admittance to a hospital for observation for up to a month,[48] and for treatment for a longer period.[49] A compulsory hospital order was also available after, or instead of, conviction for a criminal offence.[50] Without such powers, it is unlikely that suicide would have been decriminalised without alternative and specific detention powers to prevent suicide being enacted. Since the 1960s, the preventative powers in relation to suicide have continued to be subsumed within the broader mental health laws and, despite some significant changes to the mental health laws in order to recognise the importance of the rights of patients, the main detention provisions remain very similar to those conceived in the 1950s.

The Mental Health Act 1983 (MHA 1983) continues to provide for *removal to place of safety* under section 136 by a police constable if a person: a) *appears to be suffering from mental disorder*; b) appears to be in *immediate need of care or control*; and c) it is thought *necessary* to remove that person to a place of safety (or keep her there) in the *interests of that person* or for *the protection of other persons*.[51] There is no power to enter a person's own home under this section, and additional safeguards were put in place in the Policing and Crime Act 2017 to ensure that a police station does not serve as a 'place of safety' for anyone under 18 years of age and is

[47] MHA 1959, s 136.
[48] ibid s 25.
[49] ibid s 26.
[50] ibid s 60(1).
[51] MHA 1983, s 136.

only used for adults in 'exceptional' circumstances[52] and the length of detention under this provision was reduced from 72 hours to 24 hours.[53] If practicable to do so, the police constable is also required to consult with a healthcare professional before exercising this power. During the 24-hour detention, the patient will be seen by both a doctor and an approved mental health professional. The place of safety is likely to be a special 'section 136 suite' unless there are 'red flags', such as serious physical injury or actual and current attempts at self-harm, necessitating the use of an emergency department.[54] In 2020–21, there were over 20,000 uses of the section 136 powers where the place of safety was a hospital[55] and a significant proportion of those will relate to persons at risk of suicide.[56]

Beyond the removal to a place of safety power exercisable by the police, there are also longer-term powers exercisable by two registered medical practitioners to compulsorily *admit a person to hospital for mental health assessment*. Under the MHA 1983, section 2, this requires that a person: (a) be suffering from a *mental disorder of a nature or degree which warrants the detention* of the patient in hospital for assessment (or for assessment followed by medical treatment) for at least a limited period; and (b) that the person ought to be so detained in the interests of her *own health or safety* or with a view to the protection of other persons.[57] The 2021 White Paper on Reforming the Mental Health Act includes plans to strengthen and clarify the criteria for detention under sections 2 and 3, so that patients are only detained when it is absolutely appropriate.[58] The context and impetus for this proposed change is that the rate of compulsory detention in mental health hospitals has more than doubled since 1983 and is disproportionately higher among certain ethnic minority groups, with black people four times more likely than white people to be detained under the Act.[59] The White Paper

[52] Police and Crime Act 2017, s 80. Exceptionality is satisfied if there is an imminent risk of serious injury or death and no other place of safety in the police area can reasonably be expected to detain that person, and it is authorised by an inspector: The Mental Health Act 1983 (Places of Safety) Regulations 2017.

[53] ibid. The detention can be extended by 12 hours by RMP if necessary for assessment.

[54] Royal College of Emergency Medicine, 'A Brief Guide to Section 136 for Emergency Departments' (2017), available at rcem.ac.uk/wp-content/uploads/2021/10/A_Brief_Guide_to_Section_136_for_Emergency_Departments_Dec_2017.pdf.

[55] Mental Health Act Statistics, 'Annual Figures 2020–21', available at digital.nhs.uk/data-and-information/publications/statistical/mental-health-act-statistics-annual-figures/2020-21-annual-figures.

[56] In a small study from 2013, the reason for detention in 57 out of 70 cases was the perception of a risk of suicide or self-harm in the following study: 'A Criminal Use of Police Cells? The use of police custody as a place of safety for people with mental health needs', Joint Thematic Review (2013), available at www.justiceinspectorates.gov.uk/hmicfrs/media/a-criminal-use-of-police-cells-20130620.pdf. Another study has suggested acts or threats of self-harm existed in 55% of cases: J Laidlaw, D Pugh, G Riley and N Hovey, 'The Use of Section 136 (Mental Health Act 1983) in Gloucestershire' (2010) 50 *Medicine, Science and the Law* 29.

[57] MHA 1983, s 2(2).

[58] 'Reforming the Mental Health Act' (n 46).

[59] ibid, ch 2.

thus proposes to tighten up the language in section 2 (and 3) to require that there be 'a substantial likelihood of significant harm to the health, safety or welfare of the person, or the safety of any other person'.[60] If these grounds exist, it justifies detention for a period not exceeding 28 days.

In order to facilitate such an admission for assessment in urgent situations, section 4 permits an emergency application to be made either by an approved mental health professional[61] or by the nearest relative of the patient where it is of *urgent necessity* for the patient to be admitted and detained under section 2 and compliance with the normal requirements of that provision (eg a written statement by two doctors) would involve undesirable delay.[62] Such an emergency application can be founded on the medical recommendation of only one doctor, rather than two, and authorises detention for a period not exceeding 72 hours (by which time a second medical recommendation must be obtained if the patient is to remain detained in hospital). There are also powers under section 5 to detain persons who are already hospital in-patients for a period of 72 hours if it appears to the registered medical practitioner or approved clinician in charge of the treatment of the patient that an application ought to be made for the compulsory admission of the patient[63] (or for six hours if it appears so to a nurse and it is not practicable to secure the immediate attendance of a practitioner or clinician).[64]

All of these short-term compulsory detention powers will be of relevance to a person thought to be at risk of suicide for any such risk would clearly satisfy the requirement of detention for her own safety (and indeed would satisfy the proposed new requirement of 'substantial likelihood of significant harm'). However, these powers only have application if the person at risk of suicide is suffering from a mental disorder warranting detention. The definition of mental disorder was revised in 2007 so that it is now simply drawn as 'any disorder or disability of the mind'.[65] Given that suicide risk is most commonly associated with mental illness and that it is estimated that approximately 90 per cent of people who die by suicide have a mental illness,[66] for the vast majority of those at risk from suicide, compulsory hospital admission for assessment is likely to be relatively unproblematic. In the UK, the most common diagnoses among patient suicide deaths are affective disorders (47 per cent), schizophrenia (19 per cent), alcohol dependence (eight per cent), personality disorder (nine per cent) and drug dependence

[60] ibid.

[61] The MHA 2007 created the category of 'approved mental health professionals' (AMHPs) to replace approved social worker (ASW) as persons with power to apply for detention and thus opened up this role to a wider group of professionals.

[62] MHA 1983, s 4.

[63] ibid s 5(2).

[64] ibid s 5(4).

[65] The previous definition was more specific, but also more problematic: 'mental illness, arrested or incomplete development of mind, psychopathic disorder and any other disorder or disability of mind'.

[66] K Windfuhr and N Kapur, 'Suicide and Mental Illness: A Clinical Review of 15 Years Findings from a UK National Confidential Inquiry into Suicide' (2011) 100 *British Medical Bulletin* 101.

(four per cent).[67] While dependence on alcohol or drugs is explicitly not considered to be a disorder or disability of the mind under the MHA scheme,[68] the other diagnoses fall squarely into the category of mental disorder for which compulsory powers exist. This suggests that for the huge majority of persons at risk of suicide, legal powers exist to authorise compulsory admission to hospital.

Longer-term hospital detention is also permissible under the MHA 1983. Section 3 provides for *admission for treatment* in circumstances where: (a) a person must be suffering from a *mental disorder of a nature or degree* which makes it appropriate for her to receive medical treatment in a hospital; and (b) it is *necessary for the health and safety of the patient* or for the protection of other persons that she should receive such treatment and it *cannot be provided unless she is detained* under this section; and (c) *appropriate medical treatment is available* for her.[69] (As with section 2, the 2021 White Paper proposes tightening the wording of section 3 to require 'substantial likelihood of significant harm'.)

The latter requirement for availability of 'appropriate medical treatment' replaced the original treatability condition under the 1983 Act which required that detention and treatment on grounds of mental impairment or psychopathic disorder could be authorised only if treatment was 'likely to alleviate or prevent a deterioration' of the patient's condition.[70] The current requirement for availability of 'appropriate medical treatment', defined as including 'nursing, psychological intervention and specialist mental health habilitation, rehabilitation and care', must have the purpose to alleviate, or prevent a worsening of, the disorder or one or more of its symptoms or manifestations, but no longer needs to be likely to do so. The revised wording also implies that appropriate treatment actually be available to the patient which helps to clarify that detention under this provision is solely for the purposes of treatment and not merely for prevention of risk, including that of suicide. Furthermore, the 2021 White Paper proposes the reinstatement of an explicit therapeutic benefit requirement to the section 3 criteria.[71]

It is worth noting that suicide risk is elevated in the in-patient group, and periods of transition into and out of in-patient wards have been identified as particularly vulnerable periods for patients.[72] Indeed, the risk of suicide after discharge from mental health in-patient care has been reported to be 100 times that of the general population.[73] The 2021 White Paper notes that a quarter of the people who die by suicide while using an inpatient mental health service were absent without leave (AWOL) at the time of their death.[74] It proposes a Mental Health Safety

[67] ibid 111.
[68] MHA 1983, s 1(3).
[69] ibid s 3(2).
[70] Introduced by the MHA 2007, s 4.
[71] 'Reforming the Mental Health Act' (n 46) ch 2.
[72] Windfuhr and Kapur, 'Suicide and Mental Illness' (2011) 112.
[73] ibid.
[74] Reforming the Mental Health Act' (n 46) ch 2.

Improvement Programme (MHSIP) to focus on reducing AWOL episodes, as well as reducing the risk of suicide of healthcare staff, and suicide in acute general hospitals, and to support the adherence to national guidance for ligature anchor point management (to seek to prevent the most common means of suicide for inpatients).[75] An admission for treatment under section 3 will authorise compulsory detention for a period of up to six months. While the initial detention has to be authorised by two registered medical practitioners, a renewal of detention beyond the initial six months can be authorised by a 'responsible clinician' who need not be a doctor, but could be another authorised professional who has undertaken the necessary training. Two significant protections for the rights of a patient detained for compulsory treatment have been established by the European Court of Human Rights. The influential case of *Winterwerp* in 1979 established that a decision to detain someone on the grounds of mental disorder must be backed by objective medical evidence,[76] and *Herczegfalvy* determined that compulsory treatment must be therapeutically necessary.[77] Beyond those minimum requirements, treatment that is 'appropriate' and 'necessary' will be lawful. Unlike the treatment under the MCA scheme, the compulsory treatment powers under the MHA do not restrict treatment to that which is in the best interests of the patient. There is therefore no need to consider the broader interests of the patient beyond their specific medical need.[78] Applied to a patient at risk of suicide, it may be (subject to what was said in the previous section) that preventing the suicide is not always in the best interests of the patient, but it would certainly be appropriate to do so from a medical perspective.

Again, the 2021 White Paper proposes relevant changes in this context. It aims to strengthen the patient's right to choose and refuse treatment because it recognises that the current legislative framework 'does not place enough emphasis on empowering patients and it too readily removes their freedom and ability to express choices and preferences'.[79] The White Paper envisages a number of changes to facilitate this, including 'advance choice documents' (ACDs) to enable people to set out in advance the care and treatment they would prefer, and any treatments they wish to refuse, in the event they are detained under the Act and lack the relevant capacity to express their views at the time; 'care and treatment plans' to set out the patient's care and treatment, including how this takes into consideration the wishes and preferences of the patient, and the rationale when a person's wishes have not been followed; and an enhanced role for the Mental Health Tribunal (MHT) to provide a new route for patients to challenge their treatment in circumstances where there is specific disagreement about an individual treatment decision. In addition, a revised Part IV of the MHA1983 will provide a new legal framework

[75] ibid.

[76] *Winterwerp v Netherlands* Series A no 33 (1979).

[77] *Herczegfalvy v Austria* Series A no 244 (1992).

[78] P Bartlett, 'The Necessity Must be Convincingly Shown to Exist': Standards for Compulsory Treatment for Mental Disorder under the MHA 1983' (2011) 19 *Medical Law Review* 514, 545.

[79] 'Reforming the Mental Health Act' (n 46) ch 4.

for consent to medical treatment and, of relevance to treatment for suicide risk, this includes moving the need for a second opinion from three months to 14 days for those with capacity or an ACD, and to two months for those without.

More broadly, it can be noted that the compulsory powers of detention and treatment under the MHA 1983 do not require a lack of mental capacity. Thus, a person with decision-making capacity can still be subjected to compulsory treatment against their wishes. Despite the merits of the new treatment safeguards mentioned in the previous paragraph, nothing in the White Paper will prevent urgent treatment being provided in the face of a capacitated refusal, without the need for a second opinion, if doing so is immediately necessary to save the patient's life or (provided the treatment is not irreversible or hazardous) is immediately necessary and represents the minimum interference necessary to prevent the patient from behaving violently or being a danger to themselves (or others).[80] In the context of suicide risk, this means that someone who retains the mental capacity to make decisions, but is diagnosed with a mental disorder, is likely to face compulsory hospital admission and treatment, regardless of whether the wish to die is directly linked to the disorder.

The existence of parallel schemes in the MHA and MCA has been the subject of much comment and criticism. There is considerable overlap in the persons to whom the powers under each Act will apply – because many of those with a mental disorder will also lack capacity – but, as Richardson has emphasised, the two legislative schemes have very different aims. While the MCA seeks to empower people to make decisions for themselves and protect them if they are unable to do so, the MHA is primarily focused on the reduction of risks flowing from a mental disorder, both to the patient and to others.[81] Thus, in the suicide context, while the MCA seeks a balance between protection of autonomy and welfare, the MHA seeks only to reduce the risk of suicide. It is a somewhat blunt tool to apply to a complex scenario.

B. Application of Mental Capacity Laws for Preventing Risk of Suicide

Outside of the MHA, compulsion can also be used to prevent suicide under the Mental Capacity Act (MCA 2005). The irrelevance of decision-making capacity under the mental health laws stands in stark contrast with its pivotal role in relation to treatment for physical disorders under the MCA 2005. This means that a

[80] Nor will it prevent such treatment if (not being irreversible) it is immediately necessary to prevent a serious deterioration of their condition, although further consultation is taking place on whether a refusal should be respected for treatment (not being irreversible or hazardous) that is immediately necessary to alleviate serious suffering by the patient.

[81] G Richardson, 'Mental Capacity at the Margin: The Interface between Two Acts' (2010) 18 *Medical Law Review* 56, 57.

person retaining capacity can be treated without consent for a mental disorder but not for a physical disorder. Thus the linking of suicide risk and mental disorder facilitates the compulsory admission and treatment for persons thought to be at risk. This raises a number of concerns, however, and it has been argued that a capacity test should be applied for all compulsion under English law.[82] Arguably, not doing so discriminates against persons with a mental disorder; the two parallel schemes make the law unnecessarily complex; and, as will be discussed in the following section, it appears to violate the Convention on the Rights of Persons with Disabilities (CRPD).

A person lacks capacity under the MCA if she is unable to make a decision for herself because of an impairment of, or a disturbance in the functioning of, the mind or brain.[83] The test for being 'unable to make a decision' is found in section 3; it states that a person is unable to make a decision if she is unable to: (a) understand the information relevant to the decision; (b) retain that information; (c) use or weigh that information as part of the process of making the decision; or (d) communicate the decision.[84] If a person lacks capacity under these provisions, treatment can be provided in her best interests. The determination of what treatment is the best interests of the patient requires consideration of her own past and present wishes and feelings, and the beliefs and values that would be likely to influence her decision if she had capacity.[85] A deprivation of liberty is also permitted under the MCA (and outside of the compulsory admission powers in the MHA) in order to give life-sustaining treatment or to prevent a serious deterioration in the person's condition. This is now regulated by means of new Liberty Protection Safeguards (LPS) introduced under the Mental Capacity (Amendment) Act 2019.[86] The Wesseley review on the MHA recommended that all patients without capacity who do not object should receive care and treatment under the LPS rather than under the MHA. However, the Government did not accept this recommendation in its White Paper and chose to consult further on this issue.

The MCA scheme presents a number of opportunities for suicide prevention measures, but can be controversial in its application. First, in relation to the test for capacity, there have been arguments that it has been developed in the context of physical or cognitive disorders and is inadequate in the context of psychiatric disorders because it fails to give adequate weight to the issue of insight and the role of emotions.[87] In addition, as was discussed above, there is a clear potential

[82] J Dawson, 'A Realistic Approach to Assessing Mental Health Laws' Compliance with UNCRPD' (2015) 40 *International Journal of Law and Psychiatry* 70, 76.

[83] MCA 2005, s 2(1).

[84] ibid s 3(1).

[85] ibid s 4(6).

[86] These replace the Deprivation of Liberty Safeguards (DoLS) introduced by the MHA 2007.

[87] See G Richardson, 'Mental Capacity in the Shadow of Suicide: What Can the Law Do?' (2013) 9 *International Journal of Law in Context* 87, 90 for discussion, and ultimately rejection, of such arguments.

catch-22 issue when considering capacity to choose suicide: if a person wants to end her own life, that decision is likely affected by a depression which is impossible to set aside, and thus she is not capable of making the decision to die; but if a person does not wish to end her own life, then she is capable and rational and has the right to decide to die – until she makes that decision and is thus deemed no longer capable or rational. If this is an accurate reflection of the law's approach to the capacity of a suicidal person, it suggests that a depressed person will always be prevented from exercising an autonomous choice to die and it is possible to draw parallels with the position in respect of persons with anorexia, who may be regarded as unable to make binding decisions in respect of eating. Indeed, in *Re E*, the judge recognised that ' a person with severe anorexia may be in a Catch-22 situation regarding capacity: namely, that by deciding not to eat, she proves that she lacks capacity to decide at all'.[88]

There is clear danger in such an approach because, while a mental illness such as anorexia or depression may indeed hamper a purported exercise of autonomous choice, it will be almost impossible to separate that illness from the personality of the person concerned, especially if it is a long-standing illness. As Wilson has noted,

> it may be difficult to distinguish between situations where a person's refusal of medical treatment and wish to die is purely springing from their mental impairment or is a person's true authentic wish (especially where a person's long-term impairment has become enmeshed into their personality). The result being that persons with certain kinds of impairments are effectively prevented from ever making particular decisions based on their diagnosis or status, the classic example being the inability of persons with anorexia nervosa being able to refuse food.[89]

It may be, however, that the second step of determining what is in the best interests of the person who lacks capacity can compensate for these concerns. Under the MCA, a person who lacks capacity is still entitled to have their wishes, feelings, beliefs and values taken into account in determining their future care and treatment. Although this requirement has been within the MCA since its enactment, it is only in more recent years that the courts have given greater emphasis to a subjective approach to best interests. Thus, the Supreme Court's decision in *Aintree University Hospitals NHS Foundation Trust v James and Others*[90] made clear that the choices of the incapacitated person are central to determinations of her best interests, with Baroness Hale noting that 'it is not for others to say that a life which the patient would regard as worthwhile is not worth living'.[91]

[88] *Re E* [2012] EWHC 1639 COP [53].
[89] Wilson, 'The Call for the Abolition of Mental Health Law' (2018) 675–76.
[90] *Aintree University Hospitals NHS Foundation Trust v James and Others* [2013] UKSC 6.
[91] ibid 44.

Of course, the circumstances of that case are very different to the context of suicide. *James* involved a minimally conscious patient where the evidence was that he would wish to fight on to continue life for as long as possible, which is a stark contrast to a mentally ill person expressing a desire to die by means of suicide. Indeed, while the *James* judgment champions a subjective approach to best interests, it also, on the facts of the case, supports a preservation of life approach. A subjective approach in the context of addressing the question of whether suicide can ever be in a person's best interests is likely to be far more challenging. First, it would require the law, and those enforcing and interpreting it, to depart from centuries of emphasis on preserving human life. While this is tolerated when there is a strong and unambiguous conflicting autonomy interest, a determination of best interests by definition occurs in relation to a choice made by a person who lacks decision-making capacity and therefore there will be, at least, room for doubt about whether the choice is an autonomous one or not. Secondly, the suicide context at issue in this discussion not only applies to a person lacking decision-making capacity but also one for whom the very reason for that lack of capacity may in itself have influenced the expressed wishes of that person. In other words, by the time a determination of whether death would be in the best interests of a person is being made under the MCA, she will already have been judged to lack capacity to make a choice to die because of, for example, being depressed. And it may well be that it is the depression which is influencing a desire to end life prematurely.

Thus, while it may be possible to conceive of a suicide being in a person's own interests, along the lines of the rational suicide identified earlier in this chapter, such a suicide is highly unlikely to be one at issue under the MCA because the mere fact of a lack of decision-making capacity will undermine any weight that might be given to an enduring wish to die. This returns us to the question of whether there is discrimination in the law's tolerance of suicide for all except those with a mental impairment. As Dawson notes, discrimination can be a complex notion in this context. Is it discriminatory to take into account, or not to take into account, the effects of a person's condition on their mental functioning when making decisions?[92] The answer, Dawson proposes, is to determine what counts as a relevant difference between persons regarding the particular decision of ending one's life.[93] Blindness is relevant to an ability to drive; is mental impairment relevant to a choice to end life?[94] Given that the law does not unequivocally endorse any choice of suicide, it does seem possible that equality in this context may require special protection for the life of the vulnerable.[95]

[92] Dawson, 'A Realistic Approach' (2015) 71.
[93] ibid 73.
[94] ibid.
[95] S Callaghan, C Ryan and I Kerridge, 'Risk of Suicide is Insufficient Warrant for Coercive Treatment of Mental Illness' (2013) 36 *International Journal of Law and Psychiatry* 374, 378.

C. Problems with Both Mental Capacity and Mental Health Laws in the Suicide Context

Both the MHA and the MCA schemes raise problems in the context of suicide. One way of highlighting the problems with the two schemes in the context of suicide is to compare the law's response to suicide risk in relation to Tony Nicklinson and Melanie Rabone.[96] Both suffered from health problems that appear linked to their wish to end their own lives, but while it was Nicklinson's physical health condition that led to his wish not to continue living, for Rabone it was her mental disorder that created the risk of suicide. While Nicklinson was not granted his request for assistance to facilitate a painless suicide, no efforts were put in place to seek to prevent him from taking steps (such as refusing food and water) that would lead to his early death, and there was no question of anyone being liable for failing to prevent it. By contrast, Rabone's risk of suicide led to her compulsory admission to hospital and legal liability for the hospital in granting her the home leave which provided her with the opportunity to take her own life. The respective court cases illustrate, as Callaghan et al have pointed out, the very different moral assumptions that underpin the different legal responses: while Nicklinson was viewed as 'a middle-aged, profoundly disabled man … perhaps entitled to end his life', Rabone was viewed as 'a physically healthy but troubled young woman [who] should not have killed herself'.[97]

There are a number of potentially pertinent differences between the two persons: while Nicklinson suffered from a physical disorder, Rabone suffered from a mental disorder; while Nicklinson was asking for assistance in ending his life; Rabone's suicide was being considered in relation to potential liability for failing to prevent it; while Nicklinson's case concerned the criminal law, Rabone's involved negligence; and while both cases engaged human rights law, it was the potential interference with Nicklinson's right to autonomy that was in issue as contrasted with the failure to protect Rabone's right to life. Amidst these distinctions, one issue that could (and arguably should) have been central to both cases, and might have helped to legitimately distinguish the two situations, was that of mental capacity. It is shocking, therefore, that neither case focused on whether the person who wanted to die had the mental capacity to make such a decision. It is, no doubt, assumed that Melanie Rabone's decision to end her life was not one made by a person with decision-making capacity due to her mental illness, alongside an underlying assumption that this 'physically healthy' and 'young' woman could not have really wanted to die. Similarly, it seems to be assumed that Tony Nicklinson had the capacity to decide to end his life and that the only obstacle to implementing this regrettable, but wholly legitimate, decision was the criminal prohibition

[96] *R (Nicklinson) v Ministry of Justice; R (AM) v Director of Public Prosecutions* [2014] UKSC 38; *Rabone and another v Pennine Care NHS Trust* [2012] UKSC 2.

[97] Callaghan, Ryan and Kerridge, 'Risk of Suicide is Insufficient Warrant' (2013) 374.

on the provision of assistance by another person. Neither of these assumptions should have gone uninterrogated.

Callaghan et al have criticised this lack of focus on capacity:

> It is arguable that in both cases there should have been a rigorous assessment of decision-making capacity, followed by consideration of whether or not the person's decision – in Nicklinson, to seek directly to end his life, and in Rabone, to leave hospital – should have been honoured. In both cases though, this approach was notably absent.[98]

It is entirely possible that Nicklinson's capacity was impaired due to being depressed about his condition and that Rabone's decision to enter and subsequently leave the hospital illustrated a residual mental capacity notwithstanding her mental illness. Without a judicial focus on capacity, neither of these possibilities can be categorically ruled out. With a lack of focus on functional capacity, the law's approach to suicide in such cases instead appears to be squarely based on a status-based approach under which a mental health patient's suicide must be prevented and other persons' suicides are tolerated, provided they are not actively facilitated. Tony Nicklinson took the only steps available to him in his condition to end his life shortly after the first instance decision in his case and he was able to do so in the absence of any measures to prevent his death and, of course, with no liability arising for anyone after his death. The law's efforts to prevent suicide are not, therefore, consistent across the board and with the rejection of a capacity-based approach, the distinction does not revolve around rationality but rather mental health status.

Furthermore, it is curious that at the same time as suicide prevention has acquired a global health priority status, legal efforts to use compulsory detention and treatment powers to avert suicide face a new challenge from international law. The Convention on the Rights of Persons with Disabilities (CRPD) precludes the use of a mental disability as a justification for compulsion. The CRPD extends a social model of disability to mental impairments and prohibits discrimination on the basis of mental disability.[99] Not only does this cause problems for the current English law approach under the MHA 1983,[100] where the very existence of a mental disorder is a necessary ingredient for compulsory admission and treatment, but it also seems to deter an alternative mental capacity-based approach to the use of compulsion. Of particular significance in our context is Article 12 CRPD, which

[98] ibid 380.

[99] See G Richardson, 'Mental Disabilities and the Law: From Substitute to Supported Decision-making' (2012) 65 *Current Legal Problems* 333.

[100] In its concluding observations in 2017, the CRPD Committee recommended that the UK repeal all legislation and practices that 'authorise non-consensual involuntary, compulsory treatment and detention of persons with disabilities on the basis of actual or perceived impairment': Committee on the Rights of Persons with Disabilities, 'Concluding Observations on the Initial Report of the United Kingdom of Great Britain and Northern Ireland' (2017) para 35(a), available at digitallibrary.un.org/record/1310654.

requires legal capacity to be provided on an equal basis. This means that legal and mental capacity should not be linked. At a superficial level, this would seem to require that decisions made by persons lacking mental capacity be respected, including a decision to attempt suicide. Article 12(3) does, however, require measures to provide access to the support required to exercise legal capacity, and thus envisages a system of supported decision-making.

A decoupling of legal and mental capacity is extremely challenging for English law which has traditionally (and increasingly so in recent decades) utilised mental capacity as the gatekeeper of autonomy. This has undoubtedly placed a heavy burden on the concept of mental capacity. As Richardson has noted, 'if the test of mental capacity is set too high it will exclude our truly autonomous choices from the law's respect, but if it is set too low it may accord respect to choices that do not reflect our true wishes'.[101] This is a challenge particularly pertinent to suicide prevention, where the stakes are high: failing to respect a capacitated choice to die condemns a person to a life that is not, in her view, worth living, while respecting a choice to die that does not reflect her true wishes may lead to an unnecessary loss of life. It might be argued, however, that the best approach is clearer in relation to suicide than in relation to other choices because a failure to respect a choice to die only imposes a temporary delay on enacting that choice, whereas respecting it erroneously is a mistake that cannot be rectified. It would make sense, therefore, in a world that values the preservation of human life, and in a society committed to a right to life, for the law to err on the side of preserving life when regulating life and death decisions such as suicide. This is only justifiable, however, if the possibility exists to demonstrate capacity at a later stage.

The CRPD's approach to treatment of those with mental impairment is one of supported decision-making. This model would only enable persons with mental impairment to be provided with psychiatric treatment with their informed consent or, if that is impossible, with the best interpretation of their will and preferences. The only concession to the potential obstacle to capacitated decision-making posed by a mental impairment is the recognition of the need to offer support. What could support mean for a suicidal person? Wilson notes that it seems to involve

> trying to create a safe and comfortable space to assist them to understand what is happening and to facilitate their making a decision about whether or not to end their lives which reflects their will and preferences, whatever the result.[102]

However, Wilson also identifies a conviction for involuntary manslaughter in the United States for a person who was regarded as too encouraging in supporting a friend to complete a suicide when she believed that it was in accordance with her

[101] Richardson, 'Mental Capacity in the Shadow of Suicide' (2013) 90.
[102] Wilson (n 40) 684.

friend's will and preferences.[103] This highlights the thin line that exists between avoiding criminal liability for encouraging a suicide and respecting the wishes of a person who has made a choice to die.

Generally, when viewed from the perspective of suicide prevention, it is hard to view the CRPD approach as anything but heading in the wrong direction. At a time when the World Health Organization (WHO) regards all suicides as preventable and classifies efforts to do as a public health priority, the UN through the CRPD sends the message that decisions of those with mental impairment to die by suicide should be respected, provided that support has been provided to facilitate the making of a decision. It seems clear that if the goal is really to try to prevent all suicides (although it is not conceded here that this is an appropriate goal), the provision of compulsory psychiatric treatment will be required, in at least some circumstances. Taken together the message(s) from the CRPD and WHO are contradictory and unhelpful: all suicides should be prevented but without the provision of non-consensual assistance. Indeed, the one aspect on which both messages seem to speak with one voice is that neither mental impairment nor a lack of mental capacity are relevant distinguishing features when regulating suicide. Yet, of course, within English law, these remain central features of the law's response to suicide risk.

The CRPD approach presents significant challenges to the use of compulsory powers to prevent suicide. A state cannot be justified in taking no action to seek to prevent any suicides because this would leave vulnerable people at the mercy of their mental states and would run directly counter to the WHO's claims that all suicides are preventable. Perhaps most importantly, however, it is also hard to see how such an approach would comply with the CRPD's own provision requiring that states take all necessary measures to ensure the effective enjoyment of the right to life by persons with disabilities on an equal basis with others.[104] While this provision has not yet been substantively interpreted, concluding observations by the Committee on the Rights of Persons with Disabilities have noted the need for preventive measures against suicide risk.[105] Herring has recently argued for the need to balance Article 10 CRPD's protection for the right to life with Article 14's prohibition of discrimination, which he believes 'could justify discriminatory treatment of the suicidal in a sufficiently strong case'.[106]

One solution to this dilemma that would appear to be consistent with the CRPD would be to permit state intervention to prevent suicide regardless of mental impairment or capacity.[107] While this would accord with the CRPD and

[103] ibid 684–85.
[104] CRPD, Art 10.
[105] Wilson (n 40) 667.
[106] J Herring, *The Right to be Protected from Suicide* (Oxford, Hart Publishing, 2022) 157.
[107] Herring also recognises this alternative means of circumventing Art 14's restrictions in relation to suicide, noting that if there was provision for civil detention of any suicidal person regardless of mental health status, that would arguably comply with the CRPD (ibid).

respect the WHO's goal of seeking to prevent all suicides, it can only be acceptable if we take the view either that no suicides are rational choices (which was dismissed above) or that overriding an autonomous, rational choice for a person's own good is permissible. This latter view, which violates liberal individualism, the ethos of human rights law, and JS Mill's harm principle,[108] is categorically rejected here.[109] Instead, it is argued that mental capacity should remain central to decisions about whether to respect or prevent, by compulsion if necessary, a choice to die by suicide. The justification for this, and exploration of how it might work in practice, is addressed in the following section, which will argue for a refined legal approach to capacity in relation to a choice to die.

D. A Refined Legal Approach with Capacity at its Core

While it is recognised that determinations of capacity are complex and problematic, this remains the only approach that holds the potential to respect autonomous decision-making about dying, without risking abandoning those unable to exercise their true autonomy to the dangers of their incapacitated choices. The determination of whether a person has mental capacity is described by Craigie as ultimately being about whether a decision can be explained

> in terms of the patient's particular motivating commitments (their desires, values, projects, ideas about a good life); or whether the decision is properly explained in terms of a problem in decision-making, which is due to a dysfunction of mind or brain.[110]

Such an approach would query whether a decision, including a desire to die by suicide, is consistent with the person's identity and whether it makes sense in the context of the story of her life. This is, to an extent, simply another way of saying that serious decisions, with adverse effects for the person making them, should not be made on a whim. Or, if they are, this may be an indication that the person lacks decision-making capacity in relation to this specific issue. To avoid decision-making on a whim, the concept of 'diachronic continuity'[111] can be usefully applied. As Pickard explains, a degree of diachronic continuity is 'an

[108] JS Mill, *On Liberty* in J Gray and GW Smith (eds), *JS Mill's On Liberty in Focus* (London, Routledge, 1991): the 'only purpose for which power can rightfully be exercised over any member of a civilised community against his will is to prevent harm to others' (30). Raz has provided a more recent influential defence of the harm principle when arguing that an autonomy-based principle of freedom provides the moral foundation for this principle: J Raz, *The Morality of Freedom* (Oxford, Clarendon Press, 1986) 400. Raz defends the harm principle on the basis of the principle of autonomy because coercive interference violates the autonomy of the victim.

[109] More justification for this approach may be found in E Wicks, *The State and the Body: Legal Regulation of Bodily Autonomy* (Oxford, Hart Publishing, 2016).

[110] J Craigie, 'Capacity, Value Neutrality and the Ability to Consider the Future' (2013) 9 *International Journal of Law in Context* 4, 6.

[111] ibid 8–9.

important part of identifying the desires and values that shape autonomous decisions. Signs of ambivalence and actions that are out of character offer evidence that this condition is not met'.[112] An example of such a sign of ambivalence in the context of suicide risk might be if the person concerned voluntarily contacts a doctor or other health or social care services.[113] The idea of internal coherence is one that is often applied by courts in determining the value to place upon an expressed wish.

The requirement of diachronic continuity goes further than merely expecting continuity with previous choices and values; it also crucially looks to the future. Craigie points out that psychologists 'often assume that people are rationally required to give significant weight to the future personal consequences of choices, the strongest version being that people ought to be temporarily neutral in their decision-making'.[114] This is a particularly valuable perspective in the context of decisions about suicide. A person contemplating such a grave decision should give some weight to the implications of it for their future self. In most scenarios, this might be assumed to undermine the choice to end life prematurely, for the future self will be denied the opportunity to live. This will be particularly applicable to the suicidal tendencies that are frequently inherent in depression where the future self may not be sufficiently taken into account when a decision to die prematurely is made.[115]

It is conceivable, however, that in some contexts, the future self might be saved from further harm from the choice. Perhaps this might explain why the voluntary death of Tony Nicklinson, discussed above, was widely treated as sad but understandable, because he had explicitly referred to his future self in seeking to justify his choice to die. A diachronic perspective is already utilised within the MCA when determinations are made about a person's best interests. What is being argued here, however, is that it would also be a valuable perspective in relation to determinations about a person's decision-making capacity and, as Craigie has noted, such an approach need not undermine the value neutrality inherent in the functional approach to capacity implemented in the MCA.[116] In section 2, 'understanding' is explicitly required in order for a person to retain capacity; if the implications for the future self from a purported decision have not been taken into account, this may well signify a lack of understanding.

[112] H Pickard, 'Choice, Deliberation, Violence: Mental Capacity and Criminal Responsibility in Personality Disorder (2015) 40 *International Journal of Law and Psychiatry* 15, 21.

[113] ibid.

[114] Craigie, 'Capacity' (2013) 8.

[115] Some writers go further and suggest that a compromised ability to engage in future planning threatens not only the future self but also the self itself: see M Bratman, 'Reflection, Planning and Temporally Extended Agency' (2000) 109 *Philosophical Review* 35. This has led to suggestions that within a liberal society, that elevates the idea of self, autonomy might permit intervention in order to restore the self: Craigie (n 110) 16.

[116] Craigie (n 110) 11.

Thus, it is argued here that a refined approach to the law's response to suicide risk should focus on the issue of mental capacity, rather than mental illness, but also extend beyond its traditional boundaries. As a starting point, if a person has decision-making capacity under the MCA, the use of compulsion to prevent suicide should not be used. This, of course, would require reform of the current mental health laws under the MHA, but it is an approach that would have the benefit of preventing discriminatory treatment on the basis of a mental illness, would give great weight to autonomy for those with mental capacity and would not, of course, preclude other societal efforts to prevent suicide, ranging from the reduction of opportunities for self-harm to the provision of consensual support and treatment. Beyond this starting point, however, further refinement of how decision-making capacity is determined will further support both a goal of suicide prevention and respect for autonomy. Thus, when determining whether a person has the requisite understanding needed to make a capacitated decision, regard should be had to the concept of diachronic continuity. This should involve both consideration as to the internal coherence of a desire to die by suicide with the past and present wishes and identity of the person now expressing such a desire, as well as whether or not the implications for the future self have been sufficiently taken into account. To demonstrate the capacity to make a decision to die by suicide, a person would need to follow a decision-making process that was rational, consistent, forward-looking and reflective. Without such characteristics, the decision-making capacity would be in doubt, and the focus would turn instead to whether compulsory treatment and prevention would be in their best interests. Again, the wishes of the person in question would be highly relevant here, but their match with core identity, both past and future-looking, would be taken into account.

It might be argued that the approach outlined here would push the wording of the MCA beyond its limits and set the standard for capacitated decision-making in respect of suicide unreasonably high. However, as has been discussed throughout this chapter, there are significant concerns about the undeniable link between mental illness and suicide risk, and furthermore, a presumption in favour of saving life, in circumstances where it is unclear whether a choice to die reflects an autonomous choice or not, is consistent with long-standing legal protection for human life in the English legal system, the right to life protected at domestic, regional and international level, and the WHO's public health prioritisation of suicide prevention. These are all sound reasons why, if there is any doubt about capacity, the ambiguity should be resolved in favour of the preservation of life. Sitting alongside this cautious approach, however, should be a recognition that where capacity is not in doubt, compulsion is not justifiable, even to save life.

III. Conclusion

In this chapter, we have explored the relationship between issues of mental health, suicide and the law. It has been argued that a rational suicide is possible and that therefore an assumption that all suicides are symptoms of a mental illness is unsustainable. Even if only a very small percentage of wishes to die are rational, it requires the law to be more refined in its approach to preventing suicide. A range of legal powers under the mental health and mental capacity laws have been identified that currently serve to provide compulsory interventions, detention and/or treatment in efforts to prevent suicide.

These laws raise a number of contentious and problematic issues. Perhaps most significantly, they present both internal and external contradictions. Internally, within the English legal system, the two distinct legal schemes regulating mental health and mental capacity mean that interventions in the context of suicide are not always consistent. The mental health status of a person at risk of suicide is a crucial consideration in these schemes. Indeed, the apparent rejection of a capacity-based approach to determining when to intervene to prevent suicide means that the line is not drawn at the boundary of rationality but rather at mental health status. This rejection of the centrality of mental capacity in domestic law is adopted more formally within international law due to the CRPD under which the relevance of mental capacity to the law's reaction to suicide risk is entirely rejected.

Such an approach has not found favour in this chapter's discussion. Instead, it has been argued here that the issue of mental capacity should remain crucial to the determination of the law's appropriate response to a risk of suicide. In most cases when the suicide risk is a symptom of a mental illness, the law's primary role should be one of prevention in order to protect life and health, but when the suicide risk is a capacitated choice rather than a symptom of illness, the law's response needs to be more refined. Given the important value of human life, the need to err on the side of preserving life, and the finality of a person ending their life, this chapter has argued for a heightened test of capacity in the context of choices to die. This test would evaluate whether the decision-making process was not only a capacitated one, but also rational, consistent, forward-looking and reflective. How this more complex, but also more explicit, approach to suicide under the law can be applied within real-life scenarios where suicide risk most frequently arises will be considered in the remainder of this book, as we move on to consider some key contexts – prisons, children, universities, care homes and hospitals – in which the issue of suicide presents specific challenges to English law.

5

Suicide in Detention and the Human Rights Obligations to Prevent it

In this chapter, we will consider the specific legal issues raised by suicide in prison, or other detention contexts. The discussion will focus on the human rights obligations that exist in relation to suicide in detention. This is not intended to suggest that other legal contexts and policy decisions are not significant, but human rights law, and specifically the European Convention on Human Rights (ECHR; currently implemented in domestic law through the Human Rights Act 1998),[1] reveals a fascinating dilemma in respect of suicide prevention; one that reflects the tensions highlighted throughout this book between autonomous choices to die and the genuine need for suicide prevention measures. Article 2 ECHR's protection for the right to life imposes legally enforceable obligations on prison authorities to take reasonable steps to prevent suicide in certain circumstances and Article 3 ECHR prohibits the imposition of degrading treatment, but Article 8 ECHR also requires respect for the private life and, to some extent, the autonomy of prisoners. How are these potentially conflicting obligations to be reconciled? In addressing this question, we will engage with issues that extend beyond the detention context. After a brief introduction to the severity of the problem of suicide in detention, there will be a detailed exploration of the application of Article 2's right to life to this issue which will consider both when a duty to prevent suicide arises, and what such a duty requires. The discussion will then turn to Article 3's obligations which can supplement the protection against suicide within prison. Finally, there will be analysis of why the concept of autonomy seems to be absent from this issue and how a concept of capacity to choose to die, suggested in the previous chapter, might be of specific utility here.

[1] At the time of writing, the Government has introduced a Bill of Rights to Parliament that would radically transform the protection of human rights in domestic law. Under these proposals, the Convention rights will remain within English law and it will continue to be unlawful for public authorities to violate them (cl 12) but of particular significance is proposed cl 5 that would restrict the recognition of positive obligations under the rights, including under Arts 2 and 8 (see publications. parliament.uk/pa/bills/cbill/58-03/0117/220117.pdf).

I. Suicide in Detention

Suicide within prison or another detention context is inherently controversial. Indeed, as Liebling points out, any ending of life in custody *should* be controversial because it raises issues of accountability, legitimacy and quality of life.[2] It is a matter of grave concern, therefore, that the rate of mortality in prison is 40 per cent higher than in the general population and that suicides are one of the most frequent cause of end of life in prison.[3] For example, in the 12 months to March 2022, there were 287 deaths in prison custody in England and Wales, of which 75 were self-inflicted.[4] Since 2010, the annual number of suicides in custody have ranged from 57 to 111.[5] Liebling argues that 'While suicide rates vary, the typical institutional triggers do not seem to change over time. Where disorganization, humiliation, indifference, and violence are high, prison suicides rise'.[6] The prisoners most vulnerable to suicide include young prisoners, prisoners serving long-term and indeterminate life sentences, and remand prisoners. A disproportionate number of suicides occur amongst remand prisoners and those at the earliest stages of a custodial sentence.[7] The young are especially at risk,[8] and while men are generally much more likely to die from suicide than women, the suicide rate for female prisoners is as high as the suicide rate for male prisoners.[9] Half of all those who die from suicide in prison have previously self-harmed (and one-third have done so within prison),[10] suggesting that self-injury can present a warning indicator of suicide risk. However, it has also been suggested that a surprisingly large proportion (40 per cent) of prison suicide attempts are impulsive and not thought about for more than a few minutes.[11]

Whether specific conditions of imprisonment heighten the risk of suicide is a controversial matter.[12] Overcrowding is often argued to be associated with

[2] A Liebling, 'The Meaning of Ending Life in Prison' (2017) 23 *Journal of Correctional Health Care* 20, 20. In this article, Liebling draws parallels between suicide and murder on the basis that both are violent and 'represent forms of "death without dying" as they are often sudden and lack the kinds of preparations or support and accompaniment often associated with the process of dying' (20).

[3] ibid 21.

[4] 'Safety in Custody Statistics', available at www.gov.uk/government/collections/safety-in-custody-statistics.

[5] ibid.

[6] Liebling, 'The Meaning of Ending Life in Prison' (2017) 23. Indeed, Liebling goes so far as to say that the prison system 'is culpable in some respects for high rates of suicide'. Interestingly, corporate manslaughter legislation includes deaths in custody since 2011, although it has not yet been invoked over a prison suicide: Corporate Manslaughter and Corporate Homicide Act 2007, s 2(1)(d).

[7] A Liebling and A Ludlow, 'Suicide, Distress and the Quality of Prison Life' in Y Jewkes, B Crewe and J Bennett (eds), *Handbook on Prisons*, 2nd edn (London, Routledge, 2016) 229.

[8] ibid 229–30. This will be further discussed in the following chapter.

[9] ibid 230.

[10] ibid 233.

[11] A Rivlin, S Fazel, L Marzano and K Hawton, 'The Suicidal Process in Male Prisoners making Near-lethal Suicide Attempts' (2013)19 *Psychology, Crime and Law* 305.

[12] See for example EFJC Van Ginneken, A Sutherland and T Molleman, 'An Ecological Analysis of Prison Overcrowding and Suicide Rates in England and Wales, 2000–2014' (2017) 50 *International Journal of Law and Psychiatry* 76.

a high suicide risk,[13] although some researchers have argued that the fault lies not so much with overcrowding as with high prison turnover.[14] The Harris Review in 2015 into self-inflicted deaths in custody of 18–24-year-olds identified specific problems such as a lack of purposeful activities in prisons for young people, too much time spent locked up in cells, bullying and unsafe cell conditions as contributing to suicides amongst young prisoners.[15] This review also emphasised the importance of good staff-prisoner relationships in preventing suicides, and expressed concern about lack of appropriate training and staff shortages.[16]

There are a series of international and regional obligations in respect of the treatment of prisoners. For example, the UN Principles for the Treatment of Persons under any Form of Detention, the UN Standard Minimum Rules for the Treatment of Prisoners (the 'Nelson Mandela Rules') and the European Prison Rules all provide a minimum standard of protection.[17] While not legally enforceable, they are nonetheless influential in the field. In addition, the European Committee for the Prevention of Torture and Inhuman and Degrading Treatment or Punishment (CPT) publishes reports following country visits, as well as general annual reports and thematic reports.[18] These reports also set standards which are influential, not least upon the European Court of Human Rights.

In the domestic context, the Joint Committee on Human Rights (JCHR) in an Interim Report on Mental Health and Deaths in Prison made a series of recommendations including the creation of a statutory duty on the Secretary of State to specify and maintain a minimum ratio of prison officers to prisoners at each establishment and a prescribed legal maximum to the time a prisoner can be kept in their cell each day.[19] In this Interim Report, the JCHR also recommended a statutory provision making explicit that one of the aims of prison is to treat prisoners with humanity, fairness and respect for their dignity.[20] While this is, of course, a worthy goal, within the context of prison suicide it may not always be obvious what such principles require. Does respect for human dignity only equate to intervention to preserve life or does it also imply respect for autonomous decision-making (and, as has been queried in previous chapters, can a choice to

[13] See for example the 'Report on Self-inflicted Deaths in Prison in 2013/2014' by the Prisons and Probation Ombudsman for England and Wales (2015), which noted that 81% of prisons where suicides took place were overcrowded, whereas 48% of prisons without suicides were overcrowded.

[14] Van Ginnekan, Sutherland and Molleman, 'An Ecological Analysis of Prison Overcrowding' (2017) 80: 'Prison characteristics that are associated with increased suicide rates are: a larger population size, public management of a prison, higher security category, a male population and high turnover'.

[15] T Harris, 'Changing Prisons, Saving Lives – Report of the Independent Review into Self-inflicted Deaths in Custody of 18–24 Year Olds' (London, Ministry of Justice, 2015), available at dera.ioe.ac.uk/23552/1/moj-harris-review-web-accessible.pdf.

[16] ibid.

[17] See M Rogan, 'Human Rights Approaches to Suicide in Prison: Implications for Policy, Practice and Research' (2018) 6 *Health and Justice* 15 for further detail.

[18] The CPT's reports can be found at www.coe.int/en/web/cpt/home.

[19] JCHR's 'Mental Health and Deaths in Prison: Interim Report' (2017) 19 (it is only an interim report because a general election intervened and its inquiry subsequently closed).

[20] ibid 20.

die ever truly be an autonomous one)? The remainder of this chapter will seek to apply human rights principles to this context, beginning with the crucial protection for the right to life.

II. Suicide in Detention and the Right to Life

In his recent book arguing for a 'right to be protected from committing suicide', Jonathan Herring bases his argument in large part upon an assertion that Article 2 ECHR includes such a right.[21] He claims that 'a person who commits suicide has their Article 2 right infringed as much as the person who is killed by another'.[22] Arguably this understates the complexity of the protection for human life provided by Article 2, misunderstands the manner in which it has been interpreted by the European Court of Human Rights[23] and underplays the importance of the protections offered by Article 8 ECHR. Nonetheless, it is certainly true that Article 2's protection of the right to life extends beyond a negative obligation upon the state to avoid intentional deprivations of life and extends to some quite significant positive obligations to take reasonable steps to preserve life.[24]

These positive obligations exist at two levels. First, there is a general duty to take appropriate steps to safeguard lives. This will include, for example, regulatory measures such as criminal law provisions and hospital regulations. Secondly, and the main focus of this section, there is also a so-called 'operational duty' to take preventive operational measures to protect a specific individual whose life is at risk. This operational duty only applies in certain circumstances and, despite Herring's claims of a general right to be protected from suicide, there remains considerable ambiguity as to when this specific duty exists. A series of cases heard by the European Court of Human Rights has confirmed, however, that the operational duty does *sometimes* apply in respect of a suicide risk for persons in detention. The basic requirements for such a duty to arise in this context have been expressed clearly by the Court:

> For a positive obligation to arise regarding a prisoner with suicidal tendencies, it must be established that the authorities knew, or ought to have known at the time, of the existence of a real and immediate risk to the life of an identified individual and, if so, that they failed to take measures within the scope of their powers which, judged reasonably, might have been expected to prevent that risk from materialising.[25]

[21] J Herring, *The Right to be Protected from Suicide* (Oxford, Hart Publishing, 2022).
[22] ibid 113.
[23] Herring cites the case of *Fernandes de Oliveira v Portugal* (App 78103/14, 31 January 2019) [GC] for his claim but does not provide a paragraph reference, and while the Court in that case does take the significant step of extending the operational duty from involuntary to voluntary mental health patients, it does not appear to envisage a broader duty on the state to prevent suicide within society.
[24] *Osman v United Kingdom* ECHR 1998-VIII (1998) 29 EHRR 245.
[25] *Çoşelav v Turkey* (App 1413/07, 9 October 2012) [54].

This indicates, and it is evident in the case law, that there are two fundamental issues to be considered. The first relates to the assessment of a suicide risk and the second relates to the preventative steps to be taken to avoid violating the right to life. These two issues will now be considered in turn.

A. Assessment of Suicide Risk

i. Prisons

In *Keenan v United Kingdom*[26] in 2001, the European Court of Human Rights first had the opportunity to consider the application of Article 2 ECHR's protection of the right to life to the topic of prison suicide when hearing a case about a prisoner suffering from a mental illness who hanged himself from the bars of his cell. A significant part of the Court's judgment focused on the question of whether the prison authorities knew of the risk of this prisoner taking his own life. It found that it had been common ground that the prisoner was mentally ill (despite some dispute about a precise diagnosis) and his behaviour had exhibited suicidal tendencies. The Court was able to confirm, therefore, that the prison authorities knew that 'his mental state was such that he posed a potential risk to his own life'.[27] Interestingly, the Court took this view regardless of any doubt as to how genuine the suicidal threats were, on the basis that the risk posed was 'not only that of intentionally killing himself, but of unintentionally killing himself in an attempt to manipulate the prison authorities'.[28]

No violation of Article 2 was found in *Keenan* (as will be discussed further below), but the twin factors of the existence of a mental illness and 'suicidal tendencies' have remained central to all of the Court's case law on prison suicide. Thus, in *Renolde v France*[29] the Court again held that the prison authorities had known of the risk of suicide in respect of a prisoner because they knew he was suffering from psychotic disorders capable of causing him to commit acts of self-harm.[30] The finding in both *Keenan* and *Renolde* that the authorities knew of the risk to life seems to be reliant upon the fact that the prisoner in question suffered from mental illness. Indeed, in *Renolde*, the Court reiterated that 'the vulnerability of mentally ill persons calls for special protection'.[31] However, the Court also contrasted Keenan, who was diagnosed with a mild psychosis, from Renolde, who suffered acute psychotic disorders.[32] It appears that this distinction

[26] *Keenan v UK* ECHR 2001-III.
[27] ibid [95].
[28] ibid [96].
[29] *Renolde v France* (App 5608/05, 16 October 2008), ECHR 2008 (extracts).
[30] ibid [89].
[31] ibid [109].
[32] ibid [105].

(along with others, discussed below) may even have informed the contrast in outcomes between the two cases, with France being found in violation of Article 2 in *Renolde*.

By contrast, in the later case of *Volk v Slovenia*,[33] the Court was satisfied that the prison authorities had not known of the risk of suicide. In this case, the prisoner had not been diagnosed as suffering from any psychiatric condition, nor were there any previous suicide attempts or self-harm incidents. In those circumstances, the Court found that the authorities could not have reasonably foreseen his decision to take his own life. Furthermore, it did not find any evidence that the authorities *ought* to have known of a suicide risk, holding that there was no manifest omission which would have prevented them from making a correct assessment of the situation.[34] Given that the prisoner in question had twice expressed an intention to harm himself, and this did not suffice to import knowledge of a risk of suicide, it appears from this judgment that the Court was drawing a line between prisoners with a diagnosed mental disorder and other prisoners. Such a diagnosis seems to serve as a necessary condition for Article 2's operational duty to arise in this context. While we have previously seen the close link between mental illness and suicide, it is clear that an official diagnosis does not predate all suicides, and that some prisoners without such a diagnosis remain at risk (such as Volk himself). Indeed, in the subsequent case of *Mitic v Serbia*[35] a prisoner with no known history of mental health problems or suicidal tendencies, who showed no particular signs of physical or mental distress, took his own life by hanging. Again, the Court found that such a background meant that the authorities could not reasonably have foreseen his decision to hang himself and thus the operational duty under Article 2 to take steps to prevent the suicide did not arise.

There is no doubt that the assessment of suicide risk is extremely challenging and it is all too easy to be wise after the fact. As Thoonen and Duijst point out, 'when assessing retrospectively whether the authorities knew or ought to have known of the suicide risk, the outcome is already known. Assessing beforehand whether or not a suicide risk exists is never an easy task'.[36] The Court's approach is systematic and clear, but one might wonder whether it is too inflexible. The centrality of diagnosis in determining whether the authorities knew of the risk to life elevates the importance of psychiatric assessment. Given the particular vulnerability of prisoners during their first few days in prison, a psychiatric screening process on arrival is vital. In *Isenc v France*,[37] the finding of a violation of Article 2 in relation to a prisoner who took his own life only 12 days after being admitted to

[33] *Volk v Slovenia* (App 62120/09, 13 December 2012).

[34] ibid [91]. The authorities had provided Volk with regular psychological assistance and psychiatric and medical care ([89]).

[35] *Mitic v Serbia* (App 31963/08, 22 January 2013).

[36] E Thoonen and W Duijst, 'Suicide in Detention in the Light of the Human Rights Convention' (2014) 5 *New Journal of European Criminal Law* 121, 140.

[37] *Isenc v France* (App 58828/13, 4 February 2016).

prison was largely based upon the lack of evidence that he had been given a medical assessment to assess his mental state when arriving at the prison.

The importance of screening on arrival is also recognised in the European Prison Rules, which require that prisoners receive a medical examination as soon as possible after admission.[38] The CPT has also emphasised the importance of medical screening on arrival to a prison, and highlighted the role of the reception process in suicide prevention.[39] The United Nations Standard Minimum Rules, often referred to as the Mandela Rules, adopted in 2015, also state that a physician or other qualified healthcare professional should talk with and examine every prisoner as soon as possible following admission and thereafter as necessary.[40] In this context, it is interesting to note the findings of the Howard League for Penal Reform[41] that some processes in UK prisons are not conducive to such a screening process, such as prisoners regularly arriving to prisons in the evening. As Cluley notes, this is not conducive to alerting staff to those at risk of suicide and leaves staff feeling that 'the initial contact assessment was often not adequate for detecting vulnerabilities'.[42]

The elevation of the importance of a psychiatric diagnosis in preventing prison suicide raises the question of whether the risk of suicide is inherent in an individual prisoner, or in the prison environment, or in the combination of both. While some commentators adopt an importation model, theorising that prisoners bring with them into the prison an elevated suicide risk,[43] Liebling proposes a combined model that argues that prisons expose already vulnerable populations to additional risk.[44] In her view, levels of 'imported vulnerability', such as previous suicide attempts and psychiatric treatment, 'constitute only a relatively small part of the explanation for variations in levels of distress and suicide in prison'.[45]

It is perhaps surprising that a history of psychiatric treatment is less likely among prison suicides than among suicides in the community. Only one-third of prison suicides are found to have a psychiatric history, as compared with a much larger proportion of suicides in the general community, although a high proportion are found to have psychological and emotional difficulties falling short of a formal psychiatric diagnosis, such as drug and/or alcohol dependency,

[38] Rule 16, European Prison Rules 2006, available at www.coe.int/en/web/human-rights-rule-of-law/european-prison-rules.

[39] Third General Report and 26th General Report, available at www.coe.int/en/web/cpt/annual-reports.

[40] Rule 30, United Nations Standard Minimum Rules for the Treatment of Prisoners (the Nelson Mandela Rules) 2015, available at documents-dds-ny.un.org/doc/UNDOC/GEN/N15/443/41/PDF/N1544341.pdf.

[41] 'Preventing Prison Suicide: Staff Perspectives' (Howard League for Penal Reform, 2017), available at www.howardleague.org/publications.

[42] E Cluley, 'Preventing Prison Suicide: Staff Perspectives' (2017) 64 *Probation Journal* 158, 159.

[43] For references, see Liebling and Ludlow, 'Suicide, Distress and the Quality of Prison Life' (2016) 226.

[44] ibid.

[45] Liebling (n 2) 21–22.

borderline personality disorders or self-reported anxiety and depression.[46] This leads Liebling and Ludlow to argue that 'suicide prevention strategies that treat suicide as an exclusively medical or psychiatric problem are likely to prove ineffective'.[47] In the context of the application of Article 2's operational duty, this is a significant point because it suggests that the Strasbourg Court should look beyond psychiatric history and diagnosis in assessing whether there is an identifiable risk of suicide. It also suggests that suicide prevention should focus on the prison environment generally rather than specific preventative steps for a small selection of prisoners. Of course, such an approach raises challenging questions about the exercise of autonomous choice in a prison environment and Liebling has queried whether one can ever *choose* suicide inside a prison.[48] She points out that the fact that different prisons have 'different susceptibilities to suicide over time' makes the concept of individual choice of limited application to prison suicide.[49]

ii. Mental Health Hospitals

Beyond the prison context, the operational duty under Article 2 raises similar questions about assessment of suicide risk in other places of detention. Thus, even in a mental health hospital in relation to a patient with a clearly diagnosed psychiatric condition, the question of whether the authorities knew or ought to have known of a real and immediate risk of suicide still arises. In *Hiller v Austria*,[50] the applicant complained that her son had died from suicide as a result of the psychiatric hospital's negligence, but the Court held that his suicide 'had not been foreseeable for the hospital and was not therefore attributable to it'.[51] This was despite a court-ordered hospitalisation due, at least in part, to the risk posed to the patient himself and the fact of two previous escapes from a closed ward. A third escape, this time from an open ward, culminated in his suicide but the Court found no reason for the hospital authorities to have been aware of a risk of suicide, concluding that 'hospital staff could not at any point have had any reason to expect that [the patient] would commit suicide, either on the day of his commitment to the hospital or on any of the other days during which he remained within their sphere of responsibility'.[52]

In *Fernandes de Oliveira v Portugal*,[53] the question of whether the authorities knew or ought to have known of a risk of suicide in relation to a voluntary

[46] ibid 228.
[47] ibid.
[48] Liebling (n 2) 21.
[49] ibid 22.
[50] *Hiller v Austria* (App 1967/14, 22 November 2016).
[51] ibid [53].
[52] ibid. As will be discussed below, this judgment is also notable for a renewed emphasis on residual autonomy for mental health patients.
[53] *Fernandes de Oliveira v Portugal* (n 23).

patient in a psychiatric hospital was the distinguishing feature between judgments of a Chamber and the Grand Chamber (GC) of the Court. The Chamber unanimously found that the hospital authorities ought to have known of the risk that the patient would attempt to leave the hospital and pose a risk to his own life due to his clinical history and a previous suicide attempt.[54] The Grand Chamber disagreed. It helpfully summarised the factors previously regarded as relevant to establishing whether the authorities knew or ought to have known of a real and immediate suicide risk in detention.[55] These factors include: (i) a history of mental health problems; (ii) the gravity of the mental condition; (iii) previous suicide attempts or self-harm; (iv) suicidal thoughts or threats; and (v) signs of physical or mental distress. These factors indeed match with the Court's assessment of suicide risk in prisons. As we have seen, a psychiatric diagnosis is a crucial, and apparently necessary, condition in the Court's case law as, for example, in *Volk* and *Mitić*, while the gravity of the mental condition appeared to be relevant to the Court's judgment in *Keenan* (especially when viewed in comparison with *Renolde*). Evidence of previous suicide attempts, self-harm or suicidal thoughts or threats have understandably been used to substantiate the authorities' knowledge of a suicide risk, as in *Renolde* (self-harm) and *Çoşelav* (previous suicide attempt) and the absence of such evidence was crucial in establishing the lack of foreseeability in *Hiller*.

When applying these five factors in *Fernandes de Oliveira*, it was the last factor of 'signs of physical or mental distress' that was given the most weight. The GC admitted that the patient had suffered from serious mental health problems over a long period (thus satisfying the first two factors) and had made one previous suicide attempt three weeks earlier (thus satisfying the third factor). In other cases, and indeed for the Chamber in the present case, the existence of these factors might have sufficed for the finding of knowledge of a suicide risk, but the fact that the patient had not displayed signs of suicidal thoughts, nor any worrying signs in his behaviour, during the last days of his life was regarded as crucial for the GC and enabled it to conclude that the operational duty to prevent a suicide risk did not exist.[56] In reaching this conclusion, the GC was particularly influenced by its general policy of avoiding the imposition of disproportionate obligations on state authorities. This has been a self-imposed, but politically sensible, restraint since the first recognition of positive obligations under Article 2.[57] In the context of suicide risk, it is also an approach that acknowledges the inherent difficulty in identifying those at risk. Indeed, the GC explicitly justifies it by reference to expert evidence that admitted that complete prevention of suicide in patients such as the one in this case was 'an impossible task'.[58]

[54] *Fernandes de Oliveira v Portugal* (App 78103/14, 28 March 2017) [72].
[55] *Fernandes de Oliveira v Portugal* (n 23) [115].
[56] ibid [127]–[129].
[57] *Osman v United Kingdom* (n 24).
[58] *Fernandes de Oliveira v Portugal* (n 23) [131].

Furthermore, the GC's particular focus on whether or not there were worrying signs in the days immediately preceding the suicide which might have foreseen an immediate risk to life might be partly explained by the hospital, rather than prison, context of this case. As we have seen, the prison cases seem to strongly hinge upon the existence of a psychiatric diagnosis, alongside evidence of previous risks to self. It makes sense, however, within the context of a mental health hospital for there to be a reduced focus on diagnosis given that this inevitably exists prior to admission and that there may well be many previous suicide attempts across the patient population. Identifying a specific, and immediate, risk of suicide in relation to a particular patient, without the benefit of hindsight, will naturally be correlated to signs of distress or suicide ideation in the days preceding the incident. It might be argued, however, that such an approach would also be valuable within the prison context as it would shift the focus from psychiatric diagnosis, clinical history and medical screening on admission onto the experiences of an individual prisoner at the pertinent time. Given what we have learnt from researchers such as Liebling about the prison environment exposing prisoners to elevated risks of suicide, a greater focus on how prison authorities respond to evidence of a prisoner appearing vulnerable to suicide at any point in time would arguably strengthen the utility of Article 2 to prison suicide.

B. Preventative Steps and Reasonableness

Where the authorities know or ought to have known of a risk of suicide, they are required under Article 2 to 'take measures within the scope of their powers which, judged reasonably, might have been expected to prevent that risk from materializing'.[59] By comparing the cases in which violations of Article 2 are found with those where they are not, it is possible to identify the types of measures expected under the operational duty. In *Keenan*, for example, the prison authorities were held to have taken adequate steps, such as placing the prisoner into hospital care and under suicide watch when he evinced suicidal tendencies.[60] This was all that could reasonably be expected of the authorities in the circumstances and meant that the UK was not in violation of Article 2.[61] By contrast, in *Renolde*, while the authorities had made some efforts in response to their assessment of a suicide risk, such as calling in the psychiatric emergency team and regular monitoring, these measures were held not to be sufficient. For example, the Court pointed out that there was no discussion of whether the prisoner at risk should be admitted to a psychiatric institution. The Court refers to 'Recommendation No. R (98) 7 of the Committee of Ministers of the Council of Europe concerning the ethical

[59] *Çoşelav v Turkey* (n 25) [54].
[60] *Keenan v United Kingdom* (n 26) [99].
[61] It was, however, found to have violated Art 3, which will be discussed below.

and organisational aspects of health care in prison' which provides that prisoners suffering from serious mental disturbance should be kept and cared for in a hospital facility. The Court made clear that it attaches considerable importance to this recommendation despite it not being binding on Member States.[62] The expectation that prisoners suffering from mental disorders and at risk of suicide should be transferred to hospital care is also supported by the European Prison Rules. Rule 12.1 states that people suffering from mental illness and whose state of mental health is incompatible with detention in a prison should be detained in an establishment specially designed for that purpose, although Rule 12.2 recognises that such people are detained in prisons, and exhorts the authorities to put in place special regulations to take account of their status and needs.[63] Again, these rules are not binding on Member States, but the Strasbourg Court does regularly refer to them in judgments. A third source emphasising the importance of hospital care for those at risk of suicide is the CPT, which has stated that prisoners at serious risk of attempting self-harm or suicide should be placed in a closed hospital environment with suitable equipment and staff.[64] The fact that a transfer to hospital care was not even considered in *Renolde*, in contrast to the transfer to hospital care at certain times in *Keenan*, was extremely relevant to the finding of a violation of Article 2 in that case.

In addition, the authorities in *Renolde* were criticised for a failure to supervise medication. The Court had 'serious doubts as to the advisability of leaving it to a prisoner suffering from known psychotic disorders to administer his own daily medication without any supervision'[65] and went so far as to conclude that 'the lack of supervision of his daily taking of medication played a part in his death'.[66] A failure to supervise the taking of medication has also been a feature of the response to a suicide risk in other cases leading to a violation. In *Jasińska v Poland*,[67] for example, it was alleged that a prisoner had been able to steal the medicines used to kill himself due to negligence on the part of the prison authorities. The Court found a violation of Article 2 on the basis that merely renewing his medical prescriptions without supervising the administration of them had enabled the prisoner to gather a lethal dose of drugs without the knowledge of medical staff. The Court reiterated that there is a duty on the authorities not just to prescribe medicines but also to ensure that they are properly taken, especially in the case of prisoners with mental disorders.

A failure to provide specialist medical care or supervise medication are both clearly relevant to whether the prison authorities have taken reasonable measures

[62] *Renolde v France* (n 29) [95].
[63] European Prison Rules 2006 (n 38).
[64] 'Report to the Government of the United Kingdom on the visit to the United Kingdom carried out by the European Committee for the Prevention of Torture and Inhuman or Degrading Treatment or Punishment (CPT) from 30 March to 12 April 2016' (Strasbourg, 2017) para 68.
[65] *Renolde v France* (n 29) [104].
[66] ibid [105].
[67] *Jasińska v Poland* (App 28326/05, 1 June 2010).

to seek to prevent a suicide risk materialising. In some cases, however, the failings relate to more extreme positive steps taken by prison authorities, such as placing the at-risk prisoner into solitary confinement or a punishment cell. For example, in *Renolde*,[68] the prisoner was placed in a punishment cell and deprived of visits and activities. The Court recognised that this was likely to aggravate any existing risk of suicide.[69] The timing was particularly important here as Renolde was placed in isolation only three days after a previous suicide attempt, and thus at a time when the authorities should have been taking measures to prevent a further attempt.

An even more inappropriate response to a suicide attempt was evident in *Çoşelav v Turkey* in which a juvenile who had previously attempted suicide was detained in an adult wing of the prison (albeit at the prisoner's request).[70] Not only was he not provided with any medical care following his first attempt to take his own life in a prison courtyard, but he was also merely resuscitated and returned to his cell after the attempt.[71] As the Court explained, 'the prison authorities' only response was to threaten him with disciplinary action for "setting a bad example to other inmates" by attempting to take his own life'.[72] The ineptitude of the authorities continued when, in response to the prisoner repeatedly hitting his head against the walls of his cell, his head injury was treated in the prison infirmary and he was then returned to his cell with no supervision where, within hours, he had hanged himself.[73] The Court was robust in its criticism of the 'indifference' displayed by the Turkish prison authorities in this case, and it is no surprise that the standard fell below that required under Article 2, leading to a clear violation.

Other prison authorities have done better. *Jeanty v Belgium*[74] is a recent and unusual case that highlights the difference that can be made by prison staff when responding to a suicide risk. This case was unusual in that it was the prisoner who had attempted suicide who alleged a violation of Article 2 by the prison authorities for failing to prevent the attempt. Article 2 does indeed have application in circumstances where no death results,[75] but in this case the Court did not find a violation because the measures taken by the authorities had actually prevented the applicant from dying from his attempt – the prisoner had made several attempts on his own life and it was only because of the intervention of the prison staff, by means of surveillance and restraint, that he had not succeeded.

The Article 2 case law in relation to prison suicide is built around a recognition of the inherent vulnerability of those in detention and especially those

[68] See also *Ketreb v France* (App 38447/09, 19 July 2012).
[69] *Renolde v France* (n 29) [107].
[70] *Çoşelav v Turkey* (n 25) [69].
[71] ibid [63].
[72] ibid.
[73] ibid [67].
[74] *Jeanty v Belgium* (App 82284/17, 31 March 2020).
[75] *Makaratzis v Greece* [GC] ECHR 2004-XI (2005) 41 EHRR 49.

detained while suffering from a mental disorder.[76] The Court has noted that 'Where the authorities decide to place and maintain in detention a person with disabilities, they should demonstrate special care in guaranteeing such conditions as correspond to his special needs resulting from his disability'.[77] While the overwhelming focus on a psychiatric diagnosis as a precursor to the assessment of suicide risk raises some difficulties (both in terms of excluding from protection those without such a diagnosis, and encouraging the absence of the principle of autonomy from the Article 2 judgments), the Court has, on the whole, set appropriate standards for suicide prevention once a risk is identified. As we have seen, this has extended from the need for appropriate hospital care, to supervision of medication, to avoiding disciplinary punishments and isolation. When persons are detained within other institutions, such as mental health hospitals, further considerations will come into play. These may include appropriate accommodation to minimise opportunities for suicide,[78] sufficient security to prevent departure from the hospital (even for voluntary patients),[79] and the denial of home leave.[80] The obligations imposed under the right to life are not the only ones relevant to suicide prevention in detention, however, as Article 3's prohibition of inhuman or degrading treatment or punishment will provide additional protection to detainees.

III. Suicide in Detention and Degrading Treatment

Article 3 ECHR provides that no one shall be subjected to torture or to inhuman or degrading treatment or punishment. The provision protects against a wide spectrum of mistreatment and is unusual in the Convention in being expressed in absolute terms, with no exceptions. Nonetheless, there is a minimum level of severity required before the right applies. Conditions of detention have been found to engage Article 3 and the Court has found violations in respect of unhygienic cells, overcrowding, ill-treatment by cell mates and solitary confinement.[81]

[76] *Renolde v France* (n 29) [84].

[77] *Association for the Defence of Human Rights in Romania – Helsinki Committee on behalf of Ionel Garcea v Romania* (App 2959/11, 24 March 2015) [66].

[78] In *Reynolds v United Kingdom* (App 2694/08, 13 March 2012), there was an arguable claim of an Art 2 violation in conjunction with Art 13 when a voluntary patient in a psychiatric facility housed on the sixth floor, broke a window in his room and fell to his death.

[79] In *Fernandes de Oliveira v Portugal* (n 23), the Chamber judgment found that more safeguards should have been adopted to ensure the patient did not leave the grounds of the hospital. The Grand Chamber judgment did not consider this issue as it did not find that the authorities ought to have known of the suicide risk.

[80] In *Rabone and another v Pennine Care NHS Trust* [2012] UKSC 2, the provision of home leave which provided a voluntary mental health patient with an opportunity to end her own life led to legal liability for the hospital.

[81] *Peers v Greece* ECHR 2001-III (2001) 33 EHRR 1192; *Mursic v Croatia* (App 7334/13, 20 October 2016) [GC]; *Piechowicz v Poland* (App 20071/07, 17 April 2012).

In respect of suicide prevention, the Court has often considered Article 3 alongside Article 2 and has on occasion found a violation of the former and not the latter.

In *Keenan*, the Court held that it was not possible to determine with certainty to what extent the self-imposed death resulted from the conditions of detention imposed by the authorities but considered 'this difficulty is not determinative of the issue as to whether the authorities fulfilled their obligation under Article 3'.[82] This is because under Article 3 it is not necessary to establish the actual effect of the treatment on the prisoner: 'treatment of a mentally ill person may be incompatible with the standards imposed by Article 3 in the protection of fundamental human dignity, even though that person may not be able, or capable of, pointing to any specific ill-effects'.[83] In other words, even if the treatment of Keenan by the prison authorities could not be proved to have led to his suicide, it still fell below the standards expected under Article 3. The Court explained this distinction in clear terms:

> The lack of effective monitoring of Mark Keenan's condition and the lack of informed psychiatric input into his assessment and treatment disclose significant defects in the medical care provided to a mentally ill person known to be a suicide risk. The belated imposition on him in those circumstances of a serious disciplinary punishment … which may well have threatened his physical and moral resistance, is not compatible with the standard of treatment required in respect of a mentally ill person.[84]

The Court's judgment in *Keenan* illustrates, therefore, the importance of sensitive treatment of vulnerable prisoners beyond the need for specific steps aimed at preventing suicide. This suggests that Article 2's focus on assessment of suicide risk is not the only route to legal liability for human rights violations in respect of suicide attempts. Regardless of whether the authorities know or ought to know of a risk of suicide in respect of a particular prisoner at a specific time, the obligatory standards required in respect of detaining a mentally ill person will provide some minimal support to those most vulnerable of prisoners.

The two core requirements identified in the *Keenan* judgment, relating to monitoring and psychiatric input, and the imposition of disciplinary punishments, have been echoed in other cases. Thus in *Rivière v France*,[85] the applicant's continued detention without appropriate medical supervision was found to be in violation of Article 3 and the Court explained that prisoners with serious mental disorders and suicidal tendencies require appropriate measures suited to their condition, regardless of the seriousness of the offence of which they had been convicted. Similarly, in *Güveç v Turkey*,[86] the failure of the authorities to

[82] *Keenan v United Kingdom* (n 26) [113].
[83] ibid,
[84] ibid [116].
[85] *Rivière v France* (App 33834/03, 11 July 2006).
[86] *Güveç v Turkey* (App 70337/01, 20 January 2009) ECHR 2009 (extracts).

provide adequate medical care for the prisoner's psychological problems, as well as their failure to take appropriate steps to prevent his repeated suicide attempts, was found to violate Article 3. In *Jeanty*,[87] in which the authorities' actions were held to have effectively prevented the success of the applicant's suicide attempts (and thus did not violate Article 2), the Court nonetheless found a violation of Article 3. This was partly because the applicant was found to have suffered distress or hardship beyond the level inherent in detention, due to the lack of medical supervision and treatment during his detention. This neatly illustrates that when the Convention requirements are taken together, even adequate steps to prevent a specific suicide attempt are not enough if the general treatment of the prisoner falls short of providing the psychiatric support required. Another factor contributing to the Article 3 violation in this case was the imposition of a disciplinary punishment which placed the vulnerable prisoner in an isolation cell for three days, despite his repeated suicide attempts.

In a case note on the *Jeanty* case, Graham highlighted the significance of the Court seeming to take into account the reason why treatment is imposed upon the prisoner.[88] Where the treatment was to protect the prisoner (and therefore meet Article 2 requirements) this was acceptable and not a violation of Article 3, but when imposed for the purposes of punishment, the treatment met the threshold for treatment contrary to Article 3. Indeed, Graham has used this judgment to counter arguments that Article 3 is absolute in nature, arguing that 'the imposition of treatment that would ordinarily breach Article 3 can be mitigated by recourse to an Article 2 "defence".'[89] Certainly, as under Article 2, the Court has been consistent under Article 3 in taking very seriously any disciplinary punishments when they deprive a mentally ill prisoner from human contact and support. In *Ketreb*,[90] the placement of a mentally disturbed prisoner in a disciplinary cell for two weeks was found to violate Article 3, and in *Renolde* the penalty of 45 days' detention in a punishment cell, imposed upon a mentally ill prisoner, was recognised to be one that 'may well have threatened his physical and moral resistance' and thus was not compatible with the standard of treatment required under Article 3.[91] In its judgment in *Renolde*, the Court also reiterated more broadly that 'prisoners known to be suffering from serious mental disturbance and to pose a suicide risk require special measures geared to their condition in order to ensure compatibility with the requirements of humane treatment'.[92]

There is, nonetheless, a minimal level of severity required before a violation of Article 3 can be found. Thus, in *Kudla v Poland*,[93] the retention of the applicant

[87] *Jeanty v Belgium* (n 74).

[88] L Graham, '*Jeanty v Belgium*: Saving Lives Provides (Another) Exception to Article 3 ECHR' (2021) 21 *Human Rights Law Review* 1, 8.

[89] ibid.

[90] *Ketreb v France* (n 68).

[91] *Renolde v France* (n 29) [129].

[92] ibid [128].

[93] *Kudla v Poland* [GC] ECHR 2000-XI.

in custody during a period of nearly five months despite a psychiatric opinion that continuing detention could jeopardise his life because of the likelihood of a suicide attempt was found not to reach a sufficient level of severity to come within the scope of Article 3.[94] In general, however, the requisite level of severity will be linked to the prisoner's state of mind. As Foster has argued, 'in determining whether the ill treatment reaches the necessary threshold to constitute a violation of Article 3 the Court will place great weight on the prisoner's physical and mental state and the duty of the authorities to accommodate them'.[95]

Beyond issues of suicide linked to a mental illness, there have been cases concerning the deaths of prisoners following hunger strikes. Most famously brought to public attention in 1981 when Bobby Sands and nine other IRA prisoners died from their hunger strikes without the authorities intervening, the question of whether force-feeding to save life is lawful was later considered by both domestic and Strasbourg courts. In *Secretary of State for the Home Department v Robb*,[96] Thorpe J granted declarations that prison staff could lawfully abstain from force-feeding in the event of a continued and competent refusal to eat. He held that the principles of bodily inviolability and self-determination take precedence over other state interests such as the preservation of life.[97] The status of a prisoner was held not to change this general approach.[98] However, this judgment was criticised at the time for approaching the case from a medical law perspective as if a prisoner on hunger strike is a patient refusing medical treatment.[99] From today's perspective, and in light of the stringent obligations on prison authorities to take steps to prevent suicide, it might also be criticised for failing to engage with the important issue of suicide prevention. Furthermore, while this case held that the prison authorities would be acting lawfully in not force-feeding the prisoner, it did not make any finding on whether or not they may do so if they choose. In *Nevmerzhitsky v Ukraine*,[100] the Strasbourg Court confirmed that a measure which is of therapeutic necessity cannot in principle be regarded as inhuman and degrading and that this applies to force-feeding aimed at saving the life of a detainee who consciously refuses to take food. However, there is a requirement that 'the medical necessity has been convincingly shown to exist'.[101]

[94] ibid [99].

[95] S Foster, 'Prisoners' Rights: Suicides in Detention' (2002) 24 *Journal of Social Welfare and Family Law* 185, 191.

[96] *Home Secretary of State for the Home Department v Robb* [1995] 1 All ER 677.

[97] By contrast, in the United States the principle of preservation of life is elevated to provide justification for force feeding, as for example in Guantanamo Bay. See S Cloon, 'Competent Hunger Strikers: Applying the Lessons from Northern Ireland to the Force-Feeding in Guantanamo' (2017) 31 *Notre Dame Journal of Law, Ethics and Public Policy* 383.

[98] The old case of *Leigh v Gladstone* (1909) 26 TLR 139 from the Suffragettes era, in which force-feeding was found to be lawful, was held to have little contemporary relevance. Of course, at the time of that case, suicide was still a felony under English law.

[99] See Ian Kennedy's case note in (1995) 3 *Medical Law Review* 189.

[100] *Nevmerzhitsky v Ukraine* ECHR 2005-II (extracts) (2006) 43 EHRR 32.

[101] ibid [94].

In *Nevmerzhitsky*, the Ukrainian Government had not demonstrated a medical necessity and therefore the Court found that the force-feeding, under restraint, and resisted by the applicant, not only violated Article 3 but amounted to 'treatment of such a severe character warranting the characterisation of torture'.[102] In a subsequent case, the Turkish authorities' failure to intervene to save life during a hunger strike was found not to violate their requirements under Article 2.[103] Thus, while force-feeding is in principle permissible under the ECHR, it can only be imposed when the medical necessity to do so has been established, and not in circumstances amounting to mistreatment of the prisoner, and a failure to do so may not infringe the right to life. It seems that force-feeding is another example of an intervention that might violate Article 3 even if imposed in an effort to save life and thereby meet positive obligations under Article 2.

Taken together, it is evident that Articles 2 and 3 ECHR represent important safeguards for protecting the lives of vulnerable detainees. While compliance with the letter and spirit of both of these provisions will never be able to prevent all prison suicides, it is hard to disagree with Rogan's suggestion that 'prisons which do not fulfil their obligations under human rights law to take steps to prevent suicides and investigate them when they occur, will see higher rates of suicide'.[104] However, the right to life and the prohibition of degrading treatment are not the only relevant rights in respect of prison suicide and arguably the potential relevance of other conflicting rights, such as Article 8's right to respect for private life, have been overlooked in the Strasbourg case law to date. The overwhelming focus on a psychiatric diagnosis in relation to the assessment of a risk to life from suicide under Article 2, and on the lack of appropriate psychiatric care in relation to what is reasonable to prevent that risk materialising and what is degrading treatment, has omitted any questioning around the appropriate role of autonomy in relation to suicide while in detention. There may be very good reasons for that, but the omission of explicit consideration of the right to autonomy is unfortunate and weakens the weight of the Strasbourg, and domestic, case law. Therefore, it is to this issue of the potential relevance of autonomy in relation to suicide prevention in detention that this chapter will now turn.

IV. Suicide and Autonomy in Detention

While Article 2 ECHR protects the right to life, and Article 3 protects the quality of that life by prohibiting mistreatment, autonomy also finds protection in the ECHR within the terms of Article 8. This provision protects individual autonomy by ensuring that we are all free to live our lives as we choose unless a restriction

[102] ibid 98.
[103] *Horoz v Turkey* (App 1639/03, 31 March 2009).
[104] Rogan, 'Human Rights Approaches to Suicide in Prison' (2018).

on such freedom is lawful, necessary and proportionate under Article 8(2). This protected freedom extends to choices about the end of life. In *Haas v Switzerland*, the Court explicitly recognised that a choice to end life is protected in the Convention:

> [T]he Court considers that an individual's right to decide by what means and at what point his or her life will end, provided he or she is capable of freely reaching a decision on this question and acting in consequence, is one of the aspects of the right to respect for private life within the meaning of Article 8 of the Convention.[105]

In *Haas*, the Court also recognised, however, that this Article 8 right must be balanced against the obligations imposed by Article 2. Thus, the Court clarified that Article 2 'obliges the national authorities to prevent an individual from taking his or her own life if the decision has not been taken freely and with full understanding of what is involved'.[106] Therefore, it held that Article 2 obliges Member States to establish a procedure capable of ensuring that a decision to end one's life does indeed correspond to the free wish of the individual concerned.[107] Nonetheless, there is no doubt following *Haas* that a right to decide by what means and at what point one's life will end finds some protection in the terms of Article 8 and that a foreseeable risk of suicide does not always lead to a positive obligation to prevent it. It is clear that suicide is not just tolerated under the ECHR (as we might argue it is in domestic law) but rather is an aspect of the autonomy protected by the right to respect for private life.

The concept of autonomy is notably absent, however, from most of the Strasbourg judgments on suicide in detention.[108] In the early cases, mere lip service is paid to prisoners' autonomy-based rights. For example, in *Keenan*, the UK Government argued that the principles of dignity and autonomy mean that special considerations arise where a person takes her own life which would prohibit any oppressive removal of a person's freedom of choice and action. The Court confirmed that the prison authorities 'must discharge their duties in a manner compatible with the rights and freedoms of the individual concerned'.[109] It noted the general measures and precautions which are available to 'diminish the opportunities for self-harm without infringing on personal autonomy'.[110] However, the Court regarded the question of whether more stringent measures are necessary and reasonable in respect of a specific prisoner to be one which depends solely on the circumstances of the case[111] and the remainder of the

[105] *Haas v Switzerland* ECHR 2011 [51].
[106] ibid [54].
[107] ibid [57].
[108] It is also notably absent from the JCHR's 'Interim Report' (2017) in which its 'Human rights framework' section mentions only Art 2's duty to protect life, coupled with Art 14's prohibition of discrimination, alongside other specific obligations focused on mental health and prisons (4). There is no mention of Art 8 ECHR in the Report at all.
[109] *Keenan v United Kingdom* (n 26) [92].
[110] ibid.
[111] ibid.

Court's discussion focused entirely upon the issue of whether the prison authorities knew of the risk to life in respect of Keenan. Thus, the issue of a balance between the prisoner's life and freedom became reinterpreted as a question of whether the risk to life from suicide was detectable. Arguably, that is an entirely different question.

Subsequent Article 2 judgments placed a great deal of weight, as was discussed above, on the existence of a diagnosis of mental disorder as evidence that a risk of suicide should have been foreseen. They did not, however, clarify whether the operational duty to take preventative steps depends upon such a diagnosis. It remained unclear, therefore, whether issues of autonomous decision-making would arise in respect of a prisoner without a mental disorder. Autonomy has been a greater focus of attention in more recent Article 2 cases concerning suicide prevention for mental health patients. Thus, in *Hiller* the Court explicitly recognised the relevance of autonomy for such patients and the need to provide the maximum freedom possible:

> [T]oday's paradigm in mental health care is to give persons with mental disabilities the greatest possible personal freedom in order to facilitate their re-integration into society. The Court considers that from a Convention point of view, it is not only permissible to grant hospitalised persons the maximum freedom of movement but also desirable in order to preserve as much as possible their dignity and their right to self-determination.[112]

In this case, the Court even goes so far as to say that it would agree with the Austrian Supreme Court which found that 'if the hospital would have restricted M.K.'s liberty more than it did issues under Articles 3, 5 and 8 of the Convention might have arisen'.[113] This is an important development in the Court's reasoning in suicide prevention cases. It is the first time that the Court explicitly recognised, and its judgment reflected, the need for the authorities to balance conflicting Convention requirements when intervening to reduce the risk of suicide. On the one hand, the authorities have a duty under Article 2 to take reasonable steps to prevent a suicide if they know of an immediate risk of it; on the other hand, the authorities have a duty not to interfere with a person's right to respect for private life, nor to impose degrading treatment, nor restrict liberty more than is necessary. Given that Article 8's right to respect for private life includes a right to make autonomous decisions about life and death,[114] there is an inevitable conflict here with the operational duty under Article 2 and the Court's overdue recognition of this in *Hiller* is welcome.

In *Fernandes de Oliveira v Portugal*, a case about a voluntary mental health patient, rather than a detained prisoner, the Grand Chamber reiterated that 'the

[112] *Hiller v Austria* (n 50) [54].
[113] ibid [55].
[114] *Haas v Switzerland* (n 105).

very essence of the Convention is respect for human dignity and human freedom. In this regard, the authorities must discharge their duties in a manner compatible with the rights and freedoms of the individual concerned and in such a way as to diminish the opportunities for self-harm, without infringing personal autonomy'.[115] The Court's approach in this case, in which no substantive violation of Article 2 was found, was not without controversy, however. Two dissenting judges would have found a substantive violation and argued that the majority's opinion pursues an 'ideologically charged minimalist approach to the State's positive obligations in the sphere of health care to its limits'.[116] Judge Pinto De Albuquerque highlighted the very real debate about suicide prevention:

> [T]he majority's one-sided approach to international health law and practice is patent, since they consider the trend that favours the liberty of freedom of psychiatric inpatients, but forget to ponder the counter-voices to that trend which warrant an increased State commitment to suicide prevention, especially regarding people under State supervision, and even more regarding institutionalised psychiatric patients.[117]

On whichever side of this debate one falls, the very need to choose priorities when dealing with suicidal choices by persons without full mental health is one that is too often overlooked. The previous chapter discussed the challenges posed by a lack of mental capacity and/or the diagnosis of a mental illness. The challenges in respect of prison suicide are often of a slightly different nature but no less significant and it is notable that the Strasbourg Court's shift to focusing on autonomy-based rights has occurred in the mental health hospital context rather than the prison context.

Perhaps the most effective means of highlighting the problem in the Convention caselaw relating to suicide prevention is to make the obvious comparison between the cases of *Koch v Germany* and *Ketreb v France*. Both judgments were made on the same day and by the same section of the Court. In *Koch*, the Court confirmed that Article 8 protects 'an individual's right to decide in which way and at which time his or her life should end, provided that he or she was in a position freely to form her own will and to act accordingly'.[118] In *Ketreb*, however, it found France to be in violation of Article 2 for failing to take the necessary steps to protect the life of a prisoner who died from suicide.[119] The contexts are different, but the distinction between the two approaches to suicide is not explicit and this raises difficulties that have yet to be entirely resolved by the Court. It seems clear that the proviso mentioned in the above quotation from *Koch*, namely whether the person seeking to commit suicide is 'in a position freely to form her own will and to act accordingly', is central to the

[115] *Fernandes de Oliveira v Portugal* (n 23) [112].
[116] ibid, Dissenting Opinion of Judge Pinto De Albuquerque, joined by Judge Harutyunyan [2].
[117] ibid [56].
[118] *Koch v Germany* (App 497/09, 19 July 2012) [52].
[119] *Ketreb v France* (n 68).

requirement to take steps to prevent the suicide of prisoners such as Ketreb. But why, exactly, are such prisoners not able to freely choose to die? A number of potential answers could be provided to that question, focusing on the existence of a mental disorder, a lack of mental capacity, vulnerability in need of heightened protection, the difficulty in exercising true autonomy while in detention, a forfeiture of autonomy-based rights while in detention, and even a perception of suicide as a means of escaping justice. Some of those potential answers are more justifiable than others, as we will now see.

First, we can somewhat easily reject the explanation that prisoners forfeit their rights by committing crime, because such an approach has been explicitly rejected by the Strasbourg Court in cases such as *Hirst v United Kingdom (No 2)*.[120] While the lawful detention of a person after conviction by a competent court is a permitted limitation upon the right to liberty (protected under Article 5 ECHR), it does not in itself justify an automatic restriction of other rights. Indeed, we have already seen that not only does Article 2's right to life still apply to those in detention, but it actually imposes additional duties upon the state authorities to take steps to protect the lives of those within its control. Similarly, while some elements of Article 8's right to respect for private life are inevitably limited by lawful detention, many elements remain. For example, Article 8 remains relevant for prisoners in relation to maintaining family relationships.[121] Therefore, if there is a right to make autonomous decisions about the end of one's life (and we have seen that the Court has recognised such a right under Article 8), then that right cannot be excluded from prisoners merely because they are serving a criminal sentence. It is not, of course, an absolute right and Article 8(2) permits an interference with a right to end one's life when it is in accordance with the law, and necessary in a democratic society in order to achieve one of the specified legitimate aims, such as protecting the rights and freedoms of others, the protection of health or morals, or the prevention of crime or disorder. The prison context is not unique in requiring a balancing of rights, but it manifestly does not represent a blanket exclusion of all human rights.

A variation on this explanation is that the suicide of a prisoner must be prevented in order to ensure the prisoner does not escape justice. For example, one US case, *In re Joel Caulk*,[122] explicitly suggests that the fact that the prisoner would be evading prosecution for outstanding charges against him is part of the reason why there is a state interest in preventing his death by suicide. However, such a punitive approach is out of step with contemporary judgments that recognise

[120] *Hirst v United Kingdom (No 2)* [GC] ECHR 2005-IX [69]–[70]: 'prisoners in general continue to enjoy all the fundamental rights and freedoms guaranteed under the Convention save for the right to liberty, where lawfully imposed detention expressly falls within the scope of Article 5 of the Convention … There is no question, therefore, that a prisoner forfeits his Convention rights merely because of his status as a person detained following conviction'.

[121] See, for example, *Piechowicz v Poland* (n 81) and *Khoroshenko v Russia* ECHR 2015 [GC].

[122] *In re Joel Caulk* [1984] 125 NH 226.

residual autonomy for prisoners and with the now well-established trend towards a treatment-based approach to suicide prevention.

A more convincing argument relates to the difficulty in making autonomous decisions within a prison context. Liebling has doubted whether suicide in prison can ever be a free choice:

> Autonomy and self-determination are central to dignity. But in prison, this is double-edged … There are also questions of capability, resources, and environmental effects … Can one really be said, except in exceptional circumstances, to choose suicide in a prison environment?[123]

We have also seen that the prison environment is, at the very least, a contributing factor to many prison suicides. The high rates of suicide in prison cannot be explained solely by the importation model (ie by the mental health of those entering prison), and factors such as population size and turnover, overcrowding, prison management, staffing levels and general challenges of imprisonment may all play a role.[124] As Liebling and Ludlow argue, 'Many autobiographical and qualitative studies of prison life suggest that lack of respect and fairness are frustrating and painful. Empirical studies show that these experiences are linked to elevated levels of distress, and higher rates of suicide'.[125] It was noted above that the Strasbourg Court has also explicitly recognised the vulnerability of prisoners.[126] The loss of control, the oppressive environment, the lack of privacy and the opportunities for free choice render detainees vulnerable, and it is significant that it is the state that has created this situation and assumed control over the lives of those detained in prison (or indeed in a mental health hospital).

Is it this assumption of control, coupled with the inherent vulnerability of the detainee, that requires a focus on preventing the loss of life rather than upholding autonomous choice? Is prison an environment in which the usual mental capacity test does not suffice? As Herring and Wall remind us, it is both a terrible thing to be assessed as lacking capacity when you do not, and thus lose control over your life, but also equally terrible to be said to have capacity when you do not, and thus not be protected from harm.[127] Those writers argue that mental capacity is only one ingredient for autonomous decision-making, and that the law currently fails to take others into account, including where a person is able to understand information relevant to a decision, but the decision is driven by overriding affective attitudes, such as fears, anxieties and desires. Anxiety disorders, schizophrenia and anorexia may be examples of factors that could override the decision-making process when applied to suicide. In other words, a person with a mental disorder

[123] Liebling (n 2) 21.
[124] Liebling and Ludlow (n 7) 226.
[125] ibid 234.
[126] *Keenan v United Kingdom* (n 26) [91]; *Renolde v France* (n 29) [83].
[127] J Herring and J Wall, 'Autonomy, Capacity and Vulnerable Adults: Filling the Gaps in the Mental Capacity Act' (2015) 35 *Legal Studies* 698, 698.

might satisfy the legal capacity test in the Mental Capacity Act 2005 (MCA 2005) and yet not be making a truly autonomous decision to die. This mirrors the argument drawn in the previous chapter about the need to supplement the legal test for capacity found in the MCA 2005 in order to ensure life is adequately protected in the context of suicide. It is particularly relevant here because prisoners attempting suicide might be in just such a gap as 'vulnerable' persons potentially with capacity to make decisions but no ability to make authentic autonomous choices. There has been some judicial recognition of this potential gap between having capacity and being autonomous in the context of the controversial 'vulnerable adult' jurisdiction, which it will now be useful to explore.

V. Suicide, Detention and Vulnerability

A series of recent English cases has established a vulnerable adults jurisdiction which deals with adults who have mental capacity (according to the statutory test in the MCA 2005) but who have some kind of impairment that renders them incapable of making their own decisions.[128] Regrettably, the courts have provided no definition of 'vulnerable adult', but it is applied to people who, although having capacity under the MCA 2005, have been described as having a 'borderline lack of capacity'.[129] In *Re SA*, three different categories of vulnerable adult were identified by Munby J: (a) those under constraint; (b) those subject to coercion or undue influence; or (c) those 'for some other reason deprived of a capacity to make the relevant decision, or disabled from making a free choice, or incapacitated or disabled from giving or expressing a real and genuine consent'.[130] In the English cases thus far, vulnerability has been equated with circumstances of undue influence and oppression. However, in an Irish case, *Governor of X Prison v P McD*,[131] Baker J had to consider whether a prisoner on hunger strike was also a vulnerable adult, noting that to some extent he was because 'his powers of self-determination were constrained by his incarceration and his isolation and lack of interpersonal support'.[132] Nonetheless, it was held that the capacity of the prisoner in this case was not vitiated by his living conditions or by his personality traits. While he was likely influenced by his psychological condition in deciding to go on hunger strike, his condition did not vitiate the decision to do so, even if it was one that other people would not make.

[128] *Re SK* [2004] EWHC 3202 (Fam), [2006] 1 WLR 81; *Re SA (Vulnerable Adult with Capacity: Marriage)* [2005] EWHC 2942 (Fam), [2006] 1 FLR 867; *Re L (Vulnerable Adults with Capacity: Court's Jurisdiction) (No.2)* [2012] EWCA Civ 253, [2013] Fam 1.

[129] *DL v A Local Authority* [2012] EWCA Civ 253 (CA) [62].

[130] *Re SA* (n 128) [77].

[131] *Governor of X Prison* [2015] IEHC 259.

[132] A Mulligan, 'Self-determination, Capacity and the Right to Die by Hunger Strike: *Governor of X Prison v P McD*' (2015) 54 *Irish Jurist* 165, 166.

A major difficulty in relying upon the concept of vulnerability in respect of life and death decisions in detention is that there remains too much ambiguity in the concept of vulnerability and its interaction with autonomy. As Biggs and Jones recognise, any law that seeks to protect the vulnerable should operate 'according to a properly constructed understanding of what it means to be vulnerable and who is vulnerable under this definition'.[133] The domestic vulnerable adults jurisdiction lacks such unambiguous definition and, in the context of suicide under the ECHR, this is also precisely the Strasbourg Court's failing. While describing prisoners as vulnerable, it has not adequately explained what specific factor, or combination of factors, has rendered the individual vulnerable. Furthermore, there is nothing inherent in the concept of vulnerability that implies that life must always be preserved over autonomy when such a conflict is normally subject to much more complex considerations.

Domestic case law on suicide within mental health hospitals is also useful to explore in this context because not only has it applied Article 2's operational duty to prevent suicide into a broader context but it also goes some way towards explaining the justification for the prioritisation of this approach. In *Savage v South Essex NHS Trust*, Lord Rodger explained that the Article 2 obligation to take reasonable steps to prevent the suicide of those in detention exists 'because they are under the control of the state and placed in situations where, as experience shows, there is a heightened risk of suicide'.[134] Lord Rodger did confirm that 'the need to respect the autonomy of prisoners remains'[135] but found that where a real and immediate risk of suicide has been identified, the protection of life must take precedence over autonomy.[136] This was because of the immediacy of the danger to life. Lord Rodger suggests that there 'will be time enough' for other considerations, such as autonomy, when the danger has been averted.[137] However, this is a problematic approach because if applied to every choice to die, it would imply a priority to life over autonomy that remains unreasoned and unjustified. If an autonomous choice to die is owed respect in any circumstances at all, then such a 'save life first worry about free choice later' approach cannot be applied in an indiscriminate manner. Indeed, Lady Hale explicitly recognised in *Savage* that respect for autonomy can be particularly valuable in a mental health hospital:

> Developing a patient's capacity to make sensible choices for herself, and providing her with as good a quality of life as possible, are important components in protecting her

[133] H Biggs and C Jones, 'Legally Vulnerable: What Is Vulnerability and Who Is Vulnerable?' in M Freeman, S Hawkes and B Bennett (eds), *Law and Global Health* (Oxford, Oxford University Press, 2014) 148.

[134] *Savage v South Essex NHS Trust* [2008] UKHL 74 [39].

[135] ibid [42].

[136] ibid.

[137] Lord Rodger (ibid): 'the immediacy of the danger to life means that, for the time being, there is, in practice, little room for considering other, more general, matters concerning his treatment. There will be time enough for them, if and when the danger to life has been overcome. In the meantime, the authorities' duty is to try to prevent the suicide'.

> mental health. Keeping her absolutely safe from physical harm, by secluding or restraining her, or even by keeping her on a locked ward, may do more harm to her mental health.[138]

It is regrettable, however, that there was no explicit reconciliation of this general principle with the duty to prevent suicide in the particular circumstances of the case in the House of Lords judgment.

While *Savage* concerned the compulsory detention of a mentally ill person under the mental health legislation, in *Rabone*, the Supreme Court extended the preventive operational duty to prevent suicide to voluntarily admitted mental health patients.[139] In *Rabone*, Lord Dyson conceded that the existence of a real and immediate risk to life is 'a necessary but not sufficient condition'[140] for the existence of the operational duty, thus acknowledging that some risks to life do not need to be prevented. In considering what exactly is a 'sufficient' condition for such a duty, Lord Dyson draws attention to the Strasbourg Court's prior focus upon the 'assumption of responsibility by the state for the individual's welfare and safety (including by the exercise of control)'.[141] This assumption of control justification would apply to the prison context, as well as compulsorily detained mental health patients, although it is less obviously applicable to voluntary patients such as Melanie Rabone.[142]

An assumption of control requirement can be detected in most of the Strasbourg suicide prevention cases, even if it is not always explicit in the Court's judgment. The operational duty to prevent suicide was initially only recognised in respect of persons under the control (most commonly in detention) of the contracting state.[143] One possible variation upon this rule is the case of *Mammadov v Azerbaijan*[144] in which the applicant's wife caused her own death by pouring a flammable liquid over herself and igniting it. Although not in detention, she committed this act of self-harm in response to a police operation to evict her family from their unofficial dwelling. The Court held that, once the situation became clear, the authorities had an obligation under Article 2 to prevent

[138] ibid 100.

[139] This extension had to overcome the traditional restraints of the relationship between negligence and Art 2 under which it was established in *Powell v United Kingdom* (App 45305/99, Admissibility, 4 May 2000) that deaths caused by negligence in the health care context do not amount to a violation of the right to life.

[140] *Rabone and another v Pennine Care NHS Trust* (n 80) [21].

[141] ibid [22].

[142] Lord Dyson seeks to expand the operational obligations to 'those who are especially vulnerable by reason of their physical or mental condition' (ibid [22]). In doing so, he seeks to rely upon *Z and Others v United Kingdom* ECHR 2001-V [GC] but this is an Art 3 case about protecting a child from abuse and is not an easy analogy with duties under Art 2 to protect adults from their own choices.

[143] Beyond the prison context, the Strasbourg Court has recognised the same duty to prevent suicide applies to immigrants who are kept in administrative detention (*Slimani v France* ECHR 2004-IX (extracts)) and military conscripts (*Kılınç v Turkey* (App 40145/98, 7 June 2005)).

[144] *Mammadov v Azerbaijan* (App 4762/05, 17 December 2009).

the threat to life from materialising, by any means which were reasonable and feasible in the circumstances.[145]

Although no violation was found in this case because the circumstances surrounding the death were disputed and unclear, the existence of a duty to protect a person from self-harm was found to arise in this case in circumstances far removed from detention. Nonetheless, arguably the control requirement was still relevant here given that state agents were directly involved in the creation of the risk to life. Lord Dyson in *Rabone* refers to this case, in arguing that the Strasbourg Court has in recent years expanded the circumstances in which the operational duty is owed to include what may generally be described as 'dangers for which in some way the state is responsible'.[146] He also relies upon *Öneryildiz v Turkey*[147] in which an explosion at a huge rubbish tip operated by the local authorities caused a landslide engulfing part of a shanty town located on the slope beneath the tip. Although the houses destroyed had been built illegally, the state authorities were still found to have violated Article 2 because they had tolerated the breach of planning controls and failed to install the ventilation ducts which they knew were required to make the tip safe. Thus, as Lord Dyson points out, this also fits in the 'dangers for which the state is responsible' category,[148] albeit not in the suicide context. Lord Dyson concludes that:

> The operational duty will be held to exist where there has been an assumption of responsibility by the state for the individual's welfare and safety (including by the exercise of control). The paradigm example of assumption of responsibility is where the state has detained an individual, whether in prison, in a psychiatric hospital, in an immigration detention centre or otherwise. The operational obligations apply to all detainees, but are particularly stringent in relation to those who are especially vulnerable by reason of their physical or mental condition.[149]

This concept of 'an assumption of responsibility by the state for the individual's welfare and safety' is distinguished from an 'exercise of control' concept by Lord Dyson which he argues is not always required in order to engage the Article 2 operational duty. He claims that in circumstances of sufficient vulnerability, the Strasbourg Court has been prepared to find a breach of the operational duty in the absence of an assumption of control by the state.[150]

[145] Notably, included within the Court's suggested steps that could have been taken was physically preventing the applicant's wife from pursuing life-threatening actions, as well as providing immediate medical assistance (ibid [116]).

[146] *Rabone and another v Pennine Care NHS Trust* (n 80) [16].

[147] *Öneryildiz v Turkey* ECHR 2004-XII [GC].

[148] He contrasts such cases with those involving hospital deaths resulting from what can be described as 'casual acts of negligence' by medical staff. Thus, a patient undergoing major surgery may be facing a real and immediate risk of death and yet under the Powell principle there is no Art 2 operational duty to take reasonable steps to avoid the death of such a patient: *Rabone and another v Pennine Care NHS Trust* (n 80) [21].

[149] ibid [22].

[150] ibid [23].

There is some evidence in support of this from the subsequent case of *Fernandes de Oliveira v Portugal* in which the Grand Chamber confirmed that authorities do have a general operational duty with respect to voluntary psychiatric patients to take reasonable measures to protect them from a real and immediate risk of suicide, thus extending the duty to prevent suicide from detainees to voluntary patients:

> The Court considers that a psychiatric patient is particularly vulnerable even when treated on a voluntary basis. Due to the patient's mental disorder, his or her capacity to take a rational decision to end his or her life may to some degree be impaired. Further, any hospitalisation of a psychiatric patient, whether involuntary or voluntary, inevitably involves a certain level of restraint as a result of the patient's medical condition and the ensuing treatment by medical professionals. In the process of treatment, recourse to further kinds of restraint is often an option. Such restraint may take different forms, including limitation of personal liberty and privacy rights.[151]

In this judgment, the Court has clearly stepped beyond an assumption of control basis for the operational duty to prevent suicide and has recognised the relevance of vulnerability as a factor in determining the application of conflicting human rights law to the issue of suicide. The Court proceeded to note, however, that the specific measures required under Article 2 will depend on the particular circumstances of the case, 'and those specific circumstances will often differ depending on whether the patient is voluntarily or involuntarily hospitalised'.[152] Thus 'in the case of patients who are hospitalised following a judicial order, and therefore involuntarily, the Court, in its own assessment, may apply a stricter standard of scrutiny'.[153] Such a stricter standard seems likely to apply in the prison suicide context as well, as we have seen in the relevant case law.

Questions remain, however, about the role of vulnerability as distinct from a lack of mental capacity. In *Rabone*, while there is no clarity on exactly why the obligation to take reasonable steps to prevent a suicide is extended beyond the limits of those detained by the state, Lady Hale does appear to rule out a lack of capacity-based justification, claiming that Miss Rabone's 'mental disorder meant that she *might well* lack the capacity to make an autonomous decision to take her own life'.[154] The fact that capacity is not the decisive factor is clear from this wording: Miss Rabone 'might well' lack capacity, but the judge did not feel the need to conclusively establish this. Given that Lady Hale also makes clear that 'there is no general obligation on the State to prevent a person committing suicide, even if the authorities know or ought to know of a real and immediate risk that she will do so'[155] and reiterates that 'Autonomous individuals have a right to take their own

[151] *Fernandes de Oliveira v Portugal* (n 23) [124].
[152] ibid.
[153] ibid.
[154] ibid [105] (emphasis added).
[155] ibid [100].

lives if that is what they truly want',[156] it appears that it is Miss Rabone's mental illness itself that proves crucial.

This is problematic for many reasons. It was highlighted in the previous chapter that the diagnosis of mental illness, when coupled with a risk of suicide, would enable compulsory admission to hospital and compulsory treatment. It was also noted in chapter three that it was the very existence of such powers that facilitated the decriminalisation of suicide in the first place. It may not be surprising, therefore, that the appearance of these two factors (a diagnosis of mental illness and a suicide risk) within prison engage certain duties under the right to life. However, it was also discussed in chapter four that a simplistic coupling of mental disorder and suicide does not present the full picture and that a focus on the decision-making capacity of someone contemplating suicide would be a better option both to provide protection for life when a choice to die is not an autonomous one and also avoid compulsion when capacity is not in doubt.

VI. Conclusion

In conclusion, it is undeniable that Article 2 imposes legal obligations on certain authorities to take reasonable steps to prevent suicide. This obligation arises on the basis of foreseeability of risk, and applies not only to prisoners and other detainees but also to mental health patients (and perhaps others in circumstances where it is the authorities who have created the risk of suicide). By looking beyond the confines of the prison context, we can see that the lives of prisoners are protected from self-imposed risk not due to the specific onerous conditions of prisons, but due to a perception of vulnerability and the assumption of control. It remains, however, the existence of a mental disorder that seems to serve as a necessary condition for the operational duty.

For all the reasons considered in the previous chapter, this is regrettable. A focus on mental capacity, bolstered by the requirements of diachronic continuity, as argued in chapter four, would be entirely suitable for the prison context. It would shift the focus from a diagnosis of mental illness to decision-making capacity. While the usual requirement would apply to prisoners, namely the need to follow a decision-making process that is rational, consistent, forward-looking and reflective, the challenges posed by the prison environment mean that most attempts at suicide in prison would not meet this standard. Many cases will not present the internal coherence between past and present wishes and the identity of the person expressing a desire to die, nor will they sufficiently take into account the implications for their future (perhaps post-release) self. This is not to argue

[156] ibid.

that prison suicide does not pose unique challenges, but rather that those very challenges can better be resolved by means of a stringent application of the standards argued for in chapter four. This would avoid the pitfalls of relying upon an ambiguous vulnerability concept, equating mental illness with a lack of capacity, or casting doubt upon the relevance of autonomy within prison.

6

Suicide of Children and Young Persons

The law encounters issues of suicide in many diverse contexts, such as in healthcare, in prisons, in mental health care and in policing. All present challenging issues of conflict between, broadly, legal obligations to save life and legal rights to autonomous choices about the human body. Perhaps the most challenging situation of all is when these conflicts arise in relation to children and young persons where the loss of life from suicide will be greater and felt more keenly. However, a blanket approach that sets to one side the choices and preferences of the juvenile brings its own problems. Furthermore, even if a primary goal of preserving life is identified, the appropriate measures to achieve that may be ambiguous. For young persons with mental health issues, the risk to their lives from self-harm may be long-term and/or fluctuating. Given that mental health provision generally, and mental health provision for children in particular, is under-resourced, a focus on saving life is not always easy to implement in individual cases, especially if regard is to be had to other vital principles such as protecting human dignity and respecting (at least some degree of) autonomy.

This chapter will, therefore, explore the legal issues in relation to suicide risk, and attempted suicide, of children and young persons. It will adopt a broad interpretation of suicidal choices to include those typically taken in the healthcare context relating to refusal of life-sustaining medical treatment.[1] After a brief section outlining the seriousness of the issue of juvenile suicide in today's society, the focus will then turn to the meaning and relevance of autonomy in relation to choices about dying by young persons. This section will look at both judicial and academic approaches to the issue and will conclude that even the heightened 'capacity to choose to die' test established in chapter four may need further refinement in relation to persons under 18 years of age. The final section will then consider the challenges in responding to suicide risk in young persons, including current limitations of mental health support for children at risk of suicide and how concerns about confidentiality can hinder access to family support for vulnerable young adults. The chapter will end with some conclusions which identify a number of ways in which the law has failed young persons at risk of suicide and make suggestions for reform.

[1] The following chapter will interrogate this issue more thoroughly.

I. Suicide and the Young

We have already seen that suicide is a major problem in contemporary society, but that problem is intensified in the context of attempts to end life by young persons. In England and Wales in 2019, more than 500 people aged under 25 ended their own lives, of which over a third were under the age of 20.[2] Of further concern, suicide rates among young people seem to be increasing. In particular, the suicide rate for 10–24-year-old females increased significantly from 2012 to its highest level in 2019.[3] Suicide in young people has been described as 'a loss of potential that is hard to accept'.[4]

The media is often rife with reports of juvenile suicide. For example, in April 2021 BBC News reported that the police had uncovered social media groups involving teenage girls that led to suicidal crises and serious self-harm.[5] The report stated that 12 girls, aged between 12 and 16 years old, were part of an Instagram chat group with a name referring to suicide. The group was discovered when three of the girls who had been reported missing were found seriously unwell in a London street and taken by ambulance to hospital for emergency treatment.[6] This recalls one of the impetuses for reform to the offence of assisted suicide in 2009 when concerns about websites promoting suicide led to a perceived need to remove any possible confusion about the application of the offence to online activity.[7] Furthermore, another impetus for the 2009 reforms, and one which elevated suicide to a matter of public concern, was the high incidents of suicide amongst young persons in Bridgend, South Wales, which was causing considerable concern at the time.[8] There is also frequently a focus on suicide amongst University students. In 2019, the Office for National Statistics' annual figures highlight that 174 students in England and Wales had taken their own lives. The role of

[2] Suicides in England and Wales: 2020 registrations dataset, available at www.ons.gov.uk/peoplepopulationandcommunity/birthsdeathsandmarriages/deaths/datasets/suicidesintheunitedkingdomreferencetables.

[3] The rate for females in 2019 was 3.1 deaths per 100,000, while the rate for males aged 10–25 is higher, at 8.2 per 100,000: Suicides in England and Wales: 2019 registrations: Statistical Bulletin, available at www.ons.gov.uk/peoplepopulationandcommunity/birthsdeathsandmarriages/deaths/bulletins/suicidesintheunitedkingdom/2019registrations.

[4] GA Juhnke, PF Granello and DH Granello, *Suicide, Self-Injury, and Violence in the Schools: Assessment, Prevention, and Intervention Strategies* (Hoboken, John Wiley & Sons, 2010). These authors point out that in the United States, one of the ways in which suicide is represented in government statistics is through 'Years of Potential Life Lost'; each year 270,000 years of potential life are lost through child and adolescent suicide (4).

[5] N Titheradge, 'Police Uncover Teenage Girl 'Suicide' Instagram Group' BBC News (3 April 2021), available at www.bbc.co.uk/news/uk-56617838.

[6] ibid.

[7] See Byron Review Report, 'Safer Children in a Digital World: The Report of the Byron Review' (March 2008) and the discussion of the Coroners and Justice Act 2009 in ch 3 above.

[8] During 2007 and 2008, there were 26 known suicides by hanging in or from Bridgend county in South Wales: G Raynor and R Savill, 'Bridgend Suicides: A Town Tainted by Death' *The Telegraph* (23 February 2008), available at www.telegraph.co.uk/news/uknews/1579574/Bridgend-suicides-a-town-tainted-by-death.html. See also ch 3 above.

University authorities, especially the question of whether there should be a duty to inform those with parental responsibility of a suicide risk relating to their child, is constantly interrogated.[9] The problem of juvenile suicide has also been noted by the Committee on the Rights of the Child. In its 2016 Concluding Observations on the UK's fifth periodic report, the Committee expressed concern about research linking infant and child mortality in the UK, including suicide, with the level of social and economic deprivation[10] and particularly drew attention to the fact that the number of child suicides in Northern Ireland has been steadily increasing in the past 10 years.[11]

The terms 'juvenile' or 'young persons' are, of course, ambiguous. While these terms get to the crux of the issue – the additional poignancy of a life cut unnecessarily short at an early stage – there is no clear boundary for persons falling within these categories. From a legal perspective, there are three distinct categories of young persons, potentially raising different legal issues for the law's response to a suicide attempt or risk. The first category is the under 16-year-olds. There is no assumption of legal capacity for these children. While some more mature under 16-year-olds may be regarded as '*Gillick*-competent' and thus able to lawfully provide consent to medical treatment, those with parental responsibility retain rights (and, of course, responsibilities) to make decisions on their behalf, including in relation to care and treatment. The second category is the 16- and 17-year-olds, whose capacity to make decisions will be assessed under the Mental Capacity Act 2005 (MCA 2005) (as is the case with adults). Their power to refuse treatment has been constrained by the courts, as will be explained in the following section. The final category of young persons is legally distinct from the others because they are, in law, adults. Those aged between 18 and 25 will be governed by the same mental health and mental capacity laws as all other adults, which were discussed in chapter four. As the public concern and media interest in suicide amongst university students illustrates, however, there is an argument that this category of young persons should receive extra protection for their lives even when at threat from themselves. The law applying to these three categories of young persons when purporting to make choices about dying will now be considered in detail. The following section will also interrogate the meaning, and relevance, of autonomy in this context, and critique the courts' approach to the topic as incoherent and ultimately unhelpful.

[9] See, for example, S Coughlan, 'Would Universities Call Parents in a Mental Health Crisis?' BBC News (18 April 2021), available at www.bbc.co.uk/news/education-56763189: a father whose son, a 19-year-old university student, had taken his own life, complained that he had not been informed of the well-being concerns known to the university.

[10] Committee on the Rights of the Child, 'Concluding observations on the fifth periodic report of the United Kingdom of Great Britain and Northern Ireland' (2016) CRC/C/GBR/CO/5, para 28(a), available at digitallibrary.un.org/record/835015.

[11] ibid 60(b).

II. Young People, Autonomy and Choices about Dying

Regrettably, young people are not immune from facing life-and-death choices. This difficult issue has reached the court both in the context of life-sustaining or life-saving medical treatment, and self-harm. It is in the former category of cases that the courts have grappled with issues of autonomy and the extent to which a choice by a child should be respected if it will end her life. (The latter category of cases has led to concerns about the mental health support available to children and young persons, and will be considered further in the next section.)

A. Judicial Approaches to Children who Choose to Die

There has been slow progress towards legal respect for the choices of children in respect of their bodies and health. In 1969, the Family Law Reform Act (FLRA 1969) declared that consent to medical treatment should be effective from age 16 upwards, and then in the 1985 case of *Gillick*,[12] the House of Lords extended the power to consent below the age of 16 in situations where the child has sufficient understanding and maturity to make the decision. Such an approach reflects the (later) United Nations Convention on the Rights of the Child (UNCRC) 1989[13] and was also given statutory approval in the Children Act 1989.[14] However, arguably, there was soon a retreat from this approach in two cases vividly described by such prominent medical lawyers/ethicists as Ian Kennedy and John Harris as driving 'a coach and horses through Gillick'[15] and 'palpable nonsense'.[16] In *Re R (A Minor) (Wardship: Consent to Treatment)*[17] and *Re W (A Minor) (Medical Treatment: Courts Jurisdiction)*,[18] a Court of Appeal dominated by Lord Donaldson held that the child's right to consent does not entail a right to refuse treatment, and that courts or parents can override a minor's refusal. There is no doubt that the impetus for this development was to protect the lives of children, even against a competent child's own wishes. Lord Donaldson explicitly approved the argument that

[12] *Gillick v West Norfolk and Wisbech Area Health Authority* [1986] AC 112.

[13] Article 12(1) UN Convention on the Rights of the Child: 'States Parties shall assure to the child who is capable of forming his or her own views the right to express those views freely in all matters affecting the child, the views of the child being given due weight in accordance with the age and maturity of the child'.

[14] Section 44(7) recognises the right of a child 'of sufficient understanding to make an informed decision' to refuse medical or psychiatric examination.

[15] I Kennedy, 'Consent to Treatment: The Capable Person' in C Dyer (ed), *Doctors, Patients and the Law* (Oxford, Oxford University Press, 1992) 60.

[16] 'The idea that a child (or anyone) might competently consent to a treatment but not be competent to refuse it is palpable nonsense': J Harris, 'Consent and End of Life Decisions' (2003) 29 *Journal of Medical Ethics* 10, 15.

[17] *In re R (A Minor) (Wardship: Consent to Treatment)* [1992] Fam 11.

[18] *Re W (A Minor) (Medical Treatment: Courts Jurisdiction)* [1993] Fam 64.

'good parenting involves giving minors as much rope as they can handle without an unacceptable risk that they will hang themselves'.[19] His fellow judges had similar concerns in mind, with Balcombe LJ stating that 'there must come a point at which the court, while not disregarding the child's wishes, can override them in the child's own best interests, objectively considered'[20] and Nolan LJ declaring that an 'individual who has reached the age of 18 is free to do with his life what he wishes, but it is the duty of the court to ensure so far as it can that children survive to attain that age'.[21]

In *Re R (A Minor) (Wardship: Consent to Treatment)*, the Court of Appeal held that the court in the exercise of the wardship jurisdiction was entitled to override a *Gillick* competent child's decision concerning medical treatment but, on the facts, the 15-year-old minor in question was not in fact *Gillick* competent due to the fluctuating nature of her mental illness. Brazier and Bridge argue that this fluctuating competence is the key issue in the case, that it was 'hopelessly confused' in the judgment and that 'R's age confused the issue'.[22] In other words, regardless of the youth of R, her choices about dying were unreliable due to her mental illness and the lack of capacity that intermittently followed from that.

The same criticism is made of the *Re W* case, which involved a 16-year-old suffering from anorexia who was refusing treatment. The Court of Appeal held that FLRA 1969, section 8(1) did not confer on a minor who had attained the age of 16 an absolute right to determine whether or not she received medical treatment as her refusal could not override a consent by the court. While the court would take account of the child's wishes, it would override them where her best interests so required. Given the case law in respect of adult anorexic patients, and the challenges faced in proving capacity to refuse to eat when suffering from this disorder, arguably W's age need not have been the crucial element in the decision of the court.

Brazier and Bridge argue that both of these cases, and indeed many others, should have been resolved, not on basis of age but rather on the basis of mental health. However sound this argument may be in relation to specific cases brought to court, it does not address the question of how to respond to a child in good mental health who makes a decision which will end, or endanger, her life. Fundamentally, the courts seem ambiguous on whether a decision to prevent early death for a child should be based on that child lacking competence to make that specific choice, or on the need to override such a competent choice on basis of the child's welfare.

[19] ibid 81–82.

[20] ibid 88.

[21] ibid 94. Another case decided in the same year, in which a court authorised a blood transfusion against the wishes of a 15-year-old Jehovah's Witness, continued the emotive declarations with Ward J confirming the 'compelling and overwhelming force in the submission of the Official Solicitor that this court, exercising its prerogative of protection, should be very slow to allow an infant to martyr himself': *Re E (A Minor) (Wardship: Medical Treatment)* [1993] 1 FLR 386.

[22] M Brazier and C Bridge, 'Coercion or Caring: Analysing Adolescent Autonomy' (1996) 16 *Legal Studies* 84, 95.

More recent cases in which courts have overridden refusals of treatment in the context of self-harm and/or suicide risk seem to have abandoned entirely the pretence of competence, or the lack of it, being a relevant consideration. For example, in *An NHS Foundation Hospital v P*,[23] Baker J issued a short judgment to explain the reasons for an order made as the out-of-hours judge in the middle of the night authorising treatment of a 17-year-old girl following a drug overdose, who was refusing treatment. P had a history of self-harming behaviour and had been detained briefly under the Mental Health Act 1983 (MHA 1983), section 2, but was recently discharged. She was admitted to hospital having taken an overdose of paracetamol and initially refused all treatment. Her mother gave consent to treatment but the hospital nonetheless sought a court order.[24] The on-call child and adolescent consultant psychiatrist assessed P and concluded that, although she suffered from a personality disorder, she did not lack capacity to make decisions concerning her medical treatment.[25] P subsequently agreed to take the first dose of medication, but the trust solicitor nonetheless applied for a court order.[26] Baker J's judgment begins with the question of whether P has capacity under the MCA and, in light of the psychiatrist's opinion, and applying principles in MCA 1983, section 1, he concluded (using a double negative) that he is 'not satisfied that P lacks capacity within the meaning of section 3'.[27] He then turned to the question of whether to issue a declaration authorising the treatment notwithstanding her capacitated refusal, but instead of focusing upon the FLRA 1969, he inexplicably relied upon *Gillick*, even though the girl in question was over 16.[28] He declared that:

> In exercising its inherent jurisdiction, the court must have the child's welfare as its paramount consideration. The wishes and feelings of the child, in particular those of a 17-year-old young person who is almost an adult, are an important component of the analysis of her welfare. They are not, however, decisive.[29]

Baker J noted the relevance of P's Article 8 rights (to autonomy) but regarded them as outweighed by her Article 2 right to life.[30] He noted the court's 'heavy duty to take what steps it can to protect P's life which is manifestly in danger tonight'[31] and, in balancing the competing factors, he claimed to 'have no hesitation in concluding that the balance comes down firmly in favour of overriding P's wishes'.[32]

[23] *An NHS Foundation Hospital v P* [2014] EWHC 1650 (Fam).
[24] ibid [4].
[25] ibid [5]. The judge, however, noted that the physician at the hospital responsible for treating P had some doubts about the psychiatrist's opinion.
[26] ibid [6]–[7].
[27] ibid [9].
[28] Baker J refers to *Gillick* in [12] (and at no place in the judgment to the FLRA).
[29] ibid [13].
[30] ibid [15].
[31] ibid [16].
[32] ibid [15].

The judgment in *P* is an unsatisfactory one; it undermines the significance of a psychiatric assessment of capacity, incorrectly identifies the relevant law to be applied, even on the controversial aspect of overriding the wishes of a person with capacity, and pays mere lip service to the young person's wishes. Although Baker J emphasised that he had taken account of P's wishes and feelings, he admitted that he had not spoken to her directly before authorising the treatment. He explained this failure on the basis of the urgency of the risk to life.[33] There are a number of different, better, approaches that could have been taken to the difficult situation of a 17-year-old girl's attempted suicide and initial refusal of treatment. One option would have been to engage more directly with the girl herself, not least because of evidence that she consented to a first dose of medication and thus with support may have been amenable to further life-saving measures. Alternatively, a more robust version of capacity could have been applied that would have rendered the girl legally unable to make decisions regarding the treatment to save her life.[34] Indeed, the level of capacity required for refusal of medical intervention following an attempt at suicide must be a rigorous one. As was argued in chapter four, and will be discussed further below, capacity to choose to die should be set at a very high standard to ensure that such a momentous decision, and one often associated with mental illness, is truly an autonomous choice. A final alternative approach to the situation of P that would have stood on stronger legal terms would have been a clear and robust application of the FLRA 1969 rather than *Gillick* to the key issue of overriding the wishes of a 17-year-old who does not lack capacity. While it is appreciated that urgent applications present unusual challenges to judicial hearings, they are unavoidable, particularly in the context of suicide attempts, and the law on compulsory interventions to save life is only really tested when applied in emergency life and death situations.

Another such urgent hearing, with similarly unsatisfactory reasoning, is evident in *Plymouth Hospitals NHS Trust v YZ and ZZ*.[35] In this case, a 14-year-old girl took a potentially toxic overdose of pills, and then refused testing or treatment. The judge noted that the evidence about whether she was *Gillick* competent was 'equivocal'.[36] An application was made by the hospital trust to an out-of-hours service. The judge heard submissions on the phone and within an hour had authorised treatment. There was no representation for the child or her mother. The following day, the judge provided his reasons in a brief judgment which focuses almost entirely on the issue of the girl's best interests, with 'a strong presumption in favour of taking all steps to preserve life'.[37] There was no full consideration of whether she was *Gillick* competent other than a recognition that her refusal

[33] ibid [18]: 'Every minute that passed increased the risk'.

[34] This approach, unlike the previous one, would, of course (as discussed in ch 4) fall foul of the CRPD by equating mental and legal capacity.

[35] *Plymouth Hospitals NHS Trust v YZ and ZZ* [2017] EWHC 2211 (Fam).

[36] ibid [10].

[37] ibid [19].

was not unambiguous. The judge noted that YZ's views fluctuated and acknowledged a suggestion that the inconsistent refusals might be a manifestation of her 'wider tendency towards oppositional behaviour in the context of a plainly difficult period for her rather than a considered, rational objection'.[38] These are important and highly relevant points. As with the 15-year-old girl in *Re R*, the concept of fluctuating competence, and what that means in terms of the legality of compulsory intervention, is insufficiently considered and instead the court focuses on assessing her best interests, which inevitably for a young person weigh heavily in favour of preserving life. As with the earlier *P* case, better options for resolving this situation would have engaged more directly with the girl herself, or focused more on assessing capacity. On the former point, it is relevant that a postscript added to the judgment reveals that ultimately she did not resist testing and there was no paracetamol found in her system.[39] In hindsight, therefore, the case did not concern an urgent risk to life, although that could not have been known at the time. The judge made a very important point, however, when he noted that it was 'unfortunate that the matter did not come before the court until the window for optimum treatment advised by the specialists was almost closed'.[40] The actions of the hospital in creating the need for an urgent out-of-hours application is regrettable. The brief judgment makes clear, however, that the testing and treatment would be authorised regardless of the girl's capacity due to the presumption about saving life. If that is indeed the law's approach to children, it should be explicit and not merely implicit in urgent hearings.

More recently, the case of *A NHS Trust v X (In the matter of X (A Child) (No 2))* in 2021[41] provided Munby J the opportunity to review in detail the current state of the law on this topic. Never known to overlook such an opportunity, his judgment is detailed, engaging and thorough, but also arguably flawed. X was a 15-year-old Jehovah's Witness suffering from serious sickle cell syndrome and sometimes needing blood transfusions. In a previous hearing,[42] Munby J had authorised a transfusion during a medical crisis, despite arguments that X as a *Gillick* competent child of almost 16 should have her refusal respected. Recognising the 'unfortunate scramble to justice' presented by emergency hearings where treatment has become life-saving, the judge scheduled a subsequent hearing where there would be adequate time for preparation, argument and judicial reflection.[43]

In this later hearing, Munby J summarised the key issue as follows:

> Is the decision of a *Gillick* competent child determinative in the same way as the decision of a capacitous adult? If not, are there any, and if so what, circumstances in which the decision of a *Gillick* competent child is determinative?[44]

[38] ibid.
[39] ibid [22].
[40] ibid [18].
[41] *A NHS Trust v X (In the matter of X (A Child) (No 2))* [2021] EWHC 65 (Fam).
[42] *Re X* [2020] EWHC 3003 (Fam).
[43] *X (No 2)* (n 41) [21].
[44] ibid [27].

He further described the case as challenging the 'conventional wisdom' of the judicial approach in *Re R* and *Re W* in light of developments such as the Human Rights Act 1998 (HRA 1998) and the MCA 1983.[45] In his judgment, Munby J clarifies that FLRA 1969, section 8(1) is concerned only with legal capacity and does not operate so as to deem the child to have mental capacity.[46] This clarifies that anyone over the age of 16 is to be assumed to have mental capacity, but that this assumption can be disproven by the MCA incapacity test.[47]

Munby J helpfully distinguishes *Gillick* competence (for those under 16 years old) and MCA capacity (for 16-year-olds and over):

> [T]he tests of capacity and of *Gillick* competence have nothing very obvious in common, not least because they are rooted in different areas of scientific knowledge and understanding. Capacity, or, more precisely, lack of capacity, derives from … what in section 2(1) of the 2005 Act is referred to as 'impairment of, or a disturbance in the functioning of, the mind or brain.' *Gillick* competence, in contrast, is tied to the normal development over time of the typical child and teenager. In the first, one is therefore in the realm of psychiatry … In the other, one is not in the realm of psychiatry, rather that of child and adolescent psychology.[48]

Munby J's view that *Gillick* competence and MCA capacity are 'conceptually quite distinct'[49] is one shared by some commentators. Brazier and Bridge, for example, recognise that for adults, the functional test for incapacity has a 'caveat' requiring mental impairment.[50] In the absence of such an impairment, an inability to make a decision does not remove autonomous choice, whereas for children, the authors suggest, such a caveat may not be appropriate – although they note that in most of the cases that reach the courts, the children do in fact have a mental disability which has caused the lack of capacity.

Cave also notes the crucial differences between child competence and MCA capacity, which include not only that the inability to make a decision must be due to an impairment of, or a disturbance in the functioning of, the mind or brain, but also an assumption of capacity[51] and a requirement that a person 'is not to be treated as unable to make a decision unless all practicable steps to help him to do so have been taken without success'.[52] Cave notes that these differences cause

[45] ibid [3].
[46] ibid [56].
[47] Munby J summarises the current law as follows: '(1) Until the child reaches the age of 16 the relevant inquiry is as to whether the child is Gillick competent. (2) Once the child reaches the age of 16: (i) the issue of Gillick competence falls away, and (ii) the child is assumed to have legal capacity in accordance with section 8, unless (iii) the child is shown to lack mental capacity as defined in sections 2(1) and 3(1) of the Mental Capacity Act 2005': ibid [57].
[48] ibid [73].
[49] ibid [75].
[50] Brazier and Bridge, 'Coercion or Caring' (1996) 108. They are writing pre-MCA but referring to the Law Commission's recommendations, which were subsequently enacted in the MCA.
[51] MCA 1983, s 1(2).
[52] MCA 1983, s 1(3).

particular oddities for 16- and 17-year-olds because, for example, a 16-year-old who cannot make a decision because of a lack of maturity is likely to have MCA capacity but lack FLRA competence.[53] This means that competence and capacity are starkly different issues for young persons. One could have capacity to make a decision that as an adult would be respected, but not be treated as a competent minor.

This led Cave to grapple with the question of whether the MCA 1983 should be applied to all minors (and this will be considered below). However, it also led Munby J in *X (No 2)* to a very different conclusion, namely that the MCA 'has nothing to say relevant to the medical or surgical treatment of children who are not yet 16' and for 16- and 17-year-olds, 'has nothing to say except where the child lacks mental capacity'.[54] On this basis, he was able to conclude that there is nothing in the MCA which casts any doubt on the continued validity of the judicial approach in *Re R* and *Re W*, nor suggests a need for any judicial re-evaluation.[55] Munby J was similarly dismissive of arguments that the rights ethos of the HRA 1998 necessitates any strengthening of autonomy in relation to children's choices about medical treatment, finding that there is no breach of Article 3,[56] Article 8,[57] or Article 14 ECHR.[58] Any future change to the judicial position established in *Re R* and *Re W*, namely that the wishes of competent children and capacitated 16- and 17-year-olds, can be overridden to protect their welfare, is held to be ultimately a matter for Parliament rather than the courts.[59] On the facts of the case, Munby J dismisses X's application that she had the requisite decisional capacity to exclusively decide her own medical treatment by refusing consent to blood transfusions, both then at age 15 and also later upon reaching 16.[60] Until X reached the age of 18, capacity had little relevance in relation to the life-threatening choice of refusing blood transfusions. When she turned 18, it would become the only relevant factor, determining whether her choice will be respected or not. The legal position has not, it appears, moved on since Ward J cautioned that a court 'should be very slow to allow an infant to martyr himself' in the 1993 case of *Re E*.

The clear trend in these recent cases is to regard the question of competence and/or capacity as largely irrelevant when a minor seeks to end their life, either directly (as in the self-harm cases) or indirectly as a result of religious beliefs or other values. Whether this is because it is regarded as impossible for a minor to make a capacitated and autonomous choice to die at this point in their young

[53] E Cave, 'Goodbye Gillick? Identifying and Resolving Problems with the Concept of Child Competence' (2013) *Legal Studies* 103, 105.

[54] *X (No 2)* (n 41) [76].

[55] ibid [84].

[56] ibid [121].

[57] ibid [140].

[58] ibid [157].

[59] ibid [162].

[60] ibid [163].

lives or because, even if they have done so, there is no obligation to respect it, arguably remains unclear. Therefore, this discussion will proceed by investigating the concept of autonomy in relation to young persons and choices to die, before reflecting on the variety of theoretical bases by which a young person's wish to die might justifiably not be respected.

B. The Meaning of Autonomy and Capacity in Relation to Young Persons' Choices to Die

The law might be regarded as inconsistent in its approach to juveniles and responsibility to make decisions. Lyons has pointed out the irony that the criminal law would have held the 15-year-old minor in *Re E* liable for murder from the age 10 if he decided to end someone else's life, but held he was not competent at age 15 to make life-and-death decisions about himself.[61] While there may be a pertinent distinction between being held responsible for past actions and having decisions about future welfare respected, Lyons notes that the 'responsible person engages in critical reflection before making an autonomous choice, but also takes responsibility for preferring this or that option'.[62] A key question, therefore, might be whether a minor can be held responsible for a choice to end her own life.

Some psychologists have argued that 'it is neither inconsistent nor disingenuous' to suggest that the boundary between adolescence and adulthood should be drawn at different chronological ages for different policy purposes.[63] This is because, they argue, adolescents demonstrate adult levels of cognitive capability earlier than they exhibit emotional and social maturity: 'By age 16, adolescents' general cognitive abilities are essentially indistinguishable from those of adults, but adolescents' psychosocial functioning, even at the age of 18, is significantly less mature than that of individuals in their mid-20s'.[64] Van Assche et al have explained that, while adult-like levels of cognitive capacities are usually evident from age 14, levels of psychosocial maturity comparable to that of adults are generally not found under the age of 18 and therefore 'minors are more susceptible to coercive influences, impulsivity and a distorted cost–benefit calculus'.[65] Steinberg et al argue that it is reasonable to distinguish between different decision-making contexts, requiring a later stage of maturity for decisions that do not permit unhurried

[61] B Lyons, 'Dying to be Responsible: Adolescence, Autonomy and Responsibility' (2010) 30 *Legal Studies* 257, 257–58.

[62] ibid 263.

[63] L Steinberg et al, 'Are Adolescents Less Mature than Adults? Minors' Access to Abortion, the Juvenile Death Penalty, and the Alleged APA "Flip-flop"' (2009) 64 *American Psychologist Journal* 583, 592.

[64] ibid.

[65] K Van Assche, K Raus, B Vanderhaegen and S Sterckx, '"Capacity for Discernment" and Euthanasia on Minors in Belgium' (2019) 27 *Medical Law Review* 242, 253.

and logical reflection.[66] In this context, there may well be a pertinent distinction between refusal of consent for ongoing life-sustaining medical treatment by a young person and an impulsive suicide or self-harm attempt, with decisions about the former requiring greater respect. Indeed, the argument of Steinberg et al, albeit made in the US-specific context of abortion access and juvenile death penalty, might also imply that even young adults over the age of 18 have not yet acquired the emotional maturity to choose to die unilaterally without input from others.[67] This might support the argument first developed in chapter four that 'capacity to choose to die' should be set at a higher level than the standard MCA test.

The distinction between impulsive suicide and self-harm attempts and long-term reflections about an early death is also apparent in Belgian law on euthanasia. Voluntary active euthanasia (VAE) was decriminalised in Belgium in 2002.[68] Until 2014, it was only available for legally competent adults and emancipated minors, but concerns about potential discrimination in relation to non-emancipated minors,[69] as well as the existence of some evidence that VAE was nonetheless taking place for children but without their explicit request,[70] led to an amendment to extend the possibility of obtaining euthanasia to all minors, regardless of age, provided that they are found to have the 'capacity for discernment'. This requirement was one of a number of protective mechanisms introduced in order to recognise the potential vulnerability of minors. Other protective mechanisms include requirements that such capacity for discernment be certified by an independent child and adolescent psychiatrist or psychologist, and that euthanasia is only available for minors demonstrating physical, and not mental, suffering from a condition that will result in death within the foreseeable future.[71]

The Constitutional Court of Belgium has confirmed that the legislature has fulfilled its obligation to put in place increased protective measures for minors and thus found no violation of the Constitution or international human rights law from the extension of VAE to minors.[72] The 'capacity for discernment' phrase was apparently inspired by Article 12 of the French text of the CRC, which refers to *capabilite de discernement* – translated in the English text as the 'capability of a child of forming his or her own views' – but, according to Van Assche et al, the exact phrase *capacité de discernement* has only previously been used in a few Canadian and Swiss legal instruments relating to the protection of minors in healthcare contexts, as well as in the French language judgment of

[66] Steinberg et al, 'Are Adolescents Less Mature than Adults?' (2009) 592.

[67] As quoted above, the authors argue that an 18-year-old's psychosocial functioning is significantly less mature than that of individuals in their mid-20s.

[68] The Belgian Euthanasia Act 2002 defines VAE as 'intentionally terminating life by someone other than the person concerned, at the latter's request'.

[69] Van Assche et al, '"Capacity for Discernment"' (2019) 243.

[70] ibid 244.

[71] ibid 247–48.

[72] Constitutional Court of Belgium (29 October 2015) 153/2015 (English translation), available at www.const-court.be/public/e/2015/2015-153e.pdf.

the European Court of Human Rights in *Haas v Switzerland*, where it denotes a person's capacity to form her own views.[73] The phrase was interpreted by the Belgian Constitutional Court as the ability to express one's wishes and specifically as relating to 'the ability of the minor to understand the real implications of his euthanasia request and its consequences'.[74] Van Assche et al have queried, however, whether 'capacity for discernment' adds anything additional to the protection for minors if it merely requires a level of maturity already required for other medical decisions and which, they argue, seems to already be required in respect of all euthanasia requests by the general 'voluntary and well-considered request' requirement.[75]

Furthermore, they point out the apparent contradiction in Belgian law that minors with capacity for discernment still require consent from their legal representatives (parents).[76] By contrast, in the Netherlands, while minors between 12 and 16 years of age and who are capable of a reasonable assessment of their interests can obtain euthanasia only with consent of their legal representatives, those aged 16 or 17 years old, need only ensure their legal representatives are 'involved' in the decision-making process, with no requirement for them to consent.[77] The Belgian Constitutional Court held that it was not unreasonable for the legislator to require the consent of the minor's legal representatives, not only because of the right of the parents to respect for their family life and their obligation to take care of the well-being of their children, but also as a safeguard for the physician's compliance with the criteria of due care – involving the parents will help to ensure that both the suffering and the request are at the requisite level.[78]

In short, the Belgian law on euthanasia permits a child to choose an early death but only with a heightened level of capacity (or, at least, the perception of one) and with the parallel consent of her parents. Therefore, it respects something resembling a *family* decision to end life prematurely in order to relieve prolonged suffering of an inevitable early death. Such a decision is, by definition, a well-considered choice and accords respect to what may be regarded as the epitome of a choice to die. Arguably the lessons to be drawn from this approach for the types of cases brought before English courts relating to suicide attempts and/or refusals of treatment are that an autonomous and capacitated choice to die is conceivable even from a minor, but it is an extremely high threshold to meet and, crucially, it cannot be met by the child alone. In addition to the standard requirements that would, it was argued in chapter four, substantiate a choice to die, for a young person under the age of 18 additional requirements of consultation with adults in

[73] Van Assche et al (n 65) 249.
[74] Constitutional Court of Belgium (n 72) 45.
[75] Van Assche et al (n 65) 250.
[76] This is not required for some other health decisions such as refusal of consent to life-sustaining treatment (ibid 255).
[77] ibid 256.
[78] ibid 256–57.

a position of parental responsibility may well be needed in order to establish the requisite capacity to choose to die.

C. Seeking a Principled Basis for Overriding a Young Person's Choice to Die

In the literature, there are a variety of different arguments that seek to establish a principled basis for overriding a child's wish to die. These include varied reinterpretations of the meaning of autonomy in this context, as well as concern about future autonomy and an emphasis on self-interest in well-being. In Coggon's helpful analysis of autonomy, he distinguishes between three different understandings of autonomy.[79] Firstly, 'ideal desire autonomy' is a Kantian approach, also reflected in O'Neill's principled autonomy,[80] in which autonomous action requires 'responsible decision-making', judged by reference to a purportedly universal or objective standard of values.[81] Secondly, 'best desire autonomy' is a Dworkinian approach[82] which requires autonomous action to reflect a person's 'overall desire given his own values, even if this runs contrary to his immediate desire'.[83] This is closest to the form of autonomy generally argued to apply to choices to die in this book. Impulsive decisions to end one's own life which do not fit within a person's own value system and life story are not ones requiring respect and thus (compulsory) preventative measures to save life may be appropriate. Such decisions would fall within Coggon's third understanding of autonomy, namely 'current desire autonomy'. This understanding of autonomy is akin to a person's 'first-order desires', which Coggon explains 'may refer either to a person's impulsive desire, or to a person's desire that is settled and lasting but on which he has not reflected'.[84] This is the understanding of autonomy which the English courts profess to apply to adults,[85] although arguably they often manipulate assessments of capacity in order to apply in practice something closer to 'best desire autonomy'. Coggon concludes that this conception is generally to be preferred with regard to serious decision-making,[86] and the concept of a heightened 'capacity to choose to die'

[79] J Coggon, 'Varied and Principled Understandings of Autonomy in English Law: Justifiable Inconsistency or Blinkered Moralism?' (2007) 15 *Health Care Analysis* 235.

[80] O O'Neill, *Autonomy and Trust in Bioethics* (Cambridge, Cambridge University Press, 2002).

[81] Coggon, 'Varied and Principled Understandings' (2007) 240–41.

[82] In G Dworkin, *The Theory and Practice of Autonomy* (Cambridge, Cambridge University Press, 1988) he argues that distinguishing 'first-' and 'second-order desires' and being able to act in accordance with second-order desires is what makes a being autonomous.

[83] Coggon (n 79) 240.

[84] ibid 241.

[85] As Lord Donaldson MR famously stated in the 1992 case of *Re T*, that legal right of choice 'is not limited to decisions which others might regard as sensible. It exists notwithstanding that the reasons for making the choice are rational, irrational, unknown or even non-existent': *Re T (adult: refusal of treatment)* [1992] 4 All ER 649 at 652–53.

[86] Coggon (n 79) 253. He is referring only to adults, however, and does not apply his theories to children in this article.

test developed in chapter four of this book also requires more than mere current desire autonomy to be applied to choices to die for adults.

There is an argument, however, that for young persons, or at least children, an even more stringent test of autonomy would be appropriate. The 'ideal desire' standard, necessitating responsible decision-making would ensure that only choices to die that accord with objective standards would be legally respected as autonomous choices worthy of respect. One might imagine that a mature young person with experience of a long-term terminal illness, who has reflected upon the consequences of refusing life-sustaining treatment and consulted with her parents, might be an example of such an autonomous choice worthy of respect by the law; an isolated, impulsive attempt at suicide, even by a juvenile in sound mental health, would not.

An alternative interpretation of autonomy that changes the focus of the issue is that of relational autonomy. Gilmore and Herring recognise the danger, which they see as particularly pertinent in the case of children, of viewing the patient 'in isolation from the context of the relationships within which they (and we all) live'.[87] These authors argue that parents have an interest in a life-and-death decision about their child:

> They have an interest as a parent who has parental responsibilities; as a parent who has invested his or her life (emotionally and practically) in the child and his or her upbringing; and an interest as a result of the impact that that decision might have on their own personal lives.[88]

In addition, they note that the child may also wish to make such a momentous decision in consultation with her parents.[89] Relational autonomy is a controversial approach to the appropriate legal protection for an adult's autonomy,[90] but it is far less contentious in respect of children. Under 18s, in particular, may indeed be appropriately viewed as persons for whom autonomous choice cannot be seen in isolation from the interests of other family members.

Two concerns remain, however. Firstly, while a consultative approach may be well suited to decisions about refusal of medical treatment for long-term illnesses, as these will often be experiences endured by a family rather than just a child alone, it is not quite so easy to see its application to a suicide attempt or desire in a non-medical context, where the choice may be more impulsive and its reasons less transparent. This does not mean, of course, that it should not be applied in such a context, and indeed an impulsive and less understandable choice to die by a young person is all the more in need of a wider contextual appreciation of the

[87] S Gilmore and J Herring, '"No" is the Hardest Word: Consent and Children's Autonomy' (2011) 23 *Child and Family Law Quarterly* 3, 23.

[88] ibid.

[89] ibid.

[90] See discussion in E Wicks, *The State and the Body: Legal Regulation of Bodily Autonomy* (Oxford, Hart Publishing, 2016) 7–9.

implications of such a choice for others, but the framework for such a requirement may prove more challenging. Secondly, there remains a question of whether a relational approach should apply to over-18-year-olds. Gilmore and Herring, and indeed many other commentators,[91] would apply it to all adults, but it is argued here that its strongest justification is in respect of minors under 18. It may be, however, that the ongoing interests of parents in the lives of their young adult children may also justify a family-based approach beyond 18 and into the early years of adulthood. Indeed, the response to the suicide amongst university students, and the strident calls for parents to be more informed of suicide risk, highlights the arguments for continued involvement by those with parental responsibility in choices to die beyond official adulthood.

A somewhat different argument relating to the implications of respecting autonomy is that of Feinberg, who suggests intervening in the lives of children for the sake of the child's future autonomy, in situations where a child's decision or behaviour is such that it threatens her future.[92] Chico and Hagger explain that Feinberg's approach 'does not amount to saying "no, never" but simply "no, not now" or "wait", thus protecting the child's future autonomy at the expense of disrespecting it now'.[93] They argue that this is problematic because 'it assumes that the choice is one that can wait'.[94] This may indeed be a problem when considering decisions about urgent medical treatment, but is arguably less so in relation to suicide. Erring on the side of caution – the side of postponing an early death – is a sound approach where there is any doubt about whether a wish to die now is truly an autonomous one. Gilmore and Herring also suggest that one justification for overriding a child's refusal of life-sustaining treatment is that such a refusal may not accord with true autonomy because it affects the subsequent exercise of autonomy.[95] They argue that 'a weakly autonomous decision may not be sufficient to justify doing an act which will lead to serious harm'.[96] Cave also acknowledges that there are strong arguments for applying future-orientated versions of autonomy in cases where the decision would result in death or serious injury.[97]

The idea of protecting a young person's future autonomy by preventing a purportedly autonomous choice to die now is, albeit implicitly, reflected in the case law. As we have seen, in cases such as *Re E*, there is a judicial emphasis on protecting life until adulthood at which point a person's choice to end life becomes worthy of legal respect. While the judgments explicitly phrase that intervention

[91] See, for example, J Nedelsky, 'Reconceiving Autonomy: Sources, Thoughts and Possibilities' (1989) 1 *Yale Journal of Law & Feminism* 7; C Mackenzie and N Stoljar (eds), *Relational Autonomy: Feminist Perspectives on Autonomy, Agency and the Social Self* (Oxford, Oxford University Press, 2000).

[92] J Feinberg, *Freedom and Fulfilment: Philosophical Essays* (Princeton, Princeton University Press, 1992) 76–98.

[93] V Chico and L Hagger, 'The Mental Capacity Act 2005 and Mature Minors: A Missed Opportunity?' (2011) 33 *Journal of Social Welfare and Family Law* 157, 163.

[94] ibid.

[95] Gilmore and Herring, '"No" is the Hardest Word' (2011) 21–22.

[96] ibid 22.

[97] Cave, 'Goodbye Gillick?' (2013) 111.

in terms of preserving the well-being of a child until she is fully autonomous, they might also be explained in terms of preserving the possibility of future autonomous choice because without life, there can be no exercise of autonomy. It is hard to avoid a paternalistic whiff to the future autonomy argument, however. And there is also no logical reason why it would not also justify compulsory intervention to prevent *all* suicides regardless of issues of capacity and age. It is not, therefore, the refined conceptual tool most suited to legal responses to juvenile suicide.

Some writers focus less on interpreting the meaning of autonomy for juvenile choices to die and more on protecting their self-interest in terms of well-being. Eekelaar attempts to reconcile the two goals of acting towards children with the objective of furthering their best interests, with treating children as possessors of rights, and in doing so adopts a concept he labels 'dynamic self-determinism'.[98] This concept allows scope for the child to determine her own best interests, and implies that a competent child's decision should determine the outcome subject to an exception where a decision is contrary to her self-interest in terms of physical or mental well-being and integrity.[99] Applying this to the issue of juvenile suicide, it would imply that even a competent minor might not be able to make determinative decisions about ending life due to their core self-interest being at risk. This could be regarded as reflecting the judicial approach in practice (seen in the principles evident in *Re R*, *Re W* and the FLRA). It would be much harder to justify an extension of such a principle to young persons aged over 18, however, within the context of a legal system in which a right to choose against one's own self-interest is explicitly recognised, protected and valued. In respect of minors, however, it is an approach that has garnered some support. Chico and Hagger, for example, refer to Eekelaar's proposals as striking 'an appropriate balance between the empowerment and protection of children' by ensuring their wishes are a significant consideration, but recognising that where competent children's self-interests are threatened by a child's decision then it should, at least, be challenged.[100]

The relevant academic literature, therefore, reflects the two main alternative approaches to the issue of juvenile suicide: a) basing a decision to prevent suicide on a child not having competence to make an autonomous choice to die; and b) the need to override such a competent choice on the basis of the child's well-being. As was demonstrated in the previous section, the English courts have tended to emphasise the second approach and downplay questions about competence and capacity. They have been able to do so because the MCA, which protects

[98] J Eekelaar, 'The Interests of the Child and the Child's Wishes: The Role of Dynamic Self-determinism' (1994) 8 *International Journal of Law and the Family* 42.

[99] ibid 57. Eekelaar also recognises a second constraint where a decision is not compatible with the general law and the interests of others. This is a rather more vague (and contentious) exception, but one not strictly relevant to our current discussion.

[100] Chico and Hagger, 'The Mental Capacity Act 2005 and Mature Minors' (2011) 160.

the exercise of autonomy by adults with capacity, does not apply to under-16-year-olds. The Committee on the Rights of the Child has noted as a matter of concern that children under the age of 16 years are 'excluded from protection' under the MCA, including with regard to medical treatment without consent.[101] Cave argues, however, that the MCA is an unsuitable mechanism to protect those aged under 16:

> [P]artial application of the MCA is problematic because it would insufficiently protect minors' autonomy interests; full application would fail to protect their welfare interests; and altering the terms of the Act to extend the definition of incapacity to incorporate inexperience, immaturity and undue influence would limit the effectiveness of the Act in protecting adults.[102]

What Cave proposes instead is to apply the MCA to all regardless of age, but provide additional protection for the life of minors by means of the common law's inherent jurisdiction.[103] In recent years, this mechanism has been utilised to protect so-called 'vulnerable' adults. In *DL v A Local Authority*,[104] the Court of Appeal held that adults who have capacity under the MCA may nevertheless lack capacity at common law. Cave argues that extending the same principle to minors might enable the law to adopt a universal approach to capacity, while also ensuring that the welfare of minors remains protected.[105] She proposes that there would be a presumption of capacity for minors (both under the MCA and the common law), but the MCA would enable intervention in the minor's best interests in situations where a minor lacks capacity under the Act (ie resulting from 'an impairment of, or a disturbance in the functioning of, the mind or brain'), while the common law would protect the lives and wellbeing of minors who do not lack capacity under the MCA but are seeking to make decisions 'that are in no way autonomous'.[106] Cave reiterates that this proposed approach is 'not intended to overrule those who make autonomous decisions, but to recognise the reality that the MCA definition of capacity does not necessarily encapsulate all autonomous decisions or label as incapacitous all decisions that are not autonomous'.[107] In the context of suicide (although perhaps not in other contexts), this accords with the general argument developed in this book that establishing capacity to choose to die requires a more rigorous standard of autonomous decision-making than the usual MCA capacity test. For young persons, this is all the more vital, for the many reasons highlighted above.

While it is possible for a young person to make an autonomous choice to die, and there may even be some limited circumstances in which the law should respect

[101] CRC Concluding Observations (n 10) para 60(g).
[102] Cave (n 53) 119.
[103] ibid 120.
[104] *DL v A Local Authority* [2012] EWCA Civ 253.
[105] Cave (n 53) 104.
[106] ibid 120.
[107] ibid 121.

that choice, an extremely cautious legal approach is justified in this context. Such an autonomous choice would need to satisfy not only the heightened 'capacity to choose to die' test necessitating a decision-making process that is rational, consistent, forward-looking and reflective, but for minors under the age of 18, this should also involve engagement with others, specifically those with parental responsibility, to enable a more mature input into the decision. This recommendation draws from a relational approach to autonomy that has particular applicability to children's decision-making, but it also draws from other lines of reasoning such as an 'ideal desire' autonomy standard necessitating responsible decision-making when a child purports to choose to die, and a simple wish to ensure that more mature views are included in such grave decisions. A choice to die that falls short of these standards is not one that should require upholding by the law, and interventions that are in the best interests of the child should occur. Of course, in some of the tragic circumstances that come before the courts, it may be that the best interests of the child or young person does not require prolonged life. The child's views must be given great weight at that stage too. In the vast majority of situations involving juvenile suicide, however, the overwhelming interest of that young person will be in prolonged life into adulthood and beyond.

This section has focused on the issue of whether a young person can make a truly autonomous choice to die, and to what extent, and in what circumstances, the law should respect that choice. However, this might be regarded as a somewhat 'academic' pursuit; the vast majority of cases that come before the courts, and indeed of reported cases of juvenile suicide, do not fall into a category of autonomous choices to die made by a person with capacity to do so. The most weighty and pressing challenge for law and policy is not when a choice to die should be respected, but rather what interventions are available to provide support for a young person at risk of non-autonomous and non-capacitated self-imposed death. It is to this issue that we will now turn.

III. Responding to Suicide Risks in Young People

As is the case with adults, many juveniles at risk of suicide suffer from mental health issues.[108] However, the provision of appropriate care and treatment for mental illness faces two major challenges, in addition to the general point that mental health disorders often go undetected and untreated in young persons.[109] Firstly, there seems to be a judicial reluctance to deal with mental health issues directly when considering risks to life for minors. As Brazier and Bridge have

[108] See Juhnke, Granello and Granello, *Suicide, Self-Injury, and Violence in the Schools* (2010) 10: 'children and adolescents diagnosed with mental health disorders have drastically higher rates of suicidal thoughts and behaviours than those without'.

[109] ibid.

argued in relation to the crucial *Re R* and *Re W* cases, 'faced with severely disturbed young people in need of urgent treatment, judges shied away from the perceived stigma of invoking mental health legislation'.[110] They question why, in *Re W*, the girl was not treated under the MHA 1983 given that anorexia has been recognised as a mental disorder.[111] In that case, Lord Donaldson stated that 'it may be in the long term interests of the minor that if the same treatment can be secured on some other basis, this shall be done'.[112] This leads Brazier and Bridge to query whether that brief statement is not the key to the case (and to *Re R* as well):

> Both were very sick young women. Both suffered from illness which distorted their judgment, deprived them of the capacity to make a choice. In neither instance was their condition unique to their age. Their minority was fortuitous. What their age allowed was for the courts to avoid the 'stigma' of the Mental Health Acts.[113]

The courts' failure to use the MHA to protect juveniles at risk of an early death is regrettable. Tackling the perceived 'stigma' of mental health is an important goal, and progress has been made since these early cases. The recognition of increased suicide risk in young mentally ill persons and the need to appropriately treat that illness, should outweigh any such concerns.

The more recent case of *Re P (Application for Secure Accommodation)*[114] illustrates, however, some of the challenges of treating minors at risk of suicide under the mental health laws and thus it is worth restating the facts in some detail. P had a long history of self-harm and threats of suicide. She was initially admitted to hospital on a voluntary basis,[115] and then, after further attempts to self-harm in hospital, she was detained under section 2 and subsequently section 3 MHA 1983. She was then later discharged from her section, initially remaining in hospital as a voluntary patient[116] and then later discharged into a therapeutic community placement, where she continued to self-harm and ran away from the placement.[117] P's behaviour deteriorated during August 2015 with incidents of self-harm requiring hospitalisation for physical harm. However, a psychiatrist found that a section 3 MHA admission would not be appropriate as there was 'no evidence of a serious and enduring mental disorder' and instead recommended a Secure Accommodation Order under the Children Act 1989, section 25.[118]

[110] Brazier and Bridge (n 22) 85.
[111] ibid 96.
[112] *Re W (A Minor)* (n 18).
[113] Brazier and Bridge (n 22) 96.
[114] *Re P (Application for Secure Accommodation)* [2015] EWHC 2971 (Fam).
[115] ibid [4].
[116] ibid [9].
[117] ibid [10].
[118] ibid [16].

The judge expressed that he was 'concerned' about these views of the lack of a mental disorder and called the doctor to court to give evidence. The psychiatrist reiterated that, while the risk of further self-injury was high,

> in his opinion P was not suffering from either an acute or an enduring mental illness. He was unable to identify any mental disorder. In his opinion P did not require compulsory admission to hospital under the Mental Health Act.[119]

The judge remained unconvinced, however, and expressed his concern that the real issue was the scarcity of a suitable inpatient bed for P.[120] P was moved to a secure accommodation placement on 14 September, but on 23 September she absconded and was found by a passer-by 'threatening to throw herself from a bridge'.[121] The police talked her down and then, exercising their powers under MHA 1989, section 136, took her to a hospital where she was placed on an adolescent psychiatric intensive care unit (PICU).[122] At this point, a (different) psychiatrist accepted that P did require ongoing mental health treatment[123] and she was compulsorily detained under MHA 1989, section 3.[124] As the judge noted, it took five weeks from when P was admitted to hospital having inserted a biro into her arm in an act of self-harm before a mental health bed was found for her, and one was only found following her threat to throw herself from a bridge.[125] As the judge recognised, not only was this delay regrettable, but it could have had 'catastrophic consequences'.[126]

The case of *Re P* also highlights the second major challenge in the provision of appropriate care and treatment for suicide risk in young persons, and one that has come to the forefront in recent years, namely the lack of available mental health support even when the mental health issues in a case of risk to life are recognised. This was poignantly highlighted by Munby P in *Re X (A Child) (No 3)*[127] in 2017. The case involved a 17-year-old who had made numerous attempts to end her life. She was detained in secure accommodation that was not suited to her needs. In a previous case about this person,[128] Munby P had emphasised the importance of putting in place a 'realistic and above all safe plan' for X on her imminent release from the secure unit, noting that without this 'the consequences, given her suicidal ideation, do not bear thinking about'.[129]

[119] ibid [18].
[120] ibid.
[121] ibid [23].
[122] ibid.
[123] ibid [25].
[124] ibid [26].
[125] ibid [28].
[126] ibid.
[127] *Re X (A Child) (No 3)* [2017] EWHC 2036 (Fam). See also C Parker, '"We Will Have Blood on our Hands": The Judiciary Shines a Light on the Inadequacy of Adolescent Mental Health Care' (2018) 40 *Journal of Social Welfare and Family Law* 98.
[128] *Re X (A Child) (No 2)* [2017] EWHC 1585.
[129] ibid [35].

He explained that without such a plan, the only remaining hope would be 'that the police would have had occasion to take X into custody before she was able to cause herself irreparable harm. Is that really the best the care system and the family justice system can achieve?'[130] When the case came back before the judge for the third time, his patience with the system was explicitly strained and he was frustrated with the failure to achieve a care plan for X. At the time of the second case, a psychiatrist had concluded that X's suicidal tendencies were 'behavioural rather than issues of mental health'[131] although others disagreed. By the third case, it was agreed that the grounds for a MHA 1983, section 2 assessment order were met, but there were no suitable places available.

The secure unit at which X resided was self-evidently not appropriate for X's condition as it was unable to ensure her welfare. The psychiatrist noted that

> the team have no option but to primarily physically restrain [X], if she is threatening to self-harm and cannot be kept safe, as there is no ability to follow a process of rapid tranquilisation using a medication based approach since none of the staff have a nursing or medical background.[132]

The description of X's life at that time makes depressing reading:

> She is effectively nursed in her bedroom, but this bedroom has had to be stripped in order to make it secure, to the point where [X] has no personal items in the bedroom, no carpet, no mirror, her bed is a mattress on the floor and she has to be dressed in anti-ligature clothing. Even going to the bathroom or having a shower has to be closely supervised. There is a potential for concerns to arise about [X]'s consumption of food and drink, as the periods during the day when she is restrained become increasingly extensive … she is now isolated from all her peers and no longer attends education, even on a minimal basis.[133]

Despite these extreme measures, the judge noted that during X's time at the secure accommodation, not yet totalling six months, restraints had been used on 117 occasions and there had been 102 'significant' acts of self-harm.[134] Munby P did not overlook the human rights issues raised by the care being provided to this vulnerable young person. Commenting on her living conditions, he questioned how this treatment was compatible with her humanity, dignity and welfare.[135] He also explicitly questioned whether these conditions met the requirements of Article 3 ECHR's prohibition of inhuman or degrading treatment, and Article 8 ECHR's obligation to respect X's private and family life. Interestingly, he also drew attention to the state's obligations under Article 2's right to life, noting that 'given the by now well documented and repeated attempts by X to take her own

[130] ibid.
[131] ibid [17].
[132] *Re X (A Child) (No. 3)* (n 127) [17].
[133] ibid [19].
[134] ibid [20]. These self-harm attempts were coupled with 45 assaults, 25 attempted assaults, and 16 incidents of significant damage to property.
[135] ibid [36].

life, the State's positive obligations under Article 2 of the Convention are plainly engaged'.[136]

The fact is that neither X's life nor her dignity were being protected in that situation and this was a fact widely recognised by everyone involved in her care. The problem was that there was no apparent solution. The judge notes that what X needed 'as a matter of desperate urgency' was therapy in an appropriate clinical setting.[137] This could be achieved with placement in a Tier 4 (adolescent) low secure unit (LSU), but no such placement was available anywhere in the country. Furthermore, no placement of any kind at all was available for when X was to leave her current accommodation within a matter of weeks. This led Munby P to make a striking and now infamous statement:

> If, when in eleven days' time she is released from ZX, we, the system, society, the State, are unable to provide X with the supportive and safe placement she so desperately needs, and if, in consequence, she is enabled to make another attempt on her life, then I can only say, with bleak emphasis: we will have blood on our hands.[138]

The judge directed that copies of his judgment be sent to various relevant cabinet ministers and it became a front-page story in national newspapers.[139] This unusual approach worked. In a subsequent case it was revealed that a PICU unit was to be converted into an LSU unit specifically for X (and providing beds for others, too) but Munby P cautioned that the provision of care for someone like X 'should not be dependent upon judicial involvement, nor should someone like X be privileged just because her case comes before a very senior judge'.[140]

The fact that it is a broader problem is clear. A survey of inpatient admissions for children and young people with mental health problems conducted by the Royal College of Psychiatrists in 2015, revealed that 79 per cent of respondents reported safeguarding concerns while waiting for a bed and 76.5 per cent reported young people with unacceptably high-risk profiles having to be managed in the community because of a lack of beds.[141] Most worryingly, 14 per cent of respondents' comments described patient suicide attempts while waiting for a bed.[142] This highlights that the law's response to suicide risk in young persons can only be so effective without the appropriate resources and facilities to provide the necessary mental health support. The Royal College of Psychiatrists has urged

[136] ibid.
[137] ibid [24].
[138] ibid [39].
[139] See K Rawlinson, O Bowcott and D Campbell, 'Judge Warns of "Blood on our Hands" if Suicidal Girl is Forced Out of Secure Care' *The Guardian* (3 August 2017), available at www.theguardian.com/society/2017/aug/03/judge-warns-of-blood-on-our-hands-if-suicidal-girl-is-forced-out-of-secure-care.
[140] *Re X (A Child) (No 4)* [2017] EWHC 2084 (Fam) [18].
[141] Faculty of Child and Adolescent Psychiatry, The Royal College of Psychiatrists, 'Survey of Inpatient Admissions for Children and Young People with Mental Health Problems' (2015) Faculty Report, FR/CAP/01, available at www.rcpsych.ac.uk/docs/default-source/members/faculties/child-and-adolescent-psychiatry/fr-cap-01.pdf?sfvrsn=340053fd_2.
[142] ibid.

the Government to prioritise investment in crisis care services for children and young people, and has also called for adequate emergency care pathways to be put in place as a matter of urgency.[143] Recent MHA reform plans recognise the need to improve support for children and young people and a full crisis care service for children and young people is promised by 2023–24.[144] Other proposed changes to the MHA will also apply to this category of persons, meaning that, for example, care and treatment plans will be provided to all children and young persons receiving inpatient care.[145] Much more will be needed, however, in order to ensure that future young persons at risk of suicide receive more appropriate care than either P or X.

Within the context of the current limitations of mental health support for young persons at risk of suicide, the importance of familial support must also be considered. As mentioned above, the role of universities in this respect has been the subject of particular scrutiny in recent years. Most, although not all, university students are over the age of 18 and therefore legally regarded as adults, and yet universities assume supportive roles over these persons in a manner not seen in the workplace. The large number of young persons accommodated in one place, and the fact that many of these will have moved away from a family home for the first time, and may be a long way from that home and the network of support it provides, lends strength to the argument that these young persons, although adults, are particularly vulnerable. The legal duties of university authorities to respect the medical confidentiality of their students can make it more difficult for families of students at risk of suicide to be kept informed. This can cause considerable distress to parents, as demonstrated by the father of a student who took her own life at the University of Liverpool in 2018, who was quoted as being 'bewildered' that her parents were not told of a previous suicide attempt three months before and complained that 'For as long as I live, I will never understand why no-one at the university picked up the phone to us … and told us that our 19-year-old daughter was in hospital after taking an overdose'.[146]

One way around the perceived confidentiality issue which has gained considerable support in recent years is a voluntary opt-in system under which students could choose, or refuse, to allow universities to get in touch with a parent, or other adult, if there were serious concerns about their well-being.[147] The University of Bristol introduced such a system and more than 90 per cent of students opted in.[148] The students are asked when they first register, rather than at the point of

[143] ibid, and quoted by Munby P in *Re X (A Child) (No 3)* (n 127) [28].

[144] 'Reforming the Mental Health Act' White Paper (2021) ch 10, available at www.gov.uk/government/consultations/reforming-the-mental-health-act/reforming-the-mental-health-act.

[145] ibid. Advance choice documents, and the option to choose a nominated person will also be relevant to children and young persons.

[146] Coughlan, 'Would Universities Call Parents in a Mental Health Crisis?' (n 9).

[147] ibid.

[148] ibid.

crisis, enabling an advance choice before any issues of capacity may arise. The University of Bristol's so-called 'emergency response protocol' was used 36 times in its first year,[149] which illustrates the extent of the problem of suicide risk in universities. This means that 36 times in one year in a single university, parents were informed of serious well-being issues facing their children providing the opportunity for them to provide support, without any fear that the student's right to confidentiality had been violated. It is an example of good practice that should be adopted throughout the sector. There has been some ministerial support for it,[150] and in 2019, a survey from the Higher Education Policy Institute found a large majority of students agreed with the principle of universities contacting parents.[151] That same year, 174 students in England and Wales took their own lives.[152] Failing to seek advance authority from those students to involve their parents in the most difficult time of their lives is an inexcusable omission on the part of university authorities who are uniquely placed to intervene in juvenile suicide risk. This is all the more obvious when the available mental health support for university students may also be delayed. This was apparent in respect of a student found hanged in halls at University of Liverpool in May 2018. At the inquest in which her death was recorded as suicide, coroner Anita Bhardwaj described as 'unacceptable' the delay of two months between her referring herself to the university's mental health advisers and being given an appointment to see them.[153] The involvement of parental support during that period would have gone some way to reducing the isolation of a young person at risk.

One means of providing some lower levels of support to students contemplating suicide is through technological interventions. A growing number of universities, including my own institution, the University of Leicester, have introduced the R;pple browser extension onto university computers.[154] R;pple recognises if a person searches for harmful keywords or phrases related to the topic of self-harm or suicide and provides signposting to 24/7 free mental health support at a time when people are most vulnerable. Such efforts help to ensure more support is available at the time it may be most needed. It is a sensible supportive mechanism, targeted at those who may benefit from it, without imposing intrusive restrictions upon autonomy or health, and without raising confidentiality concerns.

This section has highlighted the failings of a system in which opportunities to support young persons contemplating ending their lives are repeatedly missed. Judicial hesitance to apply the mental health law framework to young persons at

[149] ibid.
[150] In 2018, the Universities Minister Sam Gyimah spoke in favour of such an opt-in system, and the education secretary Damian Hinds wrote to university leaders telling them to improve how they reached out to families, as the top line of a new mental health initiative (ibid).
[151] ibid.
[152] ibid.
[153] ibid.
[154] www.ripplesuicideprevention.com.

risk of suicide, the acute shortage of suitable mental health accommodation when they are willing to do so, and a failure on the part of some university authorities to utilise the support that would be available from families for vulnerable young adults at risk of suicide all contribute to an inadequate response to juvenile suicide that, quite literally, puts young lives at risk.

IV. Conclusion

The law has, in some ways, failed young persons who attempt suicide. The relevant law is not clear and fails to support those most at risk. The judicial response in emergency judgments is at times legally incoherent and fails to adequately engage with the thorny issue of capacity in the context of suicidal and life-threatening choices by children and young persons. Falling back upon a presumption that life should be saved does not permit the law to really engage with the problem of juvenile suicide and is a superficial response to a much more complex issue. Furthermore, while judges may recognise the importance of prioritising efforts to prolong the lives of young persons, the statutory and healthcare system does not facilitate that, at least in any long-term manner. The conditions under which young persons such as P were confined highlight the system's failure to respect the dignity inherent in her life, while the real danger that X was mere weeks away from being abandoned by the system due to bed shortages means it is hard to ignore Munby P's urgent plea to avoid 'blood on our hands'. The recent COVID-19 pandemic will, of course, have done nothing to help the shortage of resources within juvenile mental health care.

Some of the problems highlighted here are beyond the influence of the law itself, but there is much that legal reform could achieve in this field. It could start by improving the incoherent and confusing statutory framework which often hinders access to mental health treatment and support. Recent plans to reform the MHA include a welcome emphasis on issues such as autonomy and rights, but it is hard to see any concrete improvements in navigating the complex system of laws designed to protect children and young persons, but so often failing to do so. A further small, but significant, reform related to the law, but not requiring legal reform as such, would be the roll-out of a student opt-in system to sharing wellbeing information with parents. If this were to become a standard approach across the higher education sector it would do much to improve current confusion over the significance of confidentiality in relation to juvenile suicide risk. It would enable parents to provide support in the very cases where the young adults, outside of moments of crisis, would welcome such support.

A final important legal development would be clarification of the law in respect of children's choices to die. It was previously argued in chapter four that capacity to choose to die should always be a demanding standard, but for those under 18, the issues identified in this current chapter lend support for something even greater: the involvement of those with parental responsibility. While this blunt tool would need refinement in individual circumstances,[155] it would provide a practical means of ensuring that a child's choice to die is an informed and reflective one and that it is not merely a rash choice taken by an isolated child. A stringent test for capacity to choose to die for under-18-year-olds would have a number of advantages: it would encourage judges to consider whether a minor has capacity to make such a choice, and enable speedy intervention on welfare grounds when that is not the case; it would ensure the concept of autonomy still has meaning for minors in relation to life and death choices (especially perhaps in the context of long-term illnesses and refusal of medical treatment); it would enable end of life decisions to be handled in a different manner to other medical treatment choices for minors (in which a child's capacity to make the decision herself should be much easier to establish); and it would recognise that an unnecessary loss of a child's life does not only affect that child, but their family too. Getting the balance right between respecting autonomy and preventing suicide is always a challenge for the law even in respect of adults, but when it is the life of a child at stake, considerations of autonomy must be much more refined and young lives protected more transparently because a child making a truly autonomous and capacitated choice to die (outside of a healthcare context) will be very rare indeed.

[155] There are obvious issues of detail to be worked out in circumstances where minors lack parents or where the parents are abusive, pressuring, have ulterior motives or lack capacity themselves.

7

Suicide and Refusal of Treatment at the End of Life

As will be interrogated further in the following chapter, assisting suicide currently remains criminalised in absolute terms. For many people at the end of their lives, this presents an obstacle to exercising their autonomy about dying. However, suicide remains overtly present in end of life decision-making. An adult patient with capacity has the absolute legal right to refuse medical treatment, even if it is life-sustaining treatment and death will inevitably ensue from its withdrawal. Furthermore, voluntarily stopping eating and drinking (VSED) is also an option for patients who wish to bring their lives to an end,[1] and is likely to result in the provision of palliative care to ease the passing. This chapter will investigate the current law regulating these options of ending life, question whether they are appropriately labelled as suicide or not, and indeed question whether such a label continues to have utility in a legal system in which it is lawful. This chapter will then explore the legal implications for respecting a choice to die and question whether withdrawing life-sustaining treatment is 'assisting' a suicide and therefore a criminal offence, or whether legal duties might exist to prevent such a death.

I. Refusing Life-sustaining Medical Treatment and Suicide

It has long been established in English law that medical treatment requires the consent of a competent patient.[2] There have been surprisingly few cases

[1] Indeed, this appears to have been the option ultimately chosen by Tony Nicklinson following the failure of his claim for assistance in dying. It is likely that a form of assistance for this choice was nonetheless provided. See J Savulescu, 'A Simple Solution to the Puzzles of End of Life? Voluntary Palliated Starvation' (2014) 40 *Journal of Medical Ethics* 110, 111.

[2] *Re T (adult: refusal of treatment)* [1992] 4 All ER 649: 'An adult patient who, like Miss T, suffers from no mental incapacity has an absolute right to choose whether to consent to medical treatment, to refuse it or to choose one rather than another of the treatments being offered … This right of choice is not limited to decisions which others might regard as sensible. It exists notwithstanding that the reasons for making the choice are rational, irrational, unknown or even non-existent': per Lord Donaldson MR at 652–53. See also *Airedale NHS Trust v Bland* [1993] AC 789; *Re C (adult: refusal of medical treatment)* [1994] 1 All ER 819; and *St George's Healthcare NHS Trust v S; R v Collins, ex S* [1998] 3 All ER 673.

directly dealing with the consequences of this approach when consent is withdrawn in relation to life-sustaining treatment. However, the 2002 case of *Ms B v An NHS Hospital Trust*[3] is illuminating in demonstrating the consequences of the largely non-contentious right to refuse treatment. Ms B was paralysed from the neck down and was sustained on a ventilator. She requested that the ventilator be turned off. The only relevant legal issue in this situation was the question of whether she had decision-making capacity (or, in the terminology of the pre-Mental Capacity Act 2005 (MCA 2005) time, 'competence'). Although she had previously been regarded as lacking capacity due to depression, the judge pointed out that for eight months prior to the judgment, no psychiatrist had suggested that Ms B was not competent.[4] The judge attended Ms B's hospital to hear her evidence and concluded that her wishes were clear, well-expressed and well-informed.[5] In light of this, the judge had no hesitation in holding that she was 'entirely satisfied' that Ms B was competent to make all relevant decisions about her medical treatment including the decision whether to seek to withdraw from artificial ventilation, adding that her mental competence 'is commensurate with the gravity of the decision she may wish to make'.[6]

The lack of any real doubt about the patient's capacity to make decisions about her treatment highlights the mismatch between law and reality, given that Ms B's request for treatment to be withdrawn had not been respected by the hospital for some months before the court judgment. As Butler-Sloss LJ eloquently expressed it:

> The general law on mental capacity is, in my judgment, clear and easily to be understood by lawyers. Its application to individual cases in the context of a general practitioner's surgery, a hospital ward and especially in an intensive care unit is infinitely more difficult to achieve.[7]

This is largely because of a reluctance on the part of healthcare professionals to take steps to withdraw treatment knowing it will lead to an unnecessary death of the patient. While Butler-Sloss LJ explicitly confirmed in *Re B* that, in light of precedents, 'the right of the competent patient to request cessation of treatment must prevail over the natural desire of the medical and nursing profession to try to keep her alive',[8] this remains particularly challenging in the context of an intensive care unit. Indeed, the judge suggested that Ms B's request 'would have been understood in a palliative care situation' but 'appears to have been outside the experience of the ICU in relation to a mentally competent patient. It was seen by some as killing the patient or assisting the patient to die and ethically unacceptable'.[9] The hospital's

[3] *Ms B v An NHS Hospital Trust* [2002] EWHC 429 (Fam).
[4] ibid [89].
[5] ibid [53].
[6] ibid [95].
[7] ibid [14].
[8] ibid [27].
[9] ibid [97].

failure to respect Ms B's wishes, and to continue to treat her without consent for a period of months, and particularly the Trust's failure to take any steps to resolve the situation, leaving it to the patient to initiate legal proceedings, led the judge to award nominal damages against the Trust.[10]

The case of Ms B demonstrates both that the law is clear and well established that a patient with capacity has an absolute right to refuse life-sustaining treatment, and that taking steps to facilitate that refusal of consent can be ethically challenging for the healthcare professionals concerned. Part of the reason for the latter challenge is an easy perception that a patient seeking the withdrawal of life-sustaining treatment is choosing to die by means of suicide. The law has traditionally rejected such a conclusion, however. For example, Lord Goff in *Bland* stated that 'there is no question of the patient having committed suicide' in circumstances where a patient of sound mind requires that life support be discontinued.[11] But why is this? What feature(s) distinguish Ms B's desire to end her life from suicide attempts by others? There are two potential distinguishing features which will now be considered in turn relating respectively to causation and intention. If it is determined, however, that treatment refusals can properly be labelled suicide, this will lead onto an even more important question of why withdrawing treatment in such circumstances does not amount to the criminal offence of assisting suicide.

The first factor that may potentially distinguish treatment refusal from suicide is the issue of causation. English law has sought to classify the withdrawal of life-sustaining treatment as an omission, rather than an act. This has enabled doctors to evade criminal liability for withdrawal of treatment even if they know that death will ensue. Thus, in cases concerning patients who lack capacity, treatment can (and indeed must) be withdrawn when it is no longer in the patient's best interests, and those withdrawing it face no legal liability in relation to the death that follows. In cases concerning patients with capacity, the absence of informed consent for the treatment similarly requires its withdrawal (as we have seen in the *Re B* case) and there is no question of liability for the patient's death. In contrast, a patient's request to be assisted to die will not be lawfully permitted if it requires a positive act on the part of another person. This well-established legal position is, to put it lightly, convenient. As Huxtable has noted,

> the law has conceived of withdrawing treatment as 'passive' in nature, precisely because, it would seem, this will enable the legal evaluation to mirror the ethical evaluation, i.e. doctors should be free to withdraw unwanted treatments without fear of criminal or civil sanction.[12]

So, the labelling of withdrawal of life-sustaining treatment as an omission ensures that it is lawful, but does it also mean that the death that follows is not *caused*

[10] ibid [99].
[11] *Airedale NHS Trust v Bland* (n 2) at 866.
[12] R Huxtable, '*Re B (Consent to Treatment: Capacity)* A Right to Die or is it Right to Die?' (2002) 14 *Child and Family Law Quarterly* 341, 353.

by the withdrawal of treatment? Price has noted that there can be no doubt that treatment refusal is the factual cause of death and therefore the only debate must be around the question of whether it is the legal cause of death.[13] And this debate has divided commentators. For example, Miller, Truog and Brock have presented a comparison of two patients, one on a ventilator and one not, where a choice to die will be respected only for the former, purportedly because withdrawal does not cause death.[14]

A real-life example is provided by contrasting Ms B with Mrs Pretty.[15] These two women were both recognised to have decision-making capacity and both chose to die, and yet only the former was recognised as having the legal authority to require healthcare professionals to take the necessary steps to enable her death. The only pertinent distinction between the two cases – but an immense one for the law – is that only Ms B was maintained on a ventilator, a treatment for which her continued consent was legally required. The law's differentiation between these two situations does not truly seem to be based on characterising withdrawal of the ventilator as not causing death because, were such an action to be taken without consent, it would still be regarded as homicide.[16]

McGee has sought to counter the argument that withdrawal causes death[17] by suggesting that it is at least reasonable to regard withdrawal of life-sustaining treatment as allowing the patient to die from their underlying condition.[18] He queries why withdrawal should be viewed as 'the initiation of a new process, rather than as the resumption of a process that was stopped or suspended when the treatment was initially implemented?'.[19] The challenge to this argument is the rather obvious point that, unlike withholding treatment, acts are seemingly involved in the withdrawal of treatment. For example, someone has to disconnect or switch off a ventilator rather than simply doing nothing. How then can we view that as merely an omission rather than an intervening act that causes death?

One way of tackling this issue is to subtly change the action taken. For example, as Lord Browne-Wilkinson pointed out in the *Bland* case, a patient on artificial nutrition and hydration (ANH) could have treatment withdrawn either by means of withdrawal of the feeding tube or by simply refraining from providing any

[13] DPT Price, 'Assisted Suicide and Refusing Medical Treatment: Linguistics, Morals and Legal Contortions' (1997) 4 *Medical Law Review* 270. In this influential article, Price concludes that treatment refusal is both the factual and legal cause of death.

[14] F Miller, R Truog and D Brock, 'Moral Fictions and Medical Ethics' (2010) 24 *Bioethics* 453.

[15] *R (on the application of Pretty) v Director of Public Prosecutions* [2002] 1 All ER 1 (HL); *Pretty v United Kingdom* ECHR 2002-III (2002) 35 EHRR 1 (ECtHR).

[16] See A McGee, 'Does Withdrawing Life-Sustaining Treatment Cause Death Or Allow The Patient To Die?' (2014) 22 *Medical Law Review* 26, 32.

[17] Miller, Troug and Brock, for example, make such an argument, distinguishing withdrawal of treatment from withholding treatment, which they accept is an omission and does not cause death: 'Moral Fictions and Medical Ethics' (2010).

[18] McGee, 'Withdrawing Life-Sustaining Treatment?' (2014) 33.

[19] ibid 34.

further nutrition and hydration and leaving the tube in place.[20] In that latter scenario, the eventual withdrawal of the tube cannot be a cause of death.[21] A similar process of 'bagging' could be used to withdraw ventilation without a 'switching off' action causing death.[22] While these are absurd procedures to actually follow, that is entirely the point: as Lord Browne-Wilkinson noted in *Bland*, withdrawal should be classified as an omission precisely in order to avoid the need to draw such 'intolerably fine distinctions'.[23]

If we accept that withdrawal of treatment can be performed in a manner that ensures it is truly an omission, does it necessarily follow that it is not then the cause of death? McGee argues that both the provision and the cessation of life-sustaining treatment only control the timing of death, rather than cause it.[24] This is because, without the initial provision of the treatment, the patient would no longer be alive and therefore the treatment has merely postponed a death which would have occurred at an earlier stage if the treatment had not commenced. McGee takes the view that withdrawal 'should therefore not be viewed in isolation, but should be seen in the context of the initial and ongoing provision of measures to defer death'.[25] Under this argument, for example, while Ms B died because she withdrew consent for ventilation, this was only because she would have died much sooner if the treatment had never been provided at all. Thus, according to McGee, 'the reason the law regards lawful withdrawal as non-causative is that it regards the withdrawal as balanced out by the initial and ongoing provision of life-extending measures'.[26] This approach would mean that withdrawal of life-sustaining treatment owing to a refusal of consent is not the cause of death and therefore is not properly labelled as suicide.

It is worth noting that this does not amount to a more sweeping generalisation that suicide cannot be caused by an omission. Other authors have sought to distinguish the refusal of life-sustaining treatment from other steps that may be taken by a patient who chooses to end her life, such as VSED.[27] Jox et al argue that while refusal of life-sustaining treatment does not amount to suicide, on the basis that is not a sufficient condition for dying, VSED is suicide even though it is an omission.[28] They argue that:

> The cessation of the physiological influx of nutrients and water in VSED parallels the cessation of the physiological influx of oxygen that occurs in hanging or drowning.

[20] *Airedale NHS Trust v Bland* (n 2) at 882.

[21] McGee (n 16) 37.

[22] See McGee (ibid) 37 and V Ravitsky, 'Timers on Ventilators' (2005) 330 *British Medical Journal* 415, who points out that Israel opted for making the provision of ventilation periodic by providing ventilators with built in timers.

[23] *Airedale NHS Trust v Bland* (n 2) at 882.

[24] McGee (n 16) 41.

[25] ibid 42.

[26] ibid 44.

[27] RJ Jox, I Black, GD Borasio and J Anneser, 'Voluntary Stopping of Eating and Drinking: Is Medical Support Ethically Justified?' (2017) 15 *BMC Medicine* 186.

[28] ibid 2.

> By contrast, when withdrawing artificial nutrition, hydration, or ventilation, it is not a physiological everyday behaviour that is stopped but a medical treatment that technically replaces a pathologically lost organ function.[29]

There is a clear parallel here with McGee's argument that the withdrawal of treatment cannot be the cause of death because it merely restores the situation to one prior to artificial treatment commencing. It leads to an absurdity, however, in distinguishing a refusal of ventilation from a refusal of nutrition. The key issue, surely, is the intention to end life, often implemented by the most practical means lawfully available. Thus, while Ms B sought the removal of ventilation because it was within her legal right to refuse consent to the bodily intrusion, others such as Tony Nicklinson had no such option and could only exercise an element of control over nutrition and hydration. They both, however, sought to ensure that their lives were brought to an end at a time of their choosing.

This brings us to the second consideration in any effort to distinguish refusal of life-sustaining treatment from suicide, namely that of intention. It is this feature which McGee and Miller rely upon to seek to distinguish VSED from refusal of treatment, arguing that VSED is a form of suicide because 'there is unquestionably an intention to bring about one's own death' and contrasting refusal of treatment in which death could be seen as a mere foreseen side effect and as allowing nature to run its course.[30] When a patient refuses food and drink, she cannot be viewed as allowing herself to die from a condition that would kill her without a life-prolonging measure.[31] Instead, the patient seeks to bring about her death sooner than it would naturally occur. Jox et all concur with this view and classify the intention in respect of VSED as one of hastening one's death, rather than allowing death to occur naturally.[32]

Is it not a fallacy, however, to view a refusal of life-sustaining treatment as anything but implementing an intention to die? Indeed, the law goes to great efforts to ensure that a patient refusing consent to life-sustaining treatment fully understands the fatal consequences of that decision and is able to weigh that consequence in the balance.[33] If there is any doubt about that, a patient is not regarded as having the mental capacity to make such a life-and-death decision. Any effort to distinguish intention to die from foreseeing death is also doomed to failure. The law accepts foresight of a virtual certainty as intention in the criminal context and even the doctrine of double effect, which sometimes offers a healthcare-focused loophole for intention to cause death, does not seem to be applicable in the context of suicide. As Price argues, double effect cannot apply in relation to treatment

[29] ibid.

[30] A McGee and FG Miller, 'Advice and Care for Patients who Die by Voluntarily Stopping Eating and Drinking is Not Assisted Suicide' (2017) 15 *BMC Medicine* 222.

[31] ibid.

[32] Jox et al, 'Voluntary Stopping of Eating and Drinking' (2017) 2.

[33] MCA 2005, s 3(1).

refusal because death is not an unintended side-effect to such a decision, but rather is the means of achieving the good effect sought.[34]

Given the lack of a clear legal definition for suicide – owing to the fact that it is no longer a meaningful legal term other than in relation to the actions of others assisting it – it is not surprising that arguments have been raised to seek to exclude healthcare decisions at the end of life from this label. This issue is exacerbated by the contemporary focus on suicide prevention, as well as by the criminalisation of assisting suicide. Throughout this book, we have seen that there is often a conflict between the goals of preserving life and respecting autonomous decisions to die which underlies legal responses to suicide. In the healthcare context, and especially in relation to seriously or terminally ill patients, it may be easier to accept prioritisation for autonomy, not least because choices to die in this context may appear more rational and understandable by others. But in order to ensure compatibility with a general focus on seeking to prevent all suicides and treating them as symptoms of mental illness, there are efforts to avoid the label of suicide for autonomous decisions to hasten death by means of treatment refusal by patients with decision-making capacity. However, this development excludes an important category of choices to die from the label of suicide and leaves the latter as a hollow term used only for a symptom to be treated. In other words, and as suggested in the introductory chapter, suicide becomes a label used only for actions with which we disagree and not for genuine exercises of bodily autonomy. It is argued here, therefore, that patients who make a choice to bring their lives to an end, whether by refusing consent to life-sustaining treatment, or by stopping eating and drinking, or by any other means, are choosing to die by suicide, as much as the person who takes an overdose or jumps from a building. And, in case one forgets, a choice to die by suicide is a perfectly lawful choice. The issue is complicated, of course, by the fact that providing any assistance or encouragement for such a choice remains a serious criminal offence. Indeed, it is in relation to this issue that the healthcare context becomes significant because, for a patient attached to a ventilator or provided with nursing care, a choice to end life inevitably involves other persons. If refusing consent to life-sustaining treatment is indistinguishable from suicide, as is argued here, then is respecting that choice and withdrawing the treatment 'assisting' the suicide and therefore a criminal offence?

II. Is Respecting a Choice to Die Assisting a Suicide?

As Price has noted, 'Jurisdictions throughout the world have almost invariably declined to view refusals by competent patients of medical treatment which could prolong life as (physician-assisted) suicide'.[35] The justification for this uniform

[34] Price, 'Assisted Suicide and Refusing Medical Treatment' (1997) 279.
[35] ibid 272–73.

approach is far from clear, however. We have seen in the previous section that ignoring a patient's refusal of consent for continued life-sustaining treatment is unlawful, but we also know from the Suicide Act 1961 that assisting or encouraging a suicide is a serious criminal offence. These dual legal obligations undoubtedly place healthcare professionals in a difficult and sensitive situation. Indeed, this was evident in the Ms B case, discussed above, in which the judge recognised that the treating clinicians were 'deeply distressed by the dilemma which had faced them', namely that they respected and liked her and considered her to be competent but could not 'bring themselves to contemplate that they should be part of bringing Ms B's life to an end'.[36] This discomfort at taking the steps needed to facilitate their patient's request led to the proposal of a one-way weaning process which, as the judge recognised 'appears to have been designed to help the treating clinicians and the other carers and not in any way designed to help Ms B' due to it being a process that would risk Ms B dying in discomfort and possibly in pain.[37]

The law's respect for the autonomous wishes of a patient is more complicated when it necessitates involvement by another party, such as facilitating a refusal of consent by withdrawing life-sustaining treatment. It is clear that the doctors in the above case regarded the withdrawal of treatment as them in practice assisting a suicide, but this does not appear to be the view of the current law. One possible reason why respecting a refusal of consent to continued treatment may not amount to assisting suicide is that it could be viewed in legal terms as an omission. English law certainly does take the view that withdrawal of treatment is an omission rather than act, regarding it as comparable to withholding treatment.[38] As was discussed in the previous section, however, this can appear to be a fallacy given that positive steps are typically taken in order to withdraw, rather than withhold, treatment. The law's labelling of withdrawal of treatment as an omission also raises the question of whether the offence of assisting a suicide can be performed by means of an omission rather than an act. The somewhat unhelpful legal answer is that an omission would only be culpable if there is a duty to act. While this means that there is no general legal duty to prevent suicide, and thus a member of the public would not be culpable for assisting a suicide merely because they failed to stop it, healthcare professionals do have a duty of care. At times this duty of care will extend to a duty to treat, but the duty to treat ends at the point that an adult patient with decision-making capacity refuses consent.

An alternative and more convincing reason for not regarding the withdrawal of treatment following a patient request as assisting suicide is that it is legally required in order to avoid committing a battery upon the patient. As Huxtable argues, when faced with the dilemma of a patient requesting the withdrawal of life-sustaining

[36] *Ms B v An NHS Hospital Trust* (n 3) [58].
[37] ibid [98].
[38] *Airedale NHS Trust v Bland* (n 2) at 867–68 (per Lord Goff) and 882 (per Lord Browne-Wilkinson).

treatment, 'the doctor's duty to save life is trumped by a higher duty: the duty to respect the patient's autonomous wishes'.[39] In this scenario, the doctor is not lawfully permitted to continue treatment because she lacks a lawful authorisation for it (having neither consent nor an MCA justification to rely upon). To continue to provide treatment is to commit a battery upon the patient for which the hospital will be liable to pay damages. Therefore there can logically be no legal liability upon the doctor for taking steps to facilitate the patient's choice and thereby 'assisting' in the death.[40] Whether this only applies to healthcare professionals will be considered below.

These conflicting legal duties highlight why some healthcare professionals may be reluctant to facilitate a withdrawal of treatment as a fear of liability may not be entirely unreasonable. However, if the line of argument in the previous paragraph is correct and a healthcare professional is not liable for the criminal offence of assisting a suicide merely by acting to facilitate a patient's request to withdraw life-sustaining treatment, it might be queried whether there are limits to the steps that can be taken to facilitate the patient's choice to die. As discussed above, one possible means of implementing a choice to die is by a patient voluntarily stopping eating and drinking. When this occurs, it is likely that healthcare professionals will provide such palliative care as is necessary to ease the patient's suffering, which might typically involve prescribing analgesic drugs. This cannot be defined as an omission but must be an act, but may be required under the duty of care, and indeed many writers do not view this as assisting a suicide. McGee and Miller (even though they regard VSED as suicide) argue that healthcare professionals are not assisting suicide when offering standard palliative care treatment for patients undergoing VSED and 'thereby making VSED more feasible and comfortable for the patient'.[41] This latter point highlights that such provision of assistance may be the very thing that enables the patient to choose this way of dying. An unpalliated death will be a much less desirable option.

Jox et al confront this issue when they argue that assisting a suicide requires that 'the assistance is instrumental for death to occur, meaning that, without the assistance, the suicide would not (or could not) occur'.[42] If the support is a necessary condition without which suicide would not occur, as for example if the patient would not proceed without the promise of palliative drugs, then in the view of Jox et al, this amounts to assisting a suicide. These writers suggest that this conclusion is confirmed by the fact that the assisting person must have an intention to induce death in such cases because she knows that without her support the patient would not proceed with the death.[43] However, they argue that if the palliative support is

[39] R Huxtable, *Euthanasia, Ethics and the Law: From Conflict to Compromise* (London, Routledge-Cavendish, 2007) 73.

[40] ibid.

[41] McGee and Miller, 'Advice and Care for Patients' (2017) 2.

[42] Jox et al (n 27) 3.

[43] ibid.

not instrumental to the suicide, because the patient would proceed with VSED anyway, then a doctor seeking merely to relieve the patient's suffering would not be assisting a suicide.[44] Such a fine distinction, however, relies upon an assumption that is not explicit in the English law on assisted suicide. The current criminal offence will be considered in more detail in the next chapter, but there is no clear legal requirement that the suicide would not proceed without the assistance in order for criminal liability to ensue. McGee and Miller also conclude that taking steps to make a patient comfortable as they die from VSED does not amount to assisting a suicide, but instead base this on their recognition that interfering with a competent patient's decision to undertake VSED is a battery and a crime and also that 'an essential goal of medicine is to relieve suffering and physicians do no wrong when offering standard medication to relieve the suffering ensued by patients exercising their own autonomous choice'.[45] This reasoning is more consistent with current law.

A more challenging question relates to the provision of advice offering VSED as an option to a patient who may not otherwise have knowledge of it. For example, if a patient requests physician-assisted suicide and a doctor responds that it would be unlawful but presents the option of VSED and the ways in which the patient can be made comfortable during the process, is that not encouraging suicide?[46] McGee and Miller answer in the negative on the basis that the doctor 'is advising the patient about exercising a legally protected right'.[47] This seems the correct interpretation in the specific example given, in which the patient has initiated the conversation by requesting assistance in dying.[48] However, if a doctor or other healthcare professional were to broach the topic and suggest VSED as an appropriate means of dying, arguably this could amount to encouragement. Furthermore, it has been argued in previous chapters (and will be further argued in the next chapter) that encouraging suicide is the more serious of the two elements of the current English offence – and one that should survive beyond any reform of the offence – because such an act seeks to influence an individual's decision-making process and is not permissible in a society which places a high value on the preservation of human life. On the other hand, assisting suicide, as it is argued elsewhere in this book, should be permissible when to do so facilitates an exercise of autonomy by a person with capacity to choose to die (as defined elsewhere).

[44] ibid.

[45] McGee and Miller (n 30) 2.

[46] ibid 3.

[47] ibid.

[48] The GMC's guidance on this confirms that doctors should provide 'objective advice about the lawful clinical options (such as sedation and other palliative care) which would be available if a patient were to reach a settled decision to end their own life': 'Patients Seeking Advice or Information about Assistance to Die' Ethical Guidance (last updated 18 June 2015) para 6(b)(ii), available at www.gmc-uk.org/ethical-guidance/ethical-guidance-for-doctors/when-a-patient-seeks-advice-or-information-about-assistance-to-die.

The South Australian case of *H Ltd v J and Anor*[49] is relevant to this current discussion because it involved the question of the legal responsibilities of the owners of a care home in relation to a resident who intended to end her life by ceasing to take any food, water and insulin. Specifically, the Supreme Court of South Australia was asked to consider whether it would be lawful for the care home to comply with the wishes of the resident not to provide or administer nutrition or insulin, nor to provide hydration other than for the purpose of oral hygiene and to palliate pain and discomfort. The court held that this would indeed be lawful and that there is no legal duty on providers of high-care residential services to provide sustenance to a resident who refuses it.[50] The court doubted that self-starvation was properly labelled as suicide,[51] but even if it was to be regarded as suicide, the court held that respecting the resident's wishes would not amount to the offence of assisting suicide:

> Respecting the right of personal autonomy recognised by the law cannot constitute that offence. Moreover, a person who is not under a duty to prevent the commission of an offence does not aid and abet it by failing to prevent it or by communicating that he or she will not act to prevent it, unless by so doing he or she, as a matter of fact, encourages the commission of the offence.[52]

This approach is consistent with that suggested above in relation to English law and gives appropriate weight to respect for autonomy in relation to choices about dying. Interestingly, the relevant South Australia statute, the Criminal Law Consolidation Act 1936, not only sets out the criminal offences of aiding, abetting and counselling a suicide[53] and (more seriously) procuring a suicide,[54] but also includes a lawful justification for the use of reasonable force in order to prevent suicide.[55] The court in *H Ltd* was clear, however, that this provision merely provides a defence against a charge for assault if a person uses reasonable force to sustain the life of another and it does not impose a duty on a person to provide sustenance in order to prevent a suicide.[56] As stated above, any such duty must surely give way to the well-established legal duty not to provide treatment against the wishes of a patient with capacity.

[49] *H Ltd v J and Anor* [2010] SASC 176.

[50] ibid [36].

[51] The reason for this conclusion was that 'the common law regarded as "self murder" only those suicides which were the consequence of acts or omissions which if directed to another would amount to murder. If that is the basis on which the common law proceeded it is doubtful that self starvation is suicide'; ibid [57].

[52] ibid [68].

[53] Criminal Law Consolidation Act 1935, s 13(5).

[54] ibid, s 13A(7): 'A person who, by fraud, duress or undue influence, procures the suicide of another or an attempt by another to commit suicide shall (whether or not he was a party to a suicide pact with the other person) be guilty of murder or attempted murder, as the case may require'.

[55] ibid, s 13(2): a person who finds another committing or about to commit an act which he believes on reasonable grounds would, if committed or completed, result in suicide is justified in using reasonable force to prevent the commission or completion of the act'.

[56] *H Ltd v J and Anor* (n 49) [67].

In seeking to determine whether there is legal responsibility for the involvement of healthcare professionals in respecting a choice to die, it is important to distinguish the question of responsibility for an outcome from the question of criminal culpability. Price has argued that 'facilitating a patient's decision to die is an assistance in every case'.[57] In other words, regardless of whether the doctor performs an act or omission, and whether she withdraws life-sustaining treatment, refrains from providing nutrition or hydration, or provides palliative drugs to ease the suffering of a patient who is choosing to die by VSED, she is facilitating the patient's choice to die. This does not mean, however, that she is culpable for assisting suicide because she was complying with a legal duty to respect the patient's wishes. Indeed, the best view in relation to this question of whether facilitating a request to cease life-saving measures amounts to assisted suicide is that it does indeed do so but, given that not doing so will also amount to a criminal offence against the person, it is permissible under a doctrine of necessity. English law does not favour the use of such a doctrine and it is only in very rare cases that courts have succumbed to it. In *Re A (Children) (Conjoined Twins: Surgical Separation)*,[58] the difficult choice of causing the death of one twin in order to save the life of the other was only viable due to a doctrine of necessity. The conflicting duties of healthcare professionals in relation to requests to withdraw life-sustaining treatment and thereby assist in a suicide are different in nature, but the necessity of assisting a suicide in order to refrain from a battery upon the person that infringes bodily autonomy may be a useful analytical tool to resolve the dilemma. Respect for the autonomous wishes and bodily integrity of an adult with decision-making capacity must take precedence over the law's general condemnation of assistance in another person's self-caused death.

There may be objections to this proposed solution, and it is certainly a topic on which more study is needed, but some resolution to the lack of clarity in the existing law on this point is urgently required. The current law leads to judges turning a blind eye to actions that would in other circumstances amount to a serious criminal offence – and indeed an offence in which the absolute nature of the prohibition has been explicitly justified in recent case law. It also presents a significant inconsistency – something that Price called 'analytical and jurisprudential distortion'[59] – in light of the refusal to permit indisputably active steps to assist suicide for patients without the option of refusing consent to ongoing treatment. This is an old problem, but nonetheless an important one. For this reason, as well as others, the criminal offence of assisted suicide is unsustainable in its current form, as will be argued in the following chapter. In terms of refusal of life-sustaining treatment, however, a more pertinent issue would be to consider the legal duties that might exist to prevent such a death. So it is to this issue we will now turn by means of considering the requisite capacity test required and the value of bodily integrity.

[57] Price (n 13) 297.
[58] *Re A (Children) (Conjoined Twins: Surgical Separation)* (2000) 4 All ER 961.
[59] Price (n 13) 297.

III. Is there a Duty to Prevent Suicide at the End of Life?

A decision to refuse consent to continued life-sustaining treatment presents particular problems due to the importance of the principle of bodily integrity. Herring and Wall have helpfully distinguished this concept from that of bodily autonomy.[60] They explain the relevance of that distinction in our present context:

> [G]iving a patient treatment they do not want is interfering with not only their autonomy but also their right to bodily integrity, while refusing treatment to a patient who wishes it is interfering in their autonomy alone. The right to bodily integrity is seen as enhancing and giving a special strength to an autonomy claim, making it particularly hard to justify an interference.[61]

Bodily integrity, defined by Herring and Wall as 'the right not to have your body touched or your body interfered with without your consent',[62] has exclusivity as its key as it entails the power to exclude all others from one's body.[63] Recognising the important distinction between bodily autonomy and bodily integrity means that it becomes much harder to justify a failure to respect a request to withdraw life-sustaining treatment than to justify a failure to respect an autonomous wish to die more generally. Whether or not we classify such a request as suicidal, the obligation to respect it is paramount. For healthcare professionals, this will invariably mean facilitating it, as they have been responsible for the (previously lawful) imposition of the treatment. Ultimately, regardless of whether there is a right to suicide, there is certainly a right to bodily integrity, enforced by the law and requiring respect for choices to die involving the removal of medical interventions.

It is this right to bodily integrity, rather than any belief in a right to suicide, that makes the Elizabeth Bouvia case so emotive. In this American case from the early 1980s, a judge ordered the force-feeding of a woman with cerebral palsy who was refusing to eat and expressed a wish to die, even while acknowledging she was competent.[64] The judge did so on the grounds that her right to refuse treatment was

[60] J Herring and J Wall, 'The Nature and Significance of the Right to Bodily Integrity' (2017) 76 *Cambridge Law Journal* 566.

[61] ibid 568.

[62] ibid.

[63] ibid 560. For Herring and Wall, the right to bodily integrity is a stronger one than the right to bodily autonomy. They explain this as follows: 'To touch, constrain, or intrude upon the body of another person (in the absence of consent) is to ignore, or deprioritise, that person's subjective experience of the world – experiences that are located in the body – in favour of some competing value. To justify such an infringement requires the competing value to have considerable moral weight and practicable urgency. In comparison, we limit the autonomous choices that people make, and justify such limits with reference to competing values, on a much more routine basis': 583.

[64] *Bouvia v Riverside* (No 159780 (Sup Ct, Riverside Co, Cal, Dec 16, 1983), Tr 1238-12).

outweighed by four important state interests: preserving the life of a non-terminal patient; protecting the 'established ethics of the medical profession'; preventing the 'devastating effect' that her choice to die would have on other patients and 'other handicapped people'; and preventing suicide.[65] Annas discusses the judge's controversial view that the 'established ethics of the medical profession clearly outweigh and overcome her own rights of self-determination' and queries 'how long is it reasonable to force-feed a competent adult with a naso-gastric tube in the hope that the person will decide to eat voluntarily?'.[66] This question highlights the extreme violation of bodily integrity authorised by a court in this case. Thankfully, Ms Bouvia eventually won her case when in 1986 the California Court of Appeal held that all competent patients, whether terminally ill or not, have the right to refuse any and all medical treatment regardless of their motives for doing so.[67] As we have seen, this is the well-established law in England as well. The *Bouvia* case reminds us in stark terms of the justification for this law, based not just on bodily autonomy (or respecting autonomous choices to die) but on bodily integrity and respecting the right to be free from non-consensual bodily incursions.

Neither of these important principles, however, negate the need to ensure a choice to refuse consent is a capacitated one. Indeed, Annas notes that there was a middle ground ignored in the *Bouvia* litigation between simply permitting all suicidal actions and undertaking long-term intrusive battery upon the person, such as ensuring there have been reasonable steps taken 'to assess her competence and dissuade her from self-destruction'.[68] He notes that 'we do not condemn individuals who thwart suicide attempts by dragging people off ledges, preventing them from jumping off bridges, or rescuing them from drowning' and suggests that it would be similarly reasonable for health professionals at a psychiatric unit to try to prevent a suicide of a young woman who is refusing to eat.[69] It is certainly true that the law permits the taking of steps to prevent suicide and these permissible steps are not only physically restraining individuals on a temporary basis but also compulsorily detaining a person on a long-term basis under mental health legislation due to a risk of suicide attempts. However, all such preventative steps are ostensibly justified on the basis of the mental state of the person at risk of suicide.

As we saw in chapter four, mental health detention depends upon the identification of a mental disorder in addition to a risk to life, and the law's tolerance of physical restraint to prevent suicide seems likely to be based on an assumption of a lack of capacity, although that has regrettably not been made explicit. If the concept of capacity to choose to die (as argued in this book) is to be adopted, or

[65] ibid. See M Matthews, 'Suicidal Competence and the Patient's Right to Refuse Lifesaving Treatment' (1987) 75 *California Law Review* 707.

[66] G. Annas, 'When Suicide Prevention Becomes Brutality: The Case of Elizabeth Bouvia' (1984) *Hastings Center Report* 20, 46.

[67] *Bouvia v Riverside* (179 Cal.App.3d 1127, 225 Cal.Rptr. 297 (1986)).

[68] Annas, 'When Suicide Prevention Becomes Brutality' (1984) 21.

[69] ibid.

even if the usual MCA 2005 test for capacity is to be taken seriously on issues of welfare, a temporary restraint in order to ensure the choice to die is an autonomous one made by a person with decision-making capacity rather than a symptom of a mental illness, would be justifiable. Does the same not apply to a person choosing to die by means of refusing life-sustaining treatment or food and drink? Although a basic level of capacity (namely that required under the MCA) will be assured within the healthcare context, is a more stringent test required?

In *Ms B*, discussed above, one of the consultant surgeons giving evidence seemed inclined to impose a higher level of competence upon Ms B than is normally required by the law. The judge explained that this surgeon took the view that, although Ms B had mental competence, 'she was unable to give informed consent, not because of a lack of capacity in general but her specific lack of knowledge and experience of exposure to a spinal rehabilitation unit and thereafter to readjustment to life in the community'.[70] Such experience would take two years to achieve and the judge concluded that such a requirement would be unrealistic. She expressed her 'gravest doubts as to its legal validity and indeed its practicality' and pointed out that even in issues of 'the utmost significance and gravity people, including patients, have to make decisions without experience of the consequences'.[71] Members of the judiciary have previously suggested, however, that the level of capacity required for a choice to die by means of refusing consent to treatment may be higher than in respect of other choices. In *Re T*, Lord Donaldson said that what matters is whether the patient has 'a capacity which was commensurate with the gravity of the decision which he purported to make. The more serious the decision, the greater the capacity required'.[72] Although English law has changed since this case, with the shift to a statutory test for mental capacity in the MCA, the focus on a specific decision context remains. The idea of a specific capacity to choose to die test, as argued in this book, is not inconsistent with such an approach and indeed would work well within a healthcare context in relation to refusals of consent to treatment when a full assessment of the person's capacity can be taken without the urgency of other types of suicide attempt.

Writing in the US context (and some three decades ago), Matthews has proposed her own test for suicidal competence that would require the patient's refusal to be 'a reflective, settled decision, consistent with the patient's general way of life or religious or philosophical convictions' which she contrasts with 'a hasty decision made in reaction to a sudden personal catastrophe, temporary severe depression, or a mental impairment due to pain, disease, or the side effects of medication'.[73] This requirement has some similarities with the capacity test suggested in chapter four of this book. Matthews' test for suicidal competence goes further, however,

[70] *Ms B v An NHS Hospital Trust* (n 3) [63].
[71] ibid.
[72] *Re T (adult: refusal of treatment)* (n 2) [113].
[73] Matthews, 'Suicidal Competence' (1987) 754.

and would also require assessment of whether 'the patient's probable future life will be so diminished in quality that a reasonable person could conclude that it is not worth living'.[74] This requirement for an objective assessment of quality of life is not something proposed here given the inherently subjective nature of perceptions of a worthwhile life, as well as the value of both autonomous decision-making and respect for bodily integrity. Crucially, however, Matthews only supports a temporary restriction on a patient's right to refuse life-sustaining interventions,[75] and recognises that what she calls 'the state's legitimate interest in preventing rash, incompetent suicides' must be balanced against the patient's right to refuse treatment.[76] While Matthews' proposal to take into account a reasonable person's view of whether the patient's life is worth living goes too far in terms of legal interventions into the exercise of a right to bodily integrity, there is no doubt that it accords with instinctive, underlying reactions to choices to die made in the healthcare context or at the end of life. The (presumably lawful) interventions to prevent suicide attempts in other contexts seem to be based on an assumption of a lack of capacity, while an expressed wish to end life within a healthcare context, especially if by means of a request to cease life-sustaining treatment for a person with serious or terminal illness, may not be accompanied by such an assumption. The existence of objectively reasonable grounds for a choice to die may therefore be the very reason why we do not assume a lack of capacity when a person rejects continued life in this context in contrast to a suicide attempt by a young, healthy person. This is not to suggest that such an approach is desirable or should be enacted into law, but rather that the context in which a choice to die is made will in practice influence assumptions surrounding decision-making capacity.

So far in this section we have considered the duties on healthcare professionals to respect bodily integrity of patients who have made a choice to die and have the requisite capacity to do so, but it is also important to consider the legal obligations of other persons beyond the healthcare context. Huxtable highlights the case of a man who was convicted of assisted suicide for turning away a district nurse conducting a routine visit to his son-in-law, who was suffering from multiple sclerosis (MS), at a time when he knew that his daughter was administering to him an overdose of drugs at his son-in-law's request.[77] It is hard to see how this is consistent with the law's tolerance of healthcare professionals facilitating requests to die. Furthermore, even if this man's actions could be regarded as 'keeping watch' and thereby assisting the suicide, a further case highlighted by Huxtable seems to stand

[74] ibid.

[75] ibid 756. She argues, not unreasonably, that 'a delay to ensure that the patient's decision is settled and not reversible by others' efforts to help can be seen, even by a patient determined to die, as an expression of care and concern, not insensitivity to her viewpoint and desires'.

[76] ibid 758. To achieve this balance, she calls on courts to 'temporarily restrain patients whose refusals appear suicidal to ascertain whether they are clearly and calmly determined to die'.

[77] Huxtable, *Euthanasia, Ethics and the Law* (2007) 69.

in even starker contrast to the position of healthcare professionals. The parents of a 23-year-old woman found their daughter, who suffered from MS, unconscious after taking an overdose of drugs and, rather than calling for assistance, they sat with her for eight hours as she died.[78] They were convicted of complicity in suicide,[79] and yet as Huxtable points out, merely being present at the suicide attempt should not be enough to imply complicity.[80] Generally, the law does not impose an obligation to take positive steps to prevent a suicide, except where there is a corresponding duty to act (as for example in the prison context discussed in chapter five). It is not clear that the woman in this case was owed a duty of care by her parents, given that she was an adult and had the physical ability to take the overdose unaided. However, it may be relevant that she had a history of mental illness and of previous suicide attempts. Even so, this could only *justify* interventions to prevent suicide, rather than *compel* them.[81] The imposition of legal liability for failing to take steps to save her life remains hard to reconcile with the law's approach in healthcare cases such as *Re B*.

As Huxtable expresses it, 'when an individual refuses treatment in order to die, the doctor is neither lawfully permitted to intervene nor liable for failing to prevent the patient's death', but the parents in the case he cites 'appear instead to be duty-bound to call in the doctors or else risk prosecution'.[82] What are the potential justifications for this distinction? Huxtable queries if only agents of the state have the power to 'legitimise' a suicide attempt,[83] but it should not be necessary for a lawful action such as suicide to require such state approval, especially in the context of the invasion of bodily integrity that would be required in order to save the life of a person who has taken an overdose. Other potentially relevant distinctions might relate to the suicide method (overdose of pills rather than withdrawal of treatment), or the expertise of healthcare professionals to assess mental capacity and thus bypass the common assumption of a lack of capacity for those choosing to die. Certainly, doctors are the gatekeepers of capacity, but does this mean that all suicide attempts justify an assumption of incapacity? And furthermore, that all citizens are obligated to seek to prevent a suicide in order to ensure that this starting assumption can be overturned? Arguably this goes too far in seeking to preserve life even in circumstances where a rational and autonomous choice to die has been made.

What is certain is that the law is currently incoherent on these issues. On the one hand, it imposes legal liability on a hospital that declines to withdraw

[78] ibid 70.

[79] ibid.

[80] ibid.

[81] In *R (Jenkins) v HM Coroner for Portsmouth* [2009] EWHC 3229 [49], the court confirmed that the partner of a man who had refused medical treatment for a gangrenous foot was not under a duty to call for medical assistance if that man retained capacity and was able to express his own wishes in rejecting treatment.

[82] Huxtable (n 39) 73.

[83] ibid 74.

life-sustaining treatment at a patient's request; and on the other hand it imposes legal liability on family members who decline to seek to intervene in a suicide attempt. The case discussed in the previous paragraph is a rarity and too much weight should not be placed upon it,[84] but nonetheless it is not sustainable for the law to send such a mixed message on the proper response to choices to die. This is particularly so when we consider the law's strict prohibition of positive acts to assist a suicide which draws a dubious line between those able to end their own lives or decline life-sustaining treatment and those not in a position to choose either as a means of dying. If this discussion of suicide in the healthcare context has proven anything it must be that sometimes a choice to die is worthy of respect – and indeed of steps to facilitate that choice. If that is the case, then the law really ought to be more explicit on the distinction between choices to die worthy of respect, and choices to die requiring intervention. This seems to be a minimum expectation of the law on suicide and it needs to be settled before it is possible to coherently respond to calls to legalise assisted suicide in certain circumstances.

IV. Conclusion

This chapter has explored the relevance of the law on suicide to end of life decision-making. While the criminal prohibition of assisted dying is usually the main focus of such a discussion (and indeed will be considered in the next chapter), it has been highlighted in this chapter that suicide, and therefore the law regulating it, is an ever-present feature of healthcare choices towards the end of life. It has been argued that a refusal of life-sustaining medical treatment by an adult with capacity is indistinguishable from other forms of suicide. If the usual requirements of capacity and an informed choice are present, then the refusal of treatment can only accurately be regarded as a choice to die. The law's reluctance to label this as suicide reveals more about the shortcomings of that label then about the decision to bring life to an end. Whether the label of suicide has any remaining value in a society in which it is a lawful action is an issue that will be further explored in the next two chapters. The present chapter, however, has argued that facilitating a refusal of life-sustaining medical treatment has the potential to fall within the criminal offence of assisting suicide, because the resulting death is indistinguishable from other voluntary deaths, but any such liability is superseded by the legal duty to respect bodily integrity. The fact that the current law appears to impose

[84] Arguably Huxtable does place too much weight upon this single case when concluding that 'the relative has no right to conclude that they must honour their loved one's wish to die, even if this seems to have been an autonomous decision': ibid 76.

two absolute and yet conflicting requirements upon healthcare professionals when a refusal of life-sustaining treatment occurs is a sad reflection on the law's engagement with the issue of suicide in which mixed messages and ambiguous rights and duties abound. The next chapter will highlight perhaps the most common of these: the existence of a criminal offence in assisting or encouraging a lawful action. For many patients at the end of life, the option of requesting withdrawal of life-sustaining treatment is not available and therefore bodily autonomy, rather than bodily integrity, is the value to be balanced against duties to save life.

8

Assisting and/or Encouraging Suicide

This chapter shifts the focus away from the law's engagement with suicide itself and onto its controversial prohibition of assisting or encouraging suicide. The existing debate about potential legalisation of assisted dying benefits from a broader reflection upon the law's regulation of suicide itself. While the law sends mixed messages about whether all suicides should be prevented, and whether there are ever legal duties to do so, it is impossible for the law to frame coherent prohibitions on secondary involvement in suicides. After a number of chapters in which we have explored the law's messages in relation to suicide in different contexts, and drawn conclusions about necessary reforms, this chapter finally turns the focus to the enduring criminal offence, first created in 1961 simultaneously with the decriminalisation of suicide.

In the first section, the current offence will be analysed, with a particular focus (mirroring the judicial focus of recent years) on assisted dying cases. Having identified some significant problems with the current offence, the remaining two sections will focus respectively on encouraging suicide, and assisting suicide, arguing for a strengthening and clarification of the former, alongside a limited legal exception to the latter. The overriding concern throughout is to ensure that those with the capacity to choose to die (as defined previously) have their lawful exercise of autonomy respected by the law, while those unable or choosing not to make such a capacitated choice have their lives protected by an appropriate imposition of criminal liability for those who seek to endanger those lives.

I. The Current Offence of Assisting Suicide

It is hard to ignore the global trend of legalising assisted suicide, albeit in limited circumstances. Luzon describes a 'revolution' in terms of legalisation in the last two decades[1] with moves towards exempting physician-assisted suicide from criminal prohibition in the Netherlands[2] and Belgium[3] in 2002, Luxembourg

[1] G Luzon, 'The Practice of Euthanasia and Assisted Suicide Meets the Concept of Legalization' (2019) 13 *Criminal Law and Philosophy* 329, 330–31.

[2] Termination of Life on Request and Assisted Suicide (Review Procedures) Act 2001 (Netherlands).

[3] Euthanasia Act 2002 (Belgium).

in 2009,[4] Canada in 2016[5] and the Australian state of Victoria in 2017,[6] joined by Western Australia in 2019[7] and Tasmania in 2021.[8] In the United States, a similar trend has seen legalisation in Oregon in 1997, Washington in 2008, Vermont in 2013, California in 2015, Colorado in 2016, Washington DC in 2017[9] and more recently New Jersey[10] and Maine[11] in 2019 and New Mexico in 2021.[12] At the time of writing, New Zealand,[13] Austria[14] and Spain[15] have recently joined the growing list of countries with legalised assisted suicide.[16] Switzerland has arguably gone further than these other jurisdictions in only criminalising assisted suicide in circumstances where there is a 'selfish motive' regardless of whether a physician is involved.[17] This trend towards legalisation is remarkable given that is coincides with increased global recognition of the public health emergency posed by suicide itself. As noted previously, the World Health Organization (WHO) recognises suicide prevention as a public health priority and asserts that all suicides are preventable.[18] And yet courts and legislatures in many countries around the world have been taking steps towards legalising the provision of assistance in suicide. This might suggest either that criminalising assistance is not an effective means of preventing suicides and/or that not all suicides do need to be prevented, at least by means of legal intervention. A core argument of this book has been that self-imposed deaths are of varying types and that while preventative steps may be appropriate (and indeed necessary) for many, respect for autonomy may require tolerance, respect and even, perhaps, facilitation for others.

The legal position within England and Wales has steadfastly refused to join the trend of legalisation. As seen in chapter two, a criminal offence of aiding,

[4] Law on Euthanasia and Assisted Suicide 2009 (Luxembourg).

[5] Bill C-14, An Act to amend the Criminal Code and to make related amendments to other Acts (Medical Assistance in Dying) 2016 (Canada).

[6] Voluntary Assisted Dying Act 2017 (Victoria), available at www.legislation.vic.gov.au/in-force/acts/voluntary-assisted-dying-act-2017/003.

[7] Voluntary Assisted Dying Act 2019 (Western Australia), available at www.legislation.wa.gov.au/legislation/statutes.nsf/law_a147242.html.

[8] End-of-Life Choices (Voluntary Assisted Dying) Act 2021 (Tasmania), available at www.legislation.tas.gov.au/view/html/asmade/act-2021-001.

[9] See Luzon, 'The Practice of Euthanasia and Assisted Suicide' (2019) 330–31.

[10] Medical Aid in Dying for the Terminally Ill Act 2019 (New Jersey), available at www.nj.gov/health/advancedirective/maid.

[11] Death with Dignity Act 2019 (Maine).

[12] Elizabeth Whitefield End-of-Life Options Act 2021 (New Mexico).

[13] End of Life Choice Act 2019 (New Zealand, 2019 No 67), available at www.legislation.govt.nz/act/public/2019/0067/latest/DLM7285905.html.

[14] 'New Law Allowing Assisted Suicide Takes Effect in Austria' BBC News, 1 January 2022, available at www.bbc.co.uk/news/world-europe-59847371.)

[15] Organic Law 3/2021, March 24, Regulating Euthanasia, Spain, available at www.boe.es/eli/es/lo/2021/03/24/3.

[16] I am grateful to my colleague Dr Nataly Papadopoulou for keeping me up to date on these and other developments of relevance to this chapter.

[17] Swiss Criminal Code 1937, Art 115.

[18] World Health Organization, 'Preventing Suicide: A Global Imperative' (Geneva, WHO, 2014).

abetting, counselling or procuring the suicide of another, or attempt by another to commit suicide, was created within the very statute that decriminalised suicide itself. The wording of the offence was modernised in 2009 so that it is now an offence to do an act which is capable of encouraging or assisting another person to commit or attempt to commit suicide, where such act is intended to so encourage or assist. The new wording makes even more transparent the prohibition of two very different actions in relation to suicide: that of assisting a suicide, and that of encouraging one. As has been suggested in earlier chapters, this is a crucial but often overlooked distinction and one that will be at the heart of this chapter's argument.

In the remainder of this section, we will explore the challenge to the prohibition of assisting a suicide presented by the 'assisted dying' debate. This term is used here to refer to the situation where a person is suffering from a long-term or terminal illness, has made an autonomous choice to die, and is unable to take the necessary steps to bring their life to an end without assistance. The current offence of assisted suicide prevents the realisation of this autonomous choice to die and has therefore been challenged in the courts in a number of high-profile cases over the last two decades.

A. The Assisted 'Dying' Challenge

The Suicide Act 1961, section 2 offence of assisted suicide is, and has been since 1961, an absolute prohibition. The 1961 Parliament did not anticipate arguments about a right to assistance in committing suicide and subsequent parliaments have steadfastly refused to risk deviating from the absolute nature of the protection for human life even in light of such arguments. It was the case of Dianne Pretty that first brought the issue to public attention and asked the courts to consider whether the section 2 offence was compatible with the obligations imposed by the Human Rights Act 1998 (HRA 1998). Both the House of Lords and the European Court of Human Rights confirmed that the existing law was compatible.[19] While the majority of the House of Lords had doubted whether Article 8's right to respect for private life was even engaged in relation to decisions about dying, the Strasbourg Court confirmed that the absolute prohibition on assisted suicide was an interference with Mrs Pretty's right to make autonomous choices about how and when to die, but nonetheless such interference was justified under Article 8(2) because it was necessary in a democratic society in order to protect the rights of other vulnerable members of society.

Various attempts within Parliament to revise the law so as to permit a limited exception in circumstances such as Mrs Pretty's followed, but all proved

[19] *R (on the application of Pretty) v Director of Public Prosecutions* [2002] 1 All ER 1 (HL); *Pretty v United Kingdom* ECHR 2002-III (2002) 35 EHRR 1 (ECtHR).

to be unsuccessful. Lord Joffe's efforts in the Patient (Assisted Dying) Bill 2003 and the Assisted Dying for the Terminally Ill Bill 2004 both failed to find the time or support to become law and, as we saw in chapter three, Lord Falconer's proposed amendment to the Coroners and Justice Bill in 2009 was defeated in the Lords. Lord Falconer continued to pursue the issue, chairing a privately funded Commission on Assisted Dying which reported in 2012[20] and introducing the Assisted Dying Bill in 2013, 2014 and 2015, which will be discussed further below. Perhaps the most significant development, however, was the emergence of Dignitas clinics in Switzerland, which were increasingly utilised by British citizens in order to obtain assistance in ending their lives. Of course, this meant travelling abroad and, as many of the persons choosing to take this option were already seriously ill, the assistance of relatives was often essential in order to facilitate the necessary travel. However, such actions were rarely the subject of prosecution, leading Debbie Purdy to apply to the courts for information as to whether her husband would be prosecuted if he were to assist her to travel to Switzerland for the purpose of gaining assistance in ending her life.[21] While the *Pretty* case had focused on whether the absolute prohibition on assisted suicide was necessary and proportionate in order to protect other members of society, the case of Debbie Purdy focused instead on whether the absolute prohibition was in accordance with the law. Under Strasbourg jurisprudence, this requires that it be clear and accessible and reasonably foreseeable.[22] The problem for the House of Lords in deciding this case was that while the Suicide Act 1961 sets out an offence of assisting a suicide, many of those apparently doing so had not been prosecuted, suggesting that in practice there may be a tolerance of this behaviour.

The Director of Public Prosecution's (DPP) permission is required before bringing a prosecution under the section 2 offence (and many others).[23] The position of DPP was first created in the Prosecution of Offences Act 1879 and the post-holder became the head of the Crown Prosecution Service (CPS) upon its creation in 1985.[24] For centuries, however, there has been an 'expediency' principle within the criminal justice system, meaning that not every offence needs to be

[20] The Commission on Assisted Dying, 'The Current Legal Status of Assisted Dying is Inadequate and Incoherent' (London, Demos, 2011), available at www.demos.co.uk/files/476_CoAD_FinalReport_158x240_I_web_single-NEW_.pdf.

[21] *R (on the application of Purdy) v Director of Public Prosecutions* [2009] UKHL 45.

[22] *Sunday Times v United Kingdom* Series A no 30 (1979–80) 2 EHRR 245 [49]. When defining the expression 'prescribed by law' in Art 10(2), the Strasbourg Court said the following: 'Firstly, the law must be adequately accessible: the citizen must be able to have an indication that is adequate in the circumstances of the legal rules applicable to a given case. Secondly, a norm cannot be regarded as a "law" unless it is formulated with sufficient precision to enable the citizen to regulate his conduct: he must be able – if need be with appropriate advice – to foresee, to a degree that is reasonable in the circumstances, the consequences which a given action may entail.'

[23] R Daw and A Solomon, 'Assisted Suicide and Identifying the Public Interest in the Decision to Prosecute' [2010] *Criminal Law Review* 737.

[24] Prosecution of Offences Act 1985.

prosecuted, even if there is sufficient evidence to do so.[25] This was explained by the Attorney-General, Sir Hartley Shawcross, in the House of Commons in 1951 when he said that the Attorney-General and DPP 'only intervene to direct a prosecution when they consider it in the public interest so to do',[26] further clarifying that a decision not to prosecute may be due to mitigating circumstances or wider considerations of 'public policy or national, or sometimes international, concern'.[27] Assisted suicide is, therefore, not unique in involving the public interest in decisions to prosecute. The Prosecution of Offences Act 1985 required the DPP to create a Code for Crown Prosecutors which set out the principles for prosecutors to follow when making decisions. The so-called Full Code Test includes public interest factors both in favour of and against prosecution.

Generally, this guidance is thought to be sufficient but, in *Purdy*, the House of Lords found that it did not provide sufficient guidance in respect of the offence of assisted suicide, because the factors normally taken into account when determining this issue of public interest seem to have little application to this unusual offence. Lord Neuberger stated:

> The very unusual features of this crime are that it involves the offender assisting an action by a third party which is not itself a crime, the third party who is being assisted is also the victim, the victim will almost always be willing, indeed will very often be the positive instigator of the crime, and the offender will often be a relatively reluctant participator, and will often be motivated solely by love and/or sympathy. In addition, the potential offender is not the person, or at least is not the only person, whose Convention rights are engaged: it is the victim whose article 8 rights are engaged, and he or she will almost always be unusually vulnerable and sensitive.[28]

The House of Lords accepted that the Code of Practice formed part of the 'law' in accordance with which an interference with the right to respect for private life may be held to be justified, but it concluded that the Code did not provide the required accessibility and foreseeability in assessing how prosecutorial discretion is likely to be exercised in cases of assisted suicide. There was not sufficient guidance offered to persons such as Mrs Purdy about whether certain actions are likely to result in prosecution or not. Thus the Lords required the DPP to 'clarify what his position is as to the factors that he regards as relevant for and against prosecution in this very special and carefully defined class of case'.[29] It is striking that this wording suggests that it is only for *Purdy*-like cases that extra guidance is needed and so the House of Lords seemed to envisage only special guidance about prosecuting assisted suicide when the assistance is in the form of helping someone to

[25] Daw and Solomon, 'Assisted Suicide' [2010] 738. An explicit 'public interest' justification has existed since 1886.
[26] Hansard, HC (series 5) Vol 483, col 681–82 (29 January 1951).
[27] ibid 683.
[28] *R (on the application of Purdy) v Director of Public Prosecutions* (n 21) [102].
[29] ibid 54, per Lord Hope.

travel abroad in order to receive assistance in committing suicide. What resulted from this decision proved to be far broader, as we shall shortly see.

In a sense, the two cases of *Pretty* and *Purdy* present the complete picture in relation to the compatibility of the assisted suicide offence with Article 8's autonomy-based right. *Pretty* focused on whether the absolute nature of the offence is proportionate to the need to protect other members of society, while *Purdy* focused on whether the variable enforcement of that offence by means of prosecutorial discretion prevented the offence being 'in accordance with the law'. However, it could also be argued that the two cases are difficult to reconcile. In *Pretty*, in order to be satisfied that the interference with Article 8 was 'necessary in a democratic society', the Strasbourg Court regarded the flexibility in the law's enforcement as a positive element:

> It does not appear to be arbitrary to the Court for the law to reflect the importance of the right to life, by prohibiting assisted suicide while providing for a system of enforcement and adjudication which allows due regard to be given in each particular case to the public interest in bringing a prosecution, as well as to the fair and proper requirements of retribution and deterrence.[30]

If flexibility is indeed required in order to justify a blanket ban on assisted suicide, then it will prove difficult to ensure that such ban remains in accordance with the law. Baroness Hale addressed this argument in her judgment in *Purdy*, noting that if the justification for a blanket ban 'depends upon the flexibility of its operation, it cannot be "in accordance with the law" unless there is greater clarity about the factors which the DPP and his subordinates will take into account in making their decisions'.[31] Thus, Baroness Hale and the other Law Lords required the DPP to provide offence-specific guidance as to when prosecution for assisted suicide will be in the public interest. As Lord Brown explained, what was needed in terms of guidance from the DPP was

> a custom-built policy statement indicating the various factors for and against prosecution … factors designed to distinguish between those situations in which, however tempted to assist, the prospective aider and abettor should refrain from doing so, and those situations in which he or she may fairly hope to be, if not commended, at the very least forgiven, rather than condemned, for giving assistance.[32]

This reminds us of the extremely broad ambit of behaviour covered by the section 2 offence: sometimes assisted a suicide may be a serious criminal offence; at other times it may be on the brink of praiseworthy. These two extremes are challenging to adequately cover in one offence, and one set of guidance.

[30] *Pretty v United Kingdom* (ECtHR) (n 19) 76.

[31] *R (on the application of Purdy) v Director of Public Prosecutions* (n 21) 63. The argument is then accepted by Baroness Hale at [64].

[32] ibid [86].

B. Prosecutorial Tolerance of Assisting Suicide

Following *Purdy*, the DPP published an interim policy on prosecuting assisted suicide in September 2009 which was followed by a 12-week period of public consultation. There were 4,710 public responses during this period, which is the largest number of responses by the public ever received by the CPS.[33] The DPP at the time, Keir Starmer, later explained that there were two principles underpinning the interim guidelines:

> The first was that the criminal law should rarely, if ever, be used against those who compassionately assist loved ones to die at their request, so long as that person had reached a voluntary, clear, settled and informed decision to end their life. The second was that very strong safeguards are needed to protect those who might be pressurised in any number of subtle ways.[34]

One of the main themes in the responses was the public concern about victim-based public interest factors tending against prosecution, such as the clear, settled and informed intent of the victim to commit suicide. This is surprising as it suggests that many of those who responded did not regard autonomy as a relevant issue in relation to the prosecution of assisted suicide, and yet arguably in this human rights age it is crucial. The DPP remained of the view that such factors were important and they survived into the final policy.[35]

The final policy was published on 25 February 2010. It contains 16 factors which tend in favour of prosecution and six factors that tend against prosecution. It is emphasised that these lists of public interest factors are not exhaustive and that each case must be considered on its own facts and on its own merits.[36] The factors include those associated with both the victim and the offender. So, for example, any doubt about whether the decision to commit suicide is a voluntary, clear, settled and informed one made by an adult with capacity would tend towards prosecution, as would any evidence that the suspect was not wholly motivated by compassion, had pressurised the victim, or was acting in a professional capacity.

The factors tending against prosecution could be said to amount to an exception in practice for the prohibition of assisted suicide, because in circumstances where the victim has reached a voluntary, clear, settled and informed decision to commit suicide, the suspect was wholly motivated by compassion, sought to

[33] Daw and Solomon (n 23) 747. There was also at this time an early day motion in the House of Commons initiated by Ann Widdecombe which called for the withdrawal of the guidelines and garnered the support of 10% of all MPs (EDM 302, 1 December 2009).

[34] Hansard, HC (Series 6) Vol 599, col 672 (11 September 2015), speaking in the debate on the Assisted Dying Bill 2015.

[35] See Daw and Solomon (n 23) 748.

[36] 'Suicide: Policy for Prosecutors in Respect of Cases of Encouraging or Assisting Suicide' (February 2010, updated October 2014, para 47, available at www.cps.gov.uk/legal-guidance/suicide-policy-prosecutors-respect-cases-encouraging-or-assisting-suicide).

dissuade the victim from suicide, offered only minor and reluctant encouragement or assistance, and subsequently reported the victim's suicide to the police, prosecution is unlikely to follow.[37] Does this increase clarity as the House of Lords in *Purdy* requested, or does it undermine the clarity of the Suicide Act 1961? Catherine O'Sullivan has argued that the latter is true:

> The offence of assisted suicide is clear about what is prohibited and the precision of this text is compromised, not clarified, by the Policy grafted on to it. For this reason, the Purdy case did not provide clarity but, instead, created the very circumstances of uncertainty [that would later lead to further cases.][38]

It might be pointed out that such pragmatic adaptation of the strict requirements of the criminal law is not a new feature in relation to the topic of suicide. As we saw in chapter two, for centuries those involved with enforcing the law used whatever discretion or flexibility they retained to avoid implementing the strict letter of the law. The DPP guidelines are merely the latest effort to do so, this time explicitly required by the highest court in the land. This is not to say, however, that such side-stepping or palliating of the strict letter of the law is to be welcomed. It would be far better for the law to reflect the position in reality. This was true when coroner's juries were making efforts to avoid unjust punishment for the families of those who committed suicide in the eighteenth and nineteenth centuries and it is true today when prosecutors decline to enforce an offence which Parliament has recently confirmed should remain in absolute terms. When the actions of those involved in maintaining the criminal justice system are at such odds with the substance of the criminal law it is a clear sign that the law is outdated and needs to be changed.

There are a number of other criticisms that may be made of the prosecuting guidelines and the resulting tolerance of assisted suicide. Firstly, the focus on the motives of the offender sits uneasily with the usual *mens rea* requirements.[39] It is now hugely significant whether the person assisting a suicide does so out of 'compassion' and with 'reluctance'. While such considerations might generally have relevance in terms of sentencing, they would not be expected to go to the question of whether to prosecute. O'Sullivan describes this as 'the grafting of motive considerations on to the mens rea of the offence'[40] which, arguably, should be for Parliament, rather than the DPP, to do. Secondly, as suggested above, the policy goes much further than was envisaged by the House of Lords in *Purdy* because it

[37] ibid 45. Speaking in 2015, Keir Starmer, the former DPP, stated that once the guidelines were in force he 'personally oversaw about 80 cases, looking at the details in each of the files, and made decisions in 79 of those cases that no prosecution should be brought' (Hansard 11 September 2015 (n 34) col 673).

[38] C O'Sullivan, 'Mens Rea, Motive and Assisted Suicide: Does the DPP's Policy go Too Far?' (2015) 35 *Legal Studies* 96, 107.

[39] ibid 100.

[40] ibid.

is not restricted to situations where the assistance is in the form of helping someone to travel abroad to legally end their lives. Regardless of the circumstances of the assistance, if the conditions set out above apply, a prosecution is extremely unlikely. It might go too far to suggest that the offence of assisted suicide is now a dead letter, but it will very, very rarely be enforced.

This leads to the third criticism of the policy's approach which is that it does not include the types of safeguards that we might anticipate in any statutory or judicial exception to the offence. The interim policy had included a factor relating to the victim suffering from a terminal illness, severe and incurable physical disability or severe degenerative physical condition with no possibility of recovery, but this was removed from the final policy on the basis that some respondents queried whether it was discriminatory. This has led Penney Lewis to argue that 'Without any restriction based on the victim's condition or experience, the policy is more liberal in this respect than most assisted dying regimes'.[41] While, of course, the guidance for prosecutors is not intended to be a regulatory regime, it does suggest that a regulatory regime of assisted dying – a limited and tightly defined exception to the offence of assisted suicide – would be preferable, not only because it would be more transparent and compatible with the rule of law, but also because it would be likely to include just such safeguards to ensure that only those whose autonomy was infringed by the absolute offence could be granted assistance.[42] In short, the position of the law on assisted suicide post-2010 is extremely unsatisfactory and it came as no surprise that further judicial challenges soon followed.

C. The Ongoing Judicial Struggles with Assisted Dying

The current law on assisted suicide was again challenged before the Supreme Court in the *Nicklinson* litigation.[43] There were originally two claimants, both of whom had suffered strokes which left them only able to communicate through small movements of the head and eyes (in AM's case) and eyes (in Tony Nicklinson's case). Nicklinson argued that the Suicide Act 1961, section 2 was incompatible with his Article 8 rights, and he also sought a declaration that it would not be unlawful for a doctor to assist the termination of his life, on the basis of a defence of necessity. AM sought an order that the DPP should clarify his published policy so that those who might be willing to assist him to use the Dignitas Clinic in Switzerland to commit suicide (who were professionals rather

[41] P Lewis, 'Informal Legal Change on Assisted Suicide: the Policy for Prosecutors' (2011) 31 *Legal Studies* 119, 126.

[42] Indeed, it may well be that a focus on the victim's medical condition is less opportune than a focus on whether the person concerned could commit suicide without assistance, as will be discussed further later in this chapter.

[43] *R (Nicklinson) v Ministry of Justice; R (AM) v Director of Public Prosecutions* [2014] UKSC 38.

than loved ones) would know whether they would be more likely than not to face prosecution. After their defeat in the High Court, Tony Nicklinson ended his own life by refusing food and water, highlighting in his death, as he had during his life, the callousness of the law's restrictions on the choices available to him. The Court of Appeal permitted his widow to be added to the application, and an additional appellant, Paul Lamb,[44] was also added, in order to keep the argument concerning the common law defence of necessity 'in play' after Nicklinson's death. The Court of Appeal rejected the arguments based on necessity and Article 8, but a majority did uphold the complaint raised by AM ('Martin') that the DPP's policy failed to provide sufficient clarity with respect to cases where the 'helper' had no close or emotional connection with the victim, particularly in relation to healthcare professionals.

The Supreme Court then had the opportunity to consider the issue of assisted suicide for the first time. Before this court, the main argument focused on whether the absolute nature of the assisted suicide offence was a disproportionate interference with the Article 8 rights of the applicants who wished to die but were unable to take their own lives without assistance. Ultimately, the Supreme Court refused to issue a declaration of incompatibility under HRA 1998, section 4 by a 7:2 majority. However, the judgment is not as unambiguous as that summary might suggest. While only two judges (Baroness Hale and Lord Kerr) would have declared the assisted suicide offence to be incompatible with Article 8, three other judges also seemed to take the view that the offence was incompatible. However, these judges, including the President of the Court Lord Neuberger, felt that the time was not right for the issuing of a declaration of incompatibility because of the sensitive nature of the issue and the fact that Parliament was better placed to make decisions about such issues.

The Supreme Court *Nicklinson* judgment is the most sympathetic towards the legalisation of assisted dying ever seen in UK courts. Despite being in the minority, the fact that two of the highest judges in the land wanted to declare the offence of assisted suicide to be incompatible with human rights, just half a century after suicide itself was regarded as a serious criminal offence, demonstrates the rapid evolution of legal thinking on suicide. One of the dissenting judges, Lady Hale, noted that the main problem with the current law is its lack of any exception to cover the particular circumstances of cases such as the present ones. She queries whether it is 'reasonably necessary to prohibit *everyone* who might want to end their own lives in order to protect those whom we regard as *vulnerable* to undue pressure to do so?'[45] She perceived the universal ban on assisting suicide as forcing people such as Mr Nicklinson, Mr Lamb and Martin to stay alive 'not for the sake of protecting themselves, but for the sake of protecting other people'[46] and

[44] Mr Lamb had been paralysed following a road accident, which had left him immobile, save for limited movement in his right hand. He needed constant care and was in significant pain.

[45] *R (Nicklinson) v Ministry of Justice* (n 43) [312], per Lady Hale.

[46] ibid [313].

argues convincingly that it would be entirely possible for the legal system to devise a process for identifying those few people who should fall within a well-defined exception.

It is not just the dissenting judges that are critical of the current law, however. Even Lord Neuberger in the majority explicitly recognised the inherent flaws in the current approach, describing the interference with the applicants' Article 8 rights as 'grave' and the arguments in favour of the current law as 'by no means overwhelming', noting that 'the present official attitude to assisted suicide seems in practice to come close to tolerating it in certain situations'.[47] In particular, Lord Neuberger was rightly critical of a system that relies upon post-facto decisions within the criminal justice system:

> A system whereby a judge or other independent assessor is satisfied in advance that someone has a voluntary, clear, settled, and informed wish to die and for his suicide then to be organised in an open and professional way, would, at least in my current view, provide greater and more satisfactory protection for the weak and vulnerable, than a system which involves a lawyer from the DPP's office inquiring, after the event, whether the person who had killed himself had such a wish.[48]

Despite this view, Lord Neuberger and other judges concluded that it would be 'institutionally inappropriate' to formally declare the offence of assisted suicide to be incompatible with Article 8 at this time. A variety of reasons were given for this conclusion including the difficult, controversial and sensitive nature of the issue;[49] uncertainty about what could replace the existing law;[50] and the fact that Parliament was actively considering the issue at the time.[51]

The Supreme Court was also asked to consider the slightly different issues raised by AM's appeal relating to the lack of clarity in the DPP guidance. The Court seemed to be unanimous in its view that further revision of the policy was not the way forward. Lord Sumption noted 'although presented as a complaint about the lack of clarity in the published policy, it is in reality a complaint about its substance'.[52] Lord Sumption was joined by all members of the Court in dismissing further revision and specification of the DPP policy as the way forward on assisted dying. For example, Lord Neuberger noted that 'it is one thing for the court to decide that the DPP must publish a policy, and quite another for the court to dictate what should be in that policy'.[53] It was also pointed out by Lord Sumption that any lack of clarity does not arise from the terms of the policy, but rather from 'the discretionary character of the Director's decision, the variety of relevant

[47] ibid [111], per Lord Neuberger.
[48] ibid [108].
[49] ibid [116].
[50] ibid [127] (per Lord Neuberger); [177] and [188] (per Lord Mance).
[51] ibid [116], per Lord Neuberger.
[52] ibid [247], per Lord Neuberger.
[53] ibid [141], per Lord Neuberger.

factors, and the need to vary the weight to be attached to them according to the circumstances of each individual case'.[54] As Lord Sumption noted, such discretion is constitutionally proper and certainly more appropriate in constitutional terms than the exemption of a certain class of persons from criminal liability by the DPP. Indeed, Lord Sumption even made reference to the 1689 Bill of Rights' famous declaration that 'the pretended power of suspending of laws or the execution of laws by regal authority without consent of parliament is illegal' as relevant to the DPP granting exemptions from prosecution.[55] The difficulty illustrated by *Nicklinson* is that if the DPP should not exempt persons from prosecution, and the courts do not feel the time is right to declare the absolute prohibition of assisted suicide to be incompatible with the HRA 1998, all that remains is for Parliament itself to change the law. And Parliament has shown a distinct lack of willingness to do so.

At the time of the Supreme Court judgment in *Nicklinson*, Lord Falconer's Assisted Dying Bill was before Parliament. While it had significant shortcomings, not least in that it would provide no assistance to the applicants in the case, it provided a clear opportunity for Parliament to consider the issue of assisted dying. The reluctance of some of the judges to issue a declaration of incompatibility at the present time seemed to be partly based on the fact that Parliament was currently required to debate this very issue. During the 2014/15 session, the Bill reached Committee Stage in the House of Lords before a general election intervened. During the second reading debate in the Lords,[56] there was a general consensus among those who spoke in the debate that, due to the *Nicklinson* judgment, Parliament needed to properly address the issue of assisted dying, and it was for this reason that the Bill was allowed to proceed to Committee for detailed consideration without division. However, it was clear that although the Supreme Court decision was mentioned frequently in the debate, it was rarely perceived as a request to change the law. Most of the speakers seemed to regard the debate itself as a sufficient response to the judgment, while arguably the (hidden) five-four majority of the Court was willing to make a declaration of incompatibility unless exceptions to the offence of assisted suicide were introduced.

After the 2015 election, Labour MP Rob Marris, after coming first in the Private Member's Bill ballot, introduced the Assisted Dying (No 2) Bill into the House of Commons. Its second reading debate on 11 September 2015 concluded in a self-congratulatory nature when the Minister for Policing, Crime and Criminal Justice (Mike Penning) said:

> It is an honour and a privilege to be standing at the Dispatch Box today as we show the rest of the country and the world what a Parliament should be doing. We have debated

[54] ibid [249], per Lord Sumption.
[55] ibid [241], per Lord Sumption.
[56] Hansard, HL (Series 6) Vol 755, col 775 (18 July 2014).

> this important subject with passion but shown that we all have respect for each other. It is a shame that it has been 18 years since this matter was last debated, and I congratulate the hon. Member for Wolverhampton South West (Rob Marris) on bringing it here today.[57]

Despite their pride at even discussing the issue, MPs wasted less than four hours in voting down the Bill when the House divided 330-118 against the Bill. Subsequent parliamentary consideration of the issue has been similarly perfunctory. In 2021, Baroness Meacher's Assisted Dying Bill, based on the previous ones introduced by Lord Falconer and Rob Marris, received its Second Reading on 22 October 2021, but time was not found for a committee stage to be scheduled and it was not supported by the Government, rendering any further progress highly unlikely.[58]

Nicklinson seemed to represent a real move towards change in the current law. Despite the failure of the majority of the judges to formerly declare the assisted suicide offence to be incompatible with human rights, a majority of them did hint both that the current law is disproportionate under Article 8 and that Parliament should change the law. Indeed, Lords Neuberger and Wilson explicitly warn Parliament that a declaration of incompatibility may be forthcoming in future proceedings:

> Were parliament for whatever reason, to fail satisfactorily to address the issue whether to amend the subsection to permit assistance to be given to persons in the situation of Mr Nicklinson and Mr Lamb, the issue of a fresh claim for a declaration is to be anticipated … While the conclusion of the proceedings can in no way be prejudged, there is a real prospect of their success.[59]

This suggests that not only was Parliament expected to debate this issue, but also that the debate should result in a change in law, in order to ensure that these three judges would continue to refuse to declare the current law's incompatibility with Article 8. Given Parliament's steadfast refusal to change the law on assisted suicide, despite the Supreme Court's warnings about its potential disproportionality, it was inevitable that the matter would return to the courts. When it did so, the result was unsatisfactory.

After a fight to obtain permission to bring a judicial review claim,[60] a claim by Noel Conway, who was terminally ill with motor neurone disease and wanted to

[57] ibid [723].

[58] The Bill's stunted progress can be seen on the UK Parliament's website: bills.parliament.uk/bills/2875.

[59] *R (Nicklinson) v Ministry of Justice* (n 43) [202], per Lord Wilson. See also Lord Neuberger at [118]. Lord Mance does not go quite this far but does refuse to rule out the future possibility of a further application (at [190]).

[60] Initially, the Divisional Court refused permission to bring judicial review proceedings: *R (Conway) v Secretary of State for Justice* [2017] EWHC 640 (Admin). That decision was reversed by the Court of Appeal, which granted permission for Mr Conway to bring his judicial review claim: *R (Conway) v Secretary of State for Justice* [2017] EWCA Civ 275.

receive medical assistance in ending his life at a time of his choosing, was rejected by the Divisional Court[61] and the Court of Appeal.[62] The latter court, comprising Sir Terence Etherton MR, Sir Brian Leveson P and Lady Justice King, found that the Government had accepted in principle that the court has jurisdiction to consider whether the Suicide Act 1961, section 2 is compatible with Article 8 under the HRA.[63] Understandably, the Court of Appeal did not regard itself as bound by *Pretty* to find the law to be compatible with Article 8(2),[64] but also appeared not to regard itself as bound by the Supreme Court in *Nicklinson* due to differences in the facts (namely that Conway was terminally ill unlike the applicants in the earlier case, and he had proposed a new scheme to regulate the area).[65] The emphasis on a detailed analysis and critique of Conway's proposed scheme appears to be irrelevant to the core question of whether the current law is proportionate – although it follows the concern of many of the justices in *Nicklinson* that an alternative needs to be worked out before a declaration of incompatibility is issued, which has never been the case in any other field of law.

The Court of Appeal in *Conway* refused to make such a declaration but noted that the possibility of prosecution was not high given that since the publication of the DPP's policy in October 2015, there had been 117 cases of assisted suicide referred to the CPS by the police but only one successful prosecution (and that single case had involved neither a medical professional nor a victim with a medical condition).[66] It might be argued that the unlikeliness of prosecution, despite the continued absolute prohibition of assisted suicide by the criminal law, should be a factor in favour of a speedy resolution of the current situation, but it was not so regarded by the Court. On 27 November 2018, the Supreme Court refused leave to appeal this decision.[67] The Supreme Court, ironically comprising of Baroness Hale and Lord Kerr (together with Lord Reed) who had both dissented in *Nicklinson* and are willing to declare the existing law to be incompatible with Article 8, held that:

> Ultimately, the question for the panel is whether the prospects of Mr Conway's succeeding in his claim before this court are sufficient to justify our giving him permission to pursue it, with all that that would entail for him, for his family, for those on all sides of this multi-faceted debate, for the general public and for this court. Not without some reluctance, it has been concluded that in this case those prospects are not sufficient to justify giving permission to appeal.[68]

[61] *R (Conway) v Secretary of State for Justice* [2017] EWHC 2447 (Admin), [2018] 2 WLR 322.
[62] *R (on the application of Conway) v Secretary of State for Justice* [2018] EWCA Civ 1431.
[63] ibid [125].
[64] ibid [126].
[65] ibid [134].
[66] ibid [185]. The prosecution in question was *R v Howe (Kevin James)* [2014] EWCA Crim 114.
[67] *R (on the application of Conway) v Secretary of State for Justice (Application for Permission to Appeal)* (27 November 2018).
[68] ibid [8].

Conway establishes that the courts do have jurisdiction to consider the compatibility of the assisted suicide offence with Article 8, and rather side-stepped the issues of institutional competence that were so central to *Nicklinson*.

Further cases challenging the existing law have followed, therefore, but have been equally unsuccessful. In 2018, the Omid T case, involving a 55-year-old man suffering from a rare and incurable neurological disorder, known as multiple system atrophy, who was bedbound and required 24-hour care, raised a new issue for the English courts.[69] In addition to the familiar Article 8 argument, it was also argued that Article 2's right to life was infringed by the current assisted suicide offence which forced Omid T to die sooner than he would wish in order to do so while he was still able to travel abroad. Nineteen months after beginning his legal case, but before any resolution of the preliminary legal issues, Omid T travelled to Switzerland and ended his life there with assistance.

The following year, Philippe Newby, suffering from motor neurone disease, brought a further legal challenge to the offence of assisted suicide under both Article 8 and also Article 2, arguing under the latter provision that the current law may drive him to take his own life earlier than he would wish to do, since he will be unable to rely on lawful assistance at a later stage.[70] Both arguments were rejected. On the right to life issue, the court seemed to err in relying upon the finding in the *Pretty* case that the right to life was not applicable due to representing the polar opposite of the interest in the sanctity of life that Article 2 seeks to protect. That, entirely coherent, rejection of Article 2's applicability in *Pretty* was specifically in the context of an argument that the right to life protects self-determination over life and death and facilitates a choice to die, but in *Newby* the right to life was being used in an entirely different argument, namely that death comes sooner for those unable to choose to live longer and then die with assistance. This latter argument does not contradict Article 2's sanctity of life perspective and deserved a proper hearing. The Court did also, however, hold that even if the right to life was applicable, the considerations which would need to be taken into account in any balancing exercise would be the same as those applicable to Article 8 and that therefore a case formulated under Article 2 adds nothing and must fail for the same reasons as the claim under Article 8. While this is a more cogent rejection of the Article 2 argument, it remains superficial and there are undoubtedly further debates to be had on this point. However counterintuitive it might be to permit assistance in dying in order to ensure people can live for as long as they wish to do so, it is an approach that prioritises autonomous choices about the end of life and has much to recommend it. It also reflects an oft-stated sentiment by people experiencing the terror of deteriorating health: that knowing there is an option to bring life to a peaceful end if necessary is in itself a reassuring thing and can suffice to provide a coping mechanism for enduring a natural decline in health.

[69] *R (on the Application of T) v Ministry of Justice* [2018] EWHC 2615 (Admin).
[70] *R (on the Application of Newby) v Ministry of Justice* [2019] EWHC 3118 (Admin).

D. Conclusions on the Current Offence

As we have just seen, the current state of English law on assisting suicide is regrettably ambiguous. The offence is an absolute one with no legal exceptions and thus any action that is capable of, and intended to, encourage or assist another's suicide is subject to significant criminal penalties. However, the chances of prosecution are now miniscule. The development of prosecuting guidelines specific to this offence following the House of Lords' judgment in the *Purdy* case have brought much-needed official tolerance to compassionate actions that seek to support autonomous, capacitated and voluntary choices to die. But they have left the law in an uncertain state. Luzon has described the UK approach as a 'de-prioritisation approach' in which there is a 'distinction between the law on the books and the law in action, to quiet concerns about the harsh consequences of a blanket prohibition'.[71] He argues that this de-prioritisation is a de facto decriminalisation of assisted suicide because while the definition of the act as a criminal offence is not repealed, there is a clear policy of avoiding imposing sanctions on offenders.[72] This, he argues, is a version of legalisation, albeit a soft approach to legalisation in which there are no laws or regulations, but rather guidelines, and no precise, specific or clear rules about what exactly is permissible under the law.[73] Furthermore, the state delegates authority on this issue to prosecutors.[74] This de-prioritisation of the assisted suicide offence not only fails to offer legal protection to the autonomy of persons with capacity to choose to die who are unable to do so unaided (because the absolute criminal prohibition of any assistance remains on the statute books), but also arguably fails to ensure sufficiently strict legal regulation of whether or not the person assisted to die had the capacity to choose to die.[75] A harder form of legalisation, such as specific legislation, therefore has the best potential to protect autonomy by means of ensuring specific, detailed rules and safeguards. The de facto, but not de jure, legalisation of assisted suicide might be viewed as the latest in a long history of the pragmatic adaptation of the strict requirements of the criminal law in relation to suicide. As was highlighted in chapter two, for centuries those involved with enforcing the law used whatever discretion or flexibility they retained to avoid implementing the strict letter of the law.[76] However, such a discrepancy between the actions of those involved in maintaining the criminal justice system and the formal substance of the criminal law suggests that the law is outdated and should be changed.

[71] Luzon (n 1) 340.

[72] ibid.

[73] ibid 341.

[74] ibid.

[75] See Luzon (ibid) 343; Lewis, 'Informal Legal Change on Assisted Suicide' (2011) 126; and O'Sullivan, 'Mens Rea' (2015) 107.

[76] For example, the frequent verdicts of *non compos mentis* by coroner's juries in the late 18th century; see M MacDonald and TR Murphy, *Sleepless Souls: Suicide in Early Modern England* (Oxford, Clarendon Press, 1990) 133.

The UK courts have been reluctant to declare the current law to be incompatible with human rights, but have acknowledged that a patient's right to make autonomous decisions about dying has suffered interference in order to protect the rights of so-called vulnerable members of society. For some judges, that is a legitimate, proportionate interference and for some others, it is not. Any change to the statutory offence of encouraging and assisting suicide will, of course, need to be initiated by Parliament. Even if a future court declares the Suicide Act 1961, section 2(1) to be incompatible with Article 8 using its declaratory powers under HRA 1998, s 4, the offence will remain in place unless a majority within Parliament choses to amend it. The parliamentary debates on the topic that have been held in recent years do not suggest that such a change is imminent.[77] Furthermore, it would now appear to require a massive shift in perspective for a court to even go so far as to issue a declaration of incompatibility.

While *Nicklinson* revealed two senior judges stridently declaring the absolute offence to be incompatible with Article 8's protection of autonomy,[78] and at least three other senior judges, including the president of the Court, seeming to accept the weight of arguments about a lack of proportionality in the current offence,[79] more recent cases have seen judges less open to change. As Hobson and Papadopoulou have argued in the context of the *Conway* case, the courts appear to be 'working with a basic presumption of "no, unless" it is shown the concerns it raises can be assuaged'.[80] As the authors point out, this presumption 'forces those in the position of Mr Conway to accept great and known harms to avoid the risk harms that are conceded to be speculative'.[81] Therefore, they argue that *Conway* 'perpetuates the overly-cautious nature of the courts' approach to regulatory risk when discussing alternative schemes to assisted dying'.[82] The cautious approach of the courts in cases such as this exists in a vacuum however because the current position of 'de-prioritisation' of the assisted suicide offence means there is an abundance of a lack of caution in the regulation of self-chosen deaths. Without any system for ensuring a capacity to choose to die, and in the absence of any realistic prospect of prosecution for assistance, and indeed encouragement, of suicide, the law is reckless in its engagement with suicide, trusting that a mere message of moral objection with a pragmatic tolerance in most cases will suffice to discourage but not impede suicides amongst those needing or requesting assistance.

[77] See, for example, the mixed views, strongly held on both sides, evident in the House of Lords debate on Baroness Meacher's Assisted Dying Bill in October 2021: Hansard, HL (Series 6) Vol 815, col 393 (22 October 2021).

[78] Baroness Hale and Lord Kerr.

[79] *R (Nicklinson) v Ministry of Justice* (n 43), and see E Wicks, 'The Supreme Court Judgment in *Nicklinson*: One Step Forward on Assisted Dying; Two Steps Back on Human Rights' (2015) 23 *Medical Law Review* 144.

[80] C Hobson and N Papadopoulou, 'Regulating risk and autonomy in assisted suicide: *Conway v Secretary of State for Justice*' (2021) 29 *Medical Law Review* 128, 137–38.

[81] ibid 138.

[82] ibid 142.

In other countries, the courts have been far more responsive, and less cautious about the role they need to play. In Canada, for example, the Supreme Court of Canada unanimously upheld a trial judge's determination that the blanket ban on assisted suicide violated the rights to life, liberty and security of competent adults who are suffering intolerably as a result of a grievous and irremediable medical condition.[83] This landmark judgment ultimately led to the legalisation of assisted suicide in Canada in certain circumstances.

It has been argued throughout this book that there is a vital distinction between assisting and encouraging a suicide. The current legal position in England and Wales conflates the two in an unsatisfactory manner. The remainder of this chapter will discuss these two actions separately and will argue that while legal reform is needed in respect of both elements of the current offence, it is reform in two very different directions. The offence of encouraging a suicide should be clarified and strengthened, while the offence of assisting a suicide should incorporate a limited exception. Both of these arguments flow from the complexity of the issue of suicide which has been highlighted throughout this book. In the next section, we will consider the offence of encouraging suicide, which is a highly unusual and yet important criminal prohibition.

II. Encouraging Suicide – Using the Criminal Law to Protect Human Life

There are a number of difficulties with an offence of encouraging suicide. Firstly, it criminalises the act of encouraging someone to perform a lawful action. Alongside the offence of assisting suicide, it is unique in creating liability for an accessory to a lawful activity. Secondly, encouraging suicide criminalises a form of speech. Although not unique in doing so, it raises some difficult questions about infringement with a right to free speech for the encourager, and perhaps more significantly, a right to receive information for the person contemplating suicide. Thirdly, it has a complex relationship with the concept of autonomy. It may be that encouraging someone to consider the possibility of ending their lives might facilitate an autonomous choice to a greater extent than silence. For example, a person who is suffering unbearable pain may hesitate about ending their life prematurely due to the impact of such a choice upon others, and reassurance and encouragement from loved ones might enable the making of an autonomous, capacitated choice to die. On the other hand, encouragement to attempt suicide might be designed to overrule a person's own reluctance to die and thereby to undermine their autonomy. There may be a thin line between reassurance, encouragement, incitement and coercion, and the identity of the person encouraging suicide, and their relationship to the

[83] *Carter v Canada* [2015] 1 SCR 331.

person they are encouraging, may also play a significant role. As has often proved to be the case throughout this book, these issues must be considered against a backdrop in which both the legal protection of human life and respect for individual autonomy are conflicting priorities. As it has previously been argued that only persons with a capacity to choose to die should have that choice protected by the law, a key question in respect of encouraging suicide might be whether such encouragement undermines that capacity or enables it. If the former, then appropriate legal steps should be taken to prevent the suicide, and criminalising the encouragement may well be fitting; if the latter, then it may be logically incoherent to criminalise the encouragement. If the action lies somewhere between these two extremes – if it does not undermine the capacity of the person choosing to die, but nonetheless encourages them to make that decision when they may not otherwise have done so – the balance becomes much finer.

The issue of encouraging suicide often seems to be lost within a focus on assisting suicide within the UK legal system. However, in recent years there have been some interesting explorations of encouraging, short of assisting, in other jurisdictions. The most significant and well publicised of these is the Massachusetts case of *Commonwealth v Carter*[84] in which Michelle Carter, 17 years old at the time of the incident, was convicted of manslaughter after sending text messages to her boyfriend encouraging him to end his life. Her 18-year-old boyfriend, Conrad Roy III, died of carbon monoxide poisoning after locking himself in his truck. Carter was not present at the scene and did not provide any actual assistance in the death, but of particular note was a message in which she told Roy to 'get back in' the truck after he expressed reservations about continuing in his attempt. Unlike most American jurisdictions, Massachusetts does not have a statutory offence of assisting suicide and therefore Carter was charged with involuntary manslaughter and became the first American convicted of homicide for merely encouraging suicide.[85] Her appeal against conviction in which she argued that her conviction based on her words alone was a violation of her right to free speech in the First Amendment of the US Constitution was not successful.

In terms of an encouraging suicide offence, Carter's actions seem suitable for punishment as it appears that Roy would not have continued with his suicide attempt without her persuasion to do so. There is also considerable doubt that he had the capacity to choose to die in the circumstances. However, the homicide offence with which Carter was charged specifically required proof that she caused the death.[86] Binder and Chiesa sum up the dilemma of the *Carter* case

[84] *Commonwealth v Carter* 52 NE 3d 1054 (Mass, 2016).

[85] G Binder and L Chiesa, 'The Puzzle of Inciting Suicide' (2019) 56 *American Criminal Law Review* 65, 110. These authors also point out, however, that Carter could have been charged and convicted of murder rather than manslaughter and that the failure to do so may defer to 'libertarian views that speech cannot cause choice and that consensual injury is no harm' (79).

[86] ibid 74.

nicely when they ask 'if Conrad Roy killed himself, how can Michelle Carter be said to have killed him?'.[87] Beyond questions of how significant Carter's words were to the decision to die, it may be that Carter's culpability goes beyond words of encouragement and includes a failure to take steps to prevent the death. She admitted that she could have prevented Roy's death either merely by talking him out of it, or by calling the police, but she failed to do so.[88] Binder and Chiesa suggest this suffices for causation by omission.[89] This casts a new light upon her actions by focusing not upon her encouragement of suicide but rather upon her failure to prevent a suicide, when she knew she was able to do so (and, we might add, should have had some doubts about whether Roy had the capacity to choose to die). Of course, these are challenging responsibilities to impose upon a 17-year-old.

The issue of causation in relation to encouraging a suicide also proves problematic in relation to recent calls within the UK to consider the possibility of manslaughter liability for domestic abusers whose victim takes their own life.[90] Women who experience domestic abuse have been shown to be more likely to experience suicidal thoughts and/or to attempt suicide.[91] But establishing a causal link between the victim's suicide and the defendant's abusive behaviour is extremely challenging.[92] As Munro and Shah have argued, in this context,

> the abuser does not pull the trigger or provide the rope. The victim may even see the act of suicide as a form of liberation or a final expression of rebellion or subversion against a partner's control. But this does not mean that the actions of the abuser are not a significant cause of death, and nor does it mean that the act of taking one's life is a reflection of voluntary agency.[93]

The case of *R v Dhaliwal*[94] in 2006 saw an attempt to bring a charge of unlawful act manslaughter in relation to suicide following a long history of psychological abuse. The court held that 'unlawful violence on an individual with a fragile and vulnerable personality, which is proved to be a material cause of death (even if the result of suicide) would at least arguably, be capable of amounting to manslaughter'.[95] However, psychological injury alone (as distinct from psychiatric injury) would not suffice.[96]

[87] ibid 78.
[88] ibid 77.
[89] ibid.
[90] See VE Munro and R Aitken, 'Adding Insult to Injury? The Criminal Law's Response to Domestic Abuse-Related Suicide in England and Wales' (2018) 9 *Criminal Law Review* 732.
[91] ibid 733.
[92] ibid 738.
[93] V Munro and S Shah, '*R v Dhaliwal*: Reconstructing Manslaughter Cases in Domestic Violence Suicide' in C McGlynn, C Hunter and R Rackley (eds), *Feminist Judgments: From Theory to Practice* (Oxford, Hart Publishing, 2010) 270.
[94] *R v Dhaliwal* [2006] EWCA Crim 1139, [2006] 2 Cr App R 24.
[95] ibid [8].
[96] ibid [32].

Munro and Aitken have pointed out a significant development since *Dhaliwal* that might lead to a different conclusion. The criminal offence of coercive and controlling behaviour created under the Serious Crime Act 2015, section 76 includes psychological harms and therefore creates the possibility for unlawful act manslaughter to be grounded on criminally coercive and controlling behaviour, irrespective of the existence of physical violence, and 'also recognises that focusing on isolated incidents of domestic violence may distort the significance and severity of effects associated with prolonged exposure to cumulative (and often routinised) experiences of abuse'.[97] The issue of suicide following long-term domestic abuse is, of course, distinct from mere encouragement of suicide. The real issue in such cases is whether the capacity to choose to die has been undermined by continuous abuse. The suitability of a form of legal liability for the long-term abuser in such cases is hard to deny, but it is more fittingly homicide liability rather than encouraging a suicide. For example, in 2017 Nicholas Allen pleaded guilty to unlawful act manslaughter after stalking his ex-partner Justene Reece to the point where she had ender her life by means of suicide.[98] The judge, Michael Chambers QC, is quoted as saying that Allen had 'clearly caused' the suicide and that the suicide was 'a direct result' of Allen's criminal actions.[99] This is an important precedent for enabling legal liability in circumstances where a suicide results from someone else's criminal actions, and may reflect policy reasons for discouraging abusive behaviour, and it stands apart from the question of mere encouragement to end life.

When the act of encouragement is speech, it raises potential freedom of expression issues. As noted above, Carter's appeal on this ground failed, but in 2014 the Minnesota Supreme Court struck down a provision permitting liability for encouraging suicide as a violation of the protection of free speech in the US Constitution's First Amendment.[100] Binder and Chiesa have noted that while the criminalisation of encouraging suicide may be justified from a utilitarian perspective, it is less appealing from a libertarian perspective:

> Inciting suicide brings the conflict between utilitarian and libertarian perspectives into focus because of suicide's dual character as both a tragic injury and a liberty enhancing choice, and the dual character of incitement as both causal influence on harmful conduct and as liberty enhancing speech.[101]

When suicide is viewed as an intrinsic harm and a serious public health danger, then its encouragement is worthy of criminalisation from a utilitarian perspective, but when suicide is viewed as an autonomy-enhancing act, then 'neither

[97] Munro and Aitken, 'Adding Insult to Injury?' (2018) 738.

[98] 'Man Jailed for Manslaughter over Ex-girlfriend's Suicide' BBC News, 28 July 2017, available at www.bbc.co.uk/news/uk-40758095.

[99] ibid.

[100] *State v Melchert-Dinkel*, 844 N.W.2d 13 (Minn 2014).

[101] Binder and Chiesa, 'The Puzzle of Inciting Suicide' (2019) 70.

assistance nor encouragement from another person can be said to injure the suicide victim unless it impairs his or her autonomy'.[102] If suicide is accepted as not wrongful but rather justified as an exercise of autonomy, then such a justification defence should extend to those assisting or encouraging this action unless, in the words of Binder and Chiesa, 'the actor that is contemplating suicide is coerced into doing so or lacks sufficient competency or mental clarity to make such a momentous choice'.[103] This returns us to the core issue of capacity to choose to die. If another's words or actions undermine that capacity and prevent the exercise of an autonomous choice, then two legal consequences should follow. First, there should be criminal liability for the encourager who has not only undermined the value in all human life by encouraging its end, but has also impeded a person's ability to make their own capacitated and autonomous decision about the ending of life. Secondly, however, legal interventions are permissible to seek to prevent that suicide because the person attempting it has likely not made an autonomous decision to do so and thus will not have sufficient capacity to choose to die.

Given this, it might be argued that the would-be encourager should also be treated as having a legal obligation that goes beyond the duty to refrain from the encouragement and extends to a duty to take reasonable steps to prevent the suicide, for example by actively discouraging it. If a person's autonomy is compromised by the encouragement, then in such circumstances the encourager has done more than merely encourage; they have incited, motivated and caused the death. The legal duty upon them should be not only to cease encouragement but also to take practicable steps to prevent the suicide, and a failure to do so perhaps should incur criminal liability. This would be a significant change in existing law, where duties to prevent suicide are limited to certain contexts, as we have seen, but it may be justified in order to further strengthen the law's vital role in suicide prevention, in relation to non-autonomous deaths. On the other hand, if the autonomy of the person contemplating death has not been compromised by the encouragement, then the only legal liability would be in relation to the encouragement of suicide.

There is a wide spectrum between gentle words of reassurance and encouragement aimed at augmenting an autonomous decision to die, and incitement to die based upon coercion, deception or an exploitation of vulnerability and/or incapacity. The current criminal offence does not seek to engage with these distinctions and, in its combination with the offence of assisting suicide, it is often overlooked entirely. Given the importance of ensuring that there is sufficient capacity to die, as argued in earlier chapters, an unambiguous, strongly worded and robust offence to capture words and actions that undermine that capacity or seek to pervert it, is essential.

[102] ibid 69.
[103] ibid 122.

Some other jurisdictions have more specific incitement to suicide offences. For example, Spain criminalises 'instigating' someone else to commit suicide.[104] A distinction between instigation and encouragement has great potential as it focuses upon criminalising attempts to initiate a suicide that may otherwise not occur. Other states have enacted specific offences targeting abuse leading to suicide.[105] For example, Moldova has an offence of inciting suicide through psychological abuse,[106] Tajikistan has an offence of driving an individual to suicide by threat, cruel treatment or systematic degrading of their dignity[107] and Albania has an offence of causing suicide because of systematic maltreatment or other systematic misbehaviours that seriously affect the dignity of a person where there is a family or cohabitation relationship.[108] A specific incitement of suicide offence would be able to incorporate concerns about abuse leading to suicide, as well as other words or actions that overwhelmed another person's autonomy or capacity to choose whether to live or die, while leaving scope for words that augment a person's own autonomous and capacitated choice. With such a stronger offence in place, focus could then turn to a limited legalisation of assisting a capacitated suicide, as will now be discussed.

III. Legalising Assistance with a Capacitated Voluntary Death

The current law on assisted suicide is unsustainable. It relies upon official prosecutorial tolerance which means that despite the unlikelihood of prosecution, anyone who assists a capacitated and autonomous choice to die does so under the cloud of criminalisation. For some people, unable to end their own life without assistance, this represents a significant obstacle to facilitating their autonomy over life and death. Furthermore, it is hard to reconcile with the legality and widespread acceptability of the active withdrawal of life-sustaining treatment leading to death, including often without an explicit request from the patient.[109] The blanket ban on assisted suicide seems to assume that all intentional, self-caused deaths are the same and that, whether or not they should all be prevented, they should certainly not be facilitated by anyone else.

Blanket bans are notoriously problematic from a human rights perspective. As Draghici notes, in many other areas blanket bans have been found to

[104] Criminal Code, Art 143 (Spain).
[105] See Munro and Aitken (n 90) 741 for such examples.
[106] Criminal Code, Art 150 (Moldova).
[107] Criminal Code, Art 109 (Tajikistan).
[108] Criminal Code, Art 99 (Albania).
[109] For example, *Airedale NHS Trust v Bland* [1993] 1 All ER 831; *Aintree University Hospitals NHS Foundation Trust v James* [2013] UKSC 6.

be incompatible with human rights guarantees, including in relation to irreducible life sentences, the prohibition on prisoners' right to vote and prisoners' lack of access to assisted reproduction facilities.[110] She argues that the underlying tenet of such cases is that

> the law must be capable of responding fairly to different individual circumstances, and public-interest considerations cannot remove the need to assess each case on its own merits. This remains so even where the relief sought, such as criminals' right to vote or to beget children, may offend public morality.[111]

While there has been a reluctance on the part of both Parliament and the courts to move towards a change in the law, arguably such a change would not be as controversial as might be assumed. A limited exception to the offence of assisted suicide would not send a message that suicide is a good option, or that the vast majority of suicide attempts should not be prevented. This is because lawful assistance should only be contemplated where the desired suicide is an autonomous choice made by a person with sufficient capacity to choose to die. As has been argued elsewhere, this standard is a hard one to meet, and so it should remain. But where there is an autonomous and capacitated choice to die, preventing its assistance does nothing but discriminate against those unable or reluctant to act unilaterally upon their choice. Therefore, we should assess the permissibility of the suicide itself, and not the means by which it is, and can be, achieved.

As Draghici has argued, the

> ethical unease with a change in the law quite possibly stems from the conviction that it would represent an endorsement of a particular view on life and death whereas in fact it is not a decision on what is right or wrong, but a deferral to private opinion, in the same way as is currently done in the area of life-saving medical treatment.[112]

Contrary to popular arguments that legalising assisted suicide in any circumstances would endanger the important principle of the sanctity of life, it is in fact 'value-neutral' because 'it simply leaves the judgment on the quality of life that makes life worth living or the unwavering sanctity of life to the individual's own determination'.[113] Prohibiting assistance necessary to enable a person to end their life as they choose seeks to impose a uniform morality on a society with justifiably varied perspectives on questions of life and death, pain and suffering, faith and belief, autonomy and obligation. And, most significantly perhaps, it does this at an inappropriate stage, namely at the stage of assistance to die, rather than at the stage of the person's choice to die. It is this potentially final exercise of autonomy that should be the centre of any legal interventions (such as to ensure

[110] C Draghici, 'The Blanket Ban on Assisted Suicide: Between Moral Paternalism and Utilitarian Justice' (2015) 3 *European Human Rights Law Review* 286, 292.
[111] ibid 292–93.
[112] ibid 296.
[113] ibid.

sufficient capacity), rather than the actions of a third party in offering assistance. The mental condition of a person wishing to die is a crucial factor in determining whether the suicide should be respected or prevented; the physical condition, in terms of whether or not they can end life unaided, should not be relevant to the legality of that death.

Arguing for the legalisation of assisting suicide in circumstances where the suicide is not one that needs to be legally prevented is, of course, only the first step. The specific circumstances in which such assistance should no longer be a criminal offence is at least as challenging a question. As discussed above, the current prosecutorial guidelines have identified a number of factors that make prosecution 'less likely' in the words of the guidance, and not at all likely in practice. These may provide some useful guidance to the ambit of a legal exception to the offence. The factors are as follows:

1. the victim had reached a voluntary, clear, settled and informed decision to commit suicide;
2. the suspect was wholly motivated by compassion;
3. the actions of the suspect, although sufficient to come within the definition of the offence, were of only minor encouragement or assistance;
4. the suspect had sought to dissuade the victim from taking the course of action which resulted in his or her suicide;
5. the actions of the suspect may be characterised as reluctant encouragement or assistance in the face of a determined wish on the part of the victim to commit suicide;
6. the suspect reported the victim's suicide to the police and fully assisted them in their enquiries into the circumstances of the suicide or the attempt and his or her part in providing encouragement or assistance.[114]

Putting to one side the inappropriateness of the term 'victim' for a person choosing to die (and indeed the use of the word 'commit' for a lawful action), it can be seen that only one of these factors relates directly to the person choosing to die. This is the absolutely crucial requirement of a 'voluntary, clear, settled and informed' decision to die. These considerations form elements of the capacity to choose to die test supported in earlier chapters of this book, but they do not suffice to ensure this. Therefore, a more stringent test for capacity should form an essential component of any legal exception to the offence.

In chapter four, it was argued that a stringent capacity to choose to die test should be adopted which would involve consideration as to the internal coherence of a desire to die by suicide with the past and present wishes and identity of the person now expressing such a desire, as well as whether or not the implications for the future self have been sufficiently taken into account. To demonstrate

[114] 'Suicide: Policy for Prosecutors' (n 36) para 45.

the capacity to make a decision to die by suicide, a person would need to be following a decision-making process that was rational, consistent, forward-looking and reflective. The bare legal requirements of voluntary, clear, settled and informed do not suffice for this. Ensuring that the choice to die by suicide is internally consistent with the identity of the person wishing to die, and that the interests of her future self have been considered, may be challenging if the circumstances leading to the request are overwhelming.

Given the circumstances that are most likely to result in a request for assistance with dying, the issue of depression is likely to be a significant one. It cannot be denied that there is a link between suicide and mental illness, especially depression, but some writers have argued that

> there is increasing support for a more nuanced approach towards depression in clinical end-of-life settings. For example, in palliative care, while depression is screened for as a condition, which if treated, can improve quality of life at the end of life, there is also acceptance of non-pathological concepts of distress such as grief, sadness and demoralisation.[115]

Such concepts do not prevent a capacitated choice to die, but may provide the background reason for such a choice. As with any exercise of autonomy, the reasons for a choice should not be relevant to determination of whether the person making the choice has the capacity to do so, and this applies even to a choice to die, provided that such a choice has diachronic continuity. It is worth noting that the capacity to choose to die must exist both at the time of the choice, and at the time of the death. As so many elderly patients face the loss of their own autonomy and identity towards the end of life, due to Alzheimer's disease and other forms of dementia, any potential escape route via suicide, assisted or not, can be closed off to them. An advance request for assistance in dying when capacitous cannot, and probably should not, suffice for the death of a person lacking the capacity to continue to make that choice.[116] When one's very self is disrupted, decisions of the previous self on matters as significant as life and death cannot satisfy standards of diachronic continuity. Indeed, Gather and Vollmann point out that 'Simply handing out barbiturates to dementia patients at a stage when they are still capable, but without a set time for taking the drugs or requiring the presence of a physician at the suicide is problematic'.[117] In an Australian case, the assisted 'suicide' of a man

[115] C Stewart, C Peisah and B Draper, 'A Test for Mental Capacity to Request Assisted Suicide' (2011) 37 *Journal of Medical Ethics* 34, 37.

[116] J Gather and J Vollmann, 'Physician-assisted Suicide of Patients with Dementia: A Medical Ethical Analysis with a Special Focus on Patient Autonomy' (2013) 36 *International Journal of Law and Psychiatry* 444, 450: 'One essential ethical requirement in our view is that the patients must be competent at the time of decision and at the time of the execution of the suicide and thus must be able to decide and act in a competent manner'.

[117] ibid.

with dementia who lacked capacity to make an informed choice to end his life led to criminal liability for manslaughter rather than assisting a suicide.[118]

Of course, the role of psychiatrists may be an important one in determining a capacity to choose to die with assistance. This places them in a position of great influence, not only as gatekeepers of physician-assisted suicide, but also with a vital role to protect patients from non-autonomous decisions.[119] Indeed, with the vast majority of suicide attempts a symptom of a mental illness, the most common role of a psychiatrist is to provide suitable treatment in order to *prevent* suicide attempts. It might be assumed to create a conflict of interest, but Gather and Vollmann argue that the pivotal role for psychiatrists

> is not at variance with the fact that, as a rule, the psychiatrists' task is to prevent suicide. What is crucial in our view is that psychiatrists – due to their specific knowledge and clinical experience – are in the best position to distinguish clearly in the context of mental illness between the frequent cases of incompetent patients who express suicidal wishes and the certainly rare cases of competent patients who do so.[120]

It is clearly the case that it must be far better for this assessment of the capacity of the person choosing to die to take place while they are still alive, rather than in hindsight as part of a prosecutorial decision. This may be the most important benefit in legalisation of assisted suicide. It would enable accurate assessment of whether the person requesting assistance has the capacity to choose to die, or whether instead it is a symptom of depression, or a fleeting or uncharacteristic impulse. The current legal situation in which all assistance is illegal but highly unlikely to result in prosecution does not provide the opportunity for such an assessment. Unless there is clear evidence of undue pressure or mental incapacity, the sole factor focusing upon the 'victim' of the assisted suicide is inadequate. A limited exception to the criminal offence of assisting a suicide which was only available to those assessed to reach the more stringent standard of a capacity to choose to die would be much more effective at preventing deaths where this standard is not met, in addition to facilitating the provision of assistance where it is met.

Beyond this one factor focusing on the 'victim' in the current prosecutorial guidance, the other five factors in that guidance that are described as making a prosecution 'less likely' all relate to the actions and intentions of the 'suspect' or the person providing assistance. The final of these is a largely non-contentious

[118] *R v Shirley Justins* [2008] NSWSC 1194. See Stewart, Peisah and Draper, 'A Test for Mental Capacity' (2011) 34.

[119] Gather and Vollmann remind us that 'respect of self-determination also protects patients from self-harm through decisions that are not self-determined': 'Physician-assisted Suicide of Patients with Dementia' (2013) 447.

[120] ibid 451. Rather worryingly, however, they also cite a study in which a survey of forensic psychiatrists in the United States revealed that the greater the physicians' ethical reservations against physician-assisted suicide, the higher the thresholds demanded by them to validate a patient's decision-making capacity (447).

requirement that the suicide be reported to the police and full assistance provided with their enquiries. Under the current law, the involvement of the police is an inevitable but problematic element of assisting suicide. The need for a reporting mechanism would be essential under a legalised form of assisted suicide, but this could be satisfied at the stage in the process before the death, and thus involve the person central to the suicide. This would also reduce the need for police involvement with the authoritarian message that such involvement sends.

The remaining four factors are more complex. In brief, they focus on the level of involvement of the assister in the death and on her motives. So, prosecution is less likely if there was only minor encouragement or assistance. This highlights the potential ambiguity inherent in the offence of assisted suicide. In order for the action to fall within this offence rather than a homicide offence, the death must actually be caused by the person wishing to die. There may often be a very thin line between an act that assists another to end their own life and an act that causes death, albeit with the consent of the person dying. This fine distinction is particularly apparent when the person wishing to die is already seriously ill and may not be able to act unaided. The current legal position seems to suggest that there are in fact three categories of assisting in another's death: mere minor assistance falls within the ambit of the offence of assisted suicide, but is unlikely to result in prosecution; more significant assistance that does not step over into causing the death is more likely to be prosecuted as assisted suicide; and assistance that ultimately causes death falls outside the ambit of the offence and should be prosecuted as a homicide offence instead.[121] Within the prosecutorial guidance, there is no corresponding factor likely to lead to prosecution in relation to the level of assistance in the death, perhaps because it would be hard to define the more-than-minor assistance relevant. Given the legal context in which the prosecuting guidelines were first drafted, namely that of assistance for travel to Dignitas in Switzerland, it may be assumed that such assistance is categorised as minor in nature. It could be argued, however, that this might better be described as too far removed from the death to be in the public interest to prosecute.

In light of these complexities, a legal exception to the offence of assisted suicide should be framed without reference to the level of involvement in the death. If it is accepted that assisting a suicide can in certain circumstances be justified, the level of assistance will be irrelevant to the justification provided, of course, that

[121] In 2022, the Crown Prosecution Service conducted a public consultation on public interest guidance for suicide pacts and mercy killing-type cases. The proposed revision to its legal guidance on Homicide: Murder and Manslaughter would signify an extension of the policy of official prosecutorial tolerance of assisted suicide to the more serious offence of so-called mercy killing: CPS Consultation on Suicide Pacts and Mercy Killing (2022), available at www.cps.gov.uk/consultation/consultation-public-interest-guidance-suicide-pact-and-mercy-killing-type-cases.

it remains a self-caused death and not a so-called 'mercy killing'. If some choices to die should be respected by the law, then facilitating that choice by lawfully permitting voluntary assistance cannot logically require only minor assistance. While a thin, and arguably ambiguous, distinction will remain between assisting and causing a death, there is no need to entrench a second fine distinction between minor and more substantial acts of assistance.

Perhaps more controversially, the current prosecutorial factors also include three focused upon the motives of the assister, suggesting that prosecution is less likely if the assister was 'wholly motivated by compassion', had 'sought to dissuade the victim' and there was only 'reluctant encouragement or assistance in the face of a determined wish on the part of the victim to commit suicide'. The criminal law does not usually take into account the motives of the offender and yet under these guidelines, it is hugely significant whether the person assisting a suicide does so out of 'compassion' and with 'reluctance'. As mentioned above, while such considerations might generally have relevance in terms of sentencing, they would not usually be expected to go to the question of whether to prosecute. Even within the context of a legal exception to the offence, such an explicit focus on the mental state of the assister should be avoided because, once more, it removes the primary focus from the person who has made the choice to die. If that choice is a capacitated and autonomous one, and if assistance is needed to facilitate it, then the individual motive of the assister should not matter. While the stringent capacity to choose to die standard would encompass a frank discussion with the person wishing to die to ensure that it is a fully informed, reflective and individually consistent decision, there need be no obligation upon the person assisting the suicide to be the one participating in that discussion, much less an obligation to actively dissuade this exercise of autonomy.

It seems clear that a legalised version of assisting a capacitated suicide would require rather different safeguards than the factors currently tending towards a prosecutorial tolerance of assisted suicide. The requirements focused on ensuring a voluntary and capacitated choice would need to be significantly strengthened; the requirement of minor assistance and investigation of the mental state and motive of the person assisting could be removed. Most of the current factors that favour prosecution are an inverse of those against prosecution, but there is one significant addition in that prosecution is currently envisaged as more likely when the assister is acting in a capacity as a 'medical doctor, nurse, other healthcare professional, a professional carer [whether for payment or not], or as a person in authority, such as a prison officer' and, crucially, 'the victim was in his or her care'. Further clarification of this point was added in 2014 following the *Nicklinson* case and made clear that this only applies where there is 'a relationship of care between the suspect and the victims such that it will be necessary to consider whether the suspect may have exerted some influence on the victim'. While this is clearly a well-intentioned insertion, aimed at avoiding any tolerance of undue pressure or a misuse of power, its inclusion, in its current form, as a factor tending towards prosecution has the unfortunate effect of explicitly preferring what might be called 'amateur' assistance over professional. This raises a variety of issues, including concerns over whether there might be botched attempts at assisting suicide that cause more suffering, as well as still unanswered questions of what should happen if there is no family available or willing to assist. Concerns about undue pressure or misuse of power should instead be issues falling squarely within the determination of a capacity to choose to die test, as well as potentially within the scope of a strengthened criminal offence of encouraging or inciting a suicide. A legal exception to the offence of assisting suicide should enable professional assistance in appropriate cases and this is to be preferred over the current approach which, by refusing to engage with the unsatisfactory law directly, instead quietly ignores amateur suicide attempts and their equally amateur assistance.

One final point of contrast between legalising assistance with a capacitated suicide and the current prosecutorial tolerance approach is that the current policy does not include the types of safeguards that we might typically expect to see in a statutory exception to the offence of assisted suicide. Perhaps the most striking of these omissions is any qualifying condition for access to assistance with suicide. The interim policy did include a factor relating to the victim suffering from a terminal illness, severe and incurable physical disability or severe degenerative physical condition with no possibility of recovery, but this was removed from the final policy on the basis that some respondents to the public consultation queried whether it was discriminatory. Without this restriction, the policy tolerates assisted suicide along much more liberal lines than most formalised assisted dying regimes. For example, in the Netherlands, the legalisation of euthanasia and physician-assisted suicide is subject to a requirement of unbearable suffering with no prospect of improvement,[122] while the more recent legalisation of assisted suicide in Canada requires a grievous and irremediable medical condition.[123] Previous unsuccessful attempts to legalise assisted suicide within the UK have also relied upon a strict eligibility condition, typically terminal illness with a limited and defined terminal prognosis.[124]

There is considerable room for argument over the specifics of eligibility for assisted suicide and whether a focus on a physical condition or the degree of suffering is more appropriate, but it is rare to ignore such a limitation entirely. It could be argued, however, that a focus on the reason behind the choice to die is

[122] Termination of Life on Request and Assisted Suicide (Review Procedures) Act 2001.

[123] Bill C-14, An Act to amend the Criminal Code and to make related amendments to other Acts (Medical Assistance in Dying) 2016. Interestingly, a 'reasonable foreseeability of natural death' eligibility criterion was more recently declared to be unconstitutional by the Superior Court of Québec in *Truchon v Canada (Attorney General)* [2019] QCCS 3792.

[124] Most recently, the Assisted Dying Bill introduced by Baroness Meacher into the House of Lords in 2021 contains a requirement at s 2(1) of a diagnosis of 'an inevitably progressive condition which cannot be reversed by treatment' with death reasonably expected within six months; see bills.parliament.uk/publications/41676/documents/513.

inappropriate. Certainly it is not suggested here that it should be a factor in determining the capacity to choose to die in respect of an unassisted suicide. So should it be relevant to the legality of assistance with the capacitated suicide? At the heart of many arguments about legalising assisted suicide is the perceived injustice of people such as Tony Nicklinson and Dianne Pretty being unable to implement their capacitated (presumably, although it was not interrogated) choice to die because they cannot achieve this without assistance. If that is indeed an important reason in changing the law, then their physical condition is relevant, not as their motivation to choose to die, but rather because it forces them to seek assistance. In other words, a decision to end one's own life must be an autonomous one made by a person who satisfies the heightened test for capacity to choose to die, and any encouragement to make such a decision should be the subject of a serious criminal offence, but once the decision has been made, a person such as Tony Nicklinson or Dianne Pretty might find themselves unable to act upon it without another person's assistance and thus to that extent only their physical condition is relevant to the issue.

One way of determining eligibility for assistance in dying would be by limiting it to persons unable to end their lives unaided. This would not go as far as many would wish. Having to cause one's own death without assistance is a cruel and onerous obstacle. But perhaps it is right that it should be so. Throughout this book it has been argued that the vast majority of suicides should be prevented, including by the use of compulsion in some cases. Legalising the assistance of suicide in circumstances where the desire for assistance is mere preference rather than necessity might be argued to encourage choices to die more than is optimum in a search for the appropriate preservation of human life/respect for individual autonomy balance. Replacing the current criminal law blanket ban on assisted suicide with a limited exception where there is a (stringently applied) capacitated choice to die *and* an inability to achieve this result unaided (or doing it unaided would cause significant suffering), coupled with a more stringently enforced offence of encouraging or inciting suicide, strikes a reasonable balance that could support, rather than undermine, other legal efforts to prevent suicides in other circumstances.

IV. Conclusion

This final chapter has moved away from the focus on suicide itself and engaged with the more common contemporary debate about the law in relation to assisting or encouraging suicide. It has argued that legal reform is needed in respect of both elements of the current offence, but that this should be reform in two very different directions. The offence of encouraging a suicide should be clarified and strengthened, while the offence of assisting a suicide should incorporate a limited exception. Contrary to intuitive reactions, it is encouraging suicide that is the more serious of the two elements of the current English offence because such an act seeks to influence an individual's decision-making process and runs counter to the high value placed elsewhere in law and ethics on the preservation of human life. The criminal prohibition of such an action must remain and could be made even stronger with a shift towards an 'incitement' focus, alongside a greater willingness to prosecute. Assisting suicide, on the other hand, may facilitate an exercise of autonomy by a person with capacity to choose to die (as defined elsewhere) and this element of the current offence should follow the global trend towards legalisation under tightly defined circumstances with extensive and appropriate safeguards in place. Both these arguments flow from the complexity of the issue of suicide, which has been highlighted throughout this book. Choosing to die is often a symptom of a mental illness and the law should be used to prevent such suicides, but occasionally it may represent an exercise of autonomy and, in cases where there is a clear capacity to die, the law should ensure respect for that choice. In the latter situation, if a person's autonomous and capacitated choice to die is prevented by illness or disability, then, in what is admittedly a controversial argument, the law should explicitly permit the provision of assistance.

9

Conclusion and Recommendations

In this final chapter, we will reflect upon the law's engagement with the topic of suicide and explore how it can be improved in future to ensure that legal and ethical obligations to respect the right to life are protected while also ensuring compatibility with respect for bodily autonomy. The global emphasis on suicide prevention is an important element of how the law's role in relation to suicide should develop, but it is not the only consideration if we are including all self-caused and intended deaths within the label of 'suicide'. Indeed, that very label is a problematic one and there might be much to be gained from the adoption of terminology that distinguishes between potentially lethal self-harm as a symptom of a mental disorder and a controversial but capacitated choice to determine when one's own life ends. This chapter will conclude with some recommendations for the future development, interpretation and implementation of domestic law in respect of suicide. It will be argued that statutory reform is needed, but so too is a more refined awareness of the current law and, crucially, its objectives, by the persons responsible for implementing it. This is especially true in challenging scenarios such as mental health hospitals, prisons, schools and universities, and hospitals, care homes and hospices.

I. 'Suicide' and the Law – Changing the Label, Recognising the History

In chapter one of this book, 'suicide' was defined as a self-caused death with the intention to die. This is a relatively uncontroversial definition. However, the normative manner in which the label is accorded only to those self-caused deaths, or attempted deaths, which are regarded as unnecessary and to be prevented, sits in opposition to other such deaths where the intention to die is understood and potentially respected, and which are not labelled as suicide. This means that the term carries with it hidden pejorative meanings and judgment. When coupled with the fact that suicide no longer has any legal meaning, other than in relation to secondary participants, it is argued here that the label of suicide would be best avoided. Outside of the enduring criminal offence, there is no legal significance to the term and its ongoing use in some, but not all, end of life scenarios brings unnecessary confusion. The long history of the term in which it was for so long regarded as both a sin and a felony means that outdated notions of condemnation may linger in some uses of the word even today. It would be much more fitting for contemporary society to talk simply about voluntary deaths or choices to die. This then opens the door to consideration of whether a choice to die is a capacitated one or not, and this leads onto consideration of whether such a choice should be prevented or respected.

The historical development of the law's approach to suicide is significant in terms of understanding the current approach because it illustrates how the law's role in relation to suicide has progressed from one of condemnation and punishment to one of prevention. While historically the goal of condemning and punishing was best achieved through the enforcement of criminal offences, a contemporary goal of preventing suicide requires different mechanisms. The current law focuses on permitting and facilitating compulsory mental health interventions and also to some extent on the imposition of legal obligations to take reasonable steps to prevent the suicide of others. Those legal duties are limited, however, both in terms of content and reach. Increasingly some challenging questions are being asked of the law in this context. These include querying the ethical basis on which compulsory preventative measures are imposed; for example by criticisms of equating legal and mental capacity issues and (but separately) the drawing of contrasts between the treatment of those with physical and mental health disorders. Other challenging questions concern the extent to which obligations to take steps to prevent suicide might extend beyond detention contexts, and whether or not there is a legally recognised right to die and what that might mean for facilitating choices to die. 1961 was, of course, a crucial turning point for the law on suicide, but the Parliament that crossed the Rubicon in decriminalising suicide failed to engage with the other pressing issues around this topic. These include whether all suicides should be prevented, and whether there is, or ought to be, a legal duty to prevent suicide (and if so, imposed upon whom and encompassing what actions). Since 1961 the significance of these questions has only increased as suicide prevention became a global public health goal, mental health laws were forced to acknowledge human rights laws, and end of life decision-making became a pressing legal, ethical and healthcare issue.

There are two important points to make in relation to the historical development in the law's role in relation to suicide. First, it must be recognised that throughout this development, the law's approach has repeatedly been 'palliated' by those tasked with implementing it. From coroner's juries in the eighteenth century to crown prosecutors today, the people at the front line of implementing the criminal law have recognised that more refinement and flexibility is required on these issues than is provided in the law's broad-strokes criminal law approach. There are many different types of actions that potentially fall under the label of 'suicide' and each one tells a personal emotive story. If the law did a better job of recognising that complexity and responding accordingly, those involved in implementing it might not need to be so proactive in palliating the consequences.

Secondly, but closely linked to the previous point, it could be argued that a sole goal of preventing suicide is too limiting for the law in the twenty-first century. Perhaps the current law fails to reflect the extraordinary shift in suicide from a felony to a lawful choice due to the manner in which it appears to still regulate the topic *as if* deterrence (albeit not punishment) is the main goal. That ethos is contestable. Ending one's life is a lawful activity, but one that may be harmful to both the individual and wider society, and in the majority of cases is a symptom of a mental disorder. As such, considerations of welfare, access to treatment, rights to health, equality of treatment, rights to life and bodily integrity and autonomy are arguably just as important as a goal of preventing self-caused deaths. Those disparate considerations are, of course, much harder to reflect and reconcile within the law and practice than the one primary goal of prevention at all costs and regardless of consequences.

This book therefore argues that, in addition to avoiding the label of suicide, we as a society should also broaden our goals in relation to the law's involvement with self-caused deaths. In the majority of cases, providing support and treatment to protect the health and welfare of the person contemplating an end to their life will be the most important goal to be achieved by legal obligations. Such a protective approach differs albeit in a subtle way from the current preventative approach because it reminds us that preventing an attempt to end life is only one tiny aspect of the need for care and treatment for that individual. Alongside this goal, however, are other important ones such as respect for bodily integrity, autonomous choice and equality of treatment. It has been argued in this book that capacity to choose to die is a concept that holds the key to determining the respective weight of these potentially conflicting goals. In full awareness of the contestable nature of such a concept, it is to this we will now turn.

II. Capacity to Choose to Die – The Key to the Law's Proper Ambit

Although most attempts to end one's own life are linked to mental illness, there can be little doubt that rational choices to die are possible.[1] If the label of suicide obscures that point at times, then that is one further reason why the label should be removed. Despite the self-evident possibility that a rational choice to die may exist, the law currently fails to recognise that fact, or its implications for the criminal offence of assisting or encouraging suicide. As noted in the first chapter, there is a parallel between the law's old assumption that all suicides were sins to be punished and its current assumption that all suicides (alongside their attempts

[1] As discussed in ch 4.

or even contemplation) are symptoms of a mental disorder. This assumption obscures the relevance of the issue of capacity. While there has been a pushback against the dominance of mental capacity as a gatekeeper to autonomy in recent years, not least by the Convention on the Rights of Persons with Disabilities (CRPD),[2] in terms of determining whether a choice to die should be prevented or respected, it is hard to see a more fitting alternative. The gravity of a choice to die, however, in the sense of it being irreversible if successfully implemented, means that a particularly and uniquely stringent test for capacity is appropriate. It has been argued throughout this book that a new heightened capacity to choose to die test should be the central plank in the law's approach to suicide. This would build upon the standard test for mental capacity found in the Mental Capacity Act 2005 (MCA 2005), sections 2 and 3, but would also require a bit more.

It might be noted that in practice the courts and healthcare professionals already seem to set a particularly stringent standard for life-and-death decisions, recognising that capacity to make more straightforward day-to-day decisions cannot be equated with decisions to bring life to an end.[3] The additional elements argued for in this book reflect a concept of diachronic continuity.[4] They highlight the need to take into account both the past and the future self when deciding to end life, reflecting how suicide is unique in choices made because of its irreversibility. Specifically, it is proposed that there needs to be (legally mandated) consideration as to the internal coherence of a desire to die at one's own hands with the past and present wishes and identity of the person currently expressing such a desire, as well as whether or not the implications for the future self have been sufficiently taken into account. In order to demonstrate that the capacity to choose to die exists, a person would need to be following a decision-making process that was rational, consistent, forward-looking and reflective. The purpose of this, admittedly demanding, standard is that it can form a defensible boundary between preventative and respectful legal obligations. If the standard is met, the law's protection for respect for bodily autonomy will preclude any compulsion aimed at saving the life of a person who does not want it to continue. If the standard is not met, and it has to be assumed that in most cases it will not be, compulsory treatment and prevention become appropriate responses and, subject to the usual best-interests determination, should amount to obligatory requirements within health care and other settings (to be discussed further below).

It seems likely that such a capacity to choose to die test will face criticisms from two different perspectives. By recognising that there can be rational, capacitated and autonomous choices to end life and demanding that the law respect those, it may be criticised for failing in the goals of preventing suicide, protecting vulnerable persons and upholding the sanctity of life. While all these goals are important in the right context, they should not automatically trump other important values

[2] See discussion in ch 4.
[3] See, for example, *Re T (adult: refusal of treatment)* [1992] 4 All ER 649.
[4] See ch 4.

such as autonomy, freedom and individual choice. Therefore, where there is such capacity, a choice to die should be respected in legal terms without the imposition of compulsion to prevent it, although support to make a different choice to live should always be readily available. The capacity to choose to die test may also face criticism, however, due to enhancing the usual MCA capacity approach and therefore potentially permitting restrictions on autonomy to a greater extent than the current law. However, it is argued here that this is a necessary and proportionate interference with autonomy in order to protect life. The importance of protecting human life has a well-established history[5] and is entrenched in current English law through Article 2 ECHR's protection of the right to life, as well as various aspects of the common law and criminal justice system. Furthermore, while the proposed focus upon a heightened test for capacity may permit more restrictions upon autonomy than the current MCA test, it would consolidate legal interventions to compulsorily prevent self-caused deaths into one legal scheme rather than split it across two as with the current mental health and mental capacity laws. It is a vital element of the argument for the adoption of a stringent capacity to choose to die test that when such capacity exists, compulsion is not lawfully available to prevent the death, regardless of the mental health of the person making a capacitated choice to die. That is a controversial proposition, but one that enhances clarity, consistency and equality of the law, as well as seeking to respect both the right to life and the right to autonomy.

III. Suicide Prevention in Context

Although the current law does not impose any general legal duty to take steps to prevent suicide,[6] there are some such obligations in specific circumstances. These usually reflect the heightened concern about suicide in those contexts, as well as the ethical and practical ease with which preventative steps can be imposed. Thus, for example, suicide in detention is regarded as a particularly worrying problem and yet also presents a context in which preventative steps, and a legal duty to take them, is much more manageable and realistic than in society in general. Article 2 ECHR's protection for a right to life imposes a specific legal obligation (the 'operational duty') to take reasonable steps to prevent suicide when a suicide risk is known, or ought to be known, to exist.

Regrettably, the potential relevance of capacity to suicide is often overlooked in this context. The capacity to choose to die approach, identified above, with its emphasis on a stringent test for capacity as the gatekeeper of choices to die, should also apply in the context of detention. The current approach with its focus on foreseeability of risk all too often emphasises the existence of a mental disorder as the

[5] E Wicks, *The Right to Life and Conflicting Interests* (Oxford, Oxford University Press, 2010) ch 2.
[6] Contrary to arguments developed by Herring in *The Right to be Protected from Suicide* (Oxford, Hart Publishing, 2022).

key issue. As was discussed in chapter five, this raises dual problems: first, that those without such an identifiable disorder, but making a non-capacitous choice to die, are potentially left without appropriate preventative steps to protect their lives; and secondly, that those with a diagnosed mental disorder are unable to prove the relevance of capacity to their choice to die, even if it exists. It is argued, therefore, that capacity to choose to die remains relevant even within a detention context. Where it does not exist, however, it is entirely appropriate that legally enforceable duties to prevent suicide should apply. The detention context makes this particularly suitable because of the inherent vulnerability of detainees, as well as the state's assumption of control over the lives of those it detains. Adding a more explicit focus on the capacity of the person choosing to die within the detention context has the potential to ensure that autonomy is respected to the extent that is possible within detention, without undermining the particular need for obligations to protect human life when at its most vulnerable.

Another context in which suicide is a particular cause for concern, and in which legal obligations are normatively justifiable, is in relation to children and young persons. Again, in this context the law all too often skirts around the issue of capacity, but in addition there are serious practical problems in the provision of juvenile mental health care and in the array of different legal schemes seeking to protect the lives of young persons, but frequently failing to do so. Greater funding for mental health care generally, and juvenile provision in particular, would be vital components of any suicide prevention initiative, but legal reform is needed too. Most importantly, the incoherent and confusing statutory framework that currently exists often hinders access to mental health treatment and support for children and young persons, and it needs to be streamlined. In addition, the important potential role of parents in providing the support needed to prevent suicide could be given greater emphasis, in practice as well as in the law. For example, as discussed in chapter six, a student opt-in system to sharing wellbeing information with parents could help universities to avoid difficult confidentiality issues when a student is most in need of parental support.

Within the health care context, the refusal of life-sustaining treatment by a child or young person always presents challenging legal and ethical dilemmas. In addition to an emphasis upon the issue of capacity to choose to die, it is suggested here that a requirement under which those with parental responsibility are required to be involved in decisions where juveniles purport to choose to die should at least be considered. The precise details of that parental involvement will need careful analysis but a choice to die by a child or young person should only be given effect when it has formed part of a conversation and collaboration within the child's support network. Even if ultimately it is the child's decision that prevails, it will be a stronger choice when not contemplated in isolation.

More broadly, the refusal of life-sustaining treatment is indistinguishable from other choices to die. There can be no meaningful distinction between the manner in which the death results or the reasons underlying the choice. If a patient has the capacity to choose to die (and the assessment of this will be relatively easy to achieve within the health care context), then a choice to die by refusing consent to ongoing medical treatment should be treated no differently in the law than other types of choices to die. However, while the label of 'suicide' should not matter, recognising that a refusal of life-sustaining treatment is indistinguishable from other suicides does raise legal difficulties in respect of those health care professionals who are under a legal duty to respect such a choice and to facilitate the withdrawal of treatment. The importance of both individual autonomy and bodily integrity means that continuing to provide treatment to a patient who has made a capacitated choice to refuse it is not only unconscionable but also illegal. It is unfortunate that the law currently appears to impose two absolute but conflicting obligations in this context: to respect autonomy and bodily integrity by withdrawing treatment to which consent has been refused by a patient with capacity, but not to take steps that would assist a suicide. These dual legal obligations need to be urgently resolved. In chapter seven, it was suggested that a doctrine of necessity might be used in order to ensure that bodily integrity is respected. Certainly, some specific professional guidance on this issue would be useful in order to ensure that health care professionals are able to respect the rights and wishes of their patients (as the law requires them to do) without risking criminal liability for their role in facilitating an end to life.

IV. A Call for Reform of the Criminal Offence

As part of an assessment of the law's role in relation to suicide, the enduring criminal offence cannot be ignored. It is argued here that legal reform is needed of the offence in the Suicide Act 1961, section 2. Specifically, the offence of assisting a suicide should incorporate a limited exception for circumstances where an adult has made a capacitated choice to die but is unable to achieve this result unaided (or doing it unaided would cause significant suffering). Moving away from the current blanket ban on the provision of assistance in self-caused deaths would recognise the significant injustice currently caused to certain individuals forced to continue their lives against their autonomous wishes. Of course, any limited exception to the offence of assisted suicide should only be under tightly defined circumstances with extensive and appropriate safeguards in place. In order not to encourage an 'easy opt-out' of life that does not accord with the gravity of such a life-and-death decision, lawful assistance in suicide should only be permitted where the person choosing to die is unable to achieve that result unaided (or where doing it unaided would cause significant suffering). Permitting such stringently regulated assistance with self-caused deaths may then facilitate an exercise of autonomy by a person with capacity to choose to die that would otherwise be thwarted (or exercised under a cloud of criminalisation).

In parallel with such a relaxation in the law, however, it is vital that the offence of assisted suicide remain, and is appropriately enforced, for those choices to die that are not fully capacitated. The criminal prohibition of such an action is an important means of preventing unnecessary loss of life, protecting the vulnerable and recognising the inherent value in all human life. For these same reasons, the offence of encouraging suicide should be strengthened with a shift towards an 'incitement' focus, alongside a greater willingness to prosecute this offence. Only in doing so, can the law serve what should be its guiding principles in this context of both respecting bodily autonomy in end of life decisions, and upholding the right to life for those at risk. These dual recommendations, namely to permit a limited exception to the offence of assisted suicide, but otherwise strengthen the enforcement of the offence, flow from a recognition of the complexity of the issue of 'suicide' which, as we have seen in different contexts, can be either a vital exercise of autonomous choice over the biggest question of our lifetimes, or an undermining of autonomy (either by an internal or external factor) at the cost of a precious human life.

This call for reform of the law on encouraging and assisting suicide is important but should not obscure the importance of the law's approach to suicide itself which, as we have seen throughout the previous chapters, is in many ways ambiguous and incoherent. In the final section, the focus will turn to the current legal rights and duties in respect of self-caused deaths and the ways in which this law can be more appropriately implemented in order to achieve a goal of suicide prevention that does not overstep its boundaries.

V. Applying the Current Law and Preventing Suicide

The argument that 'suicide' is an unhelpful label is, at least in part, based around recognising that a desire to end one's own life can, and should, lead to a number of different responses, backed up by legal rights and duties. Therefore, the key to understanding the law's approach to suicide is to focus on the types of duties and obligations which apply in different circumstances. Most expressions of a wish to die and attempts to implement that wish, will not be capacitated choices to die and where appropriate preventative measures can be taken to prevent such a death. The first step is to ensure that it is not a capacitated choice to die. Within a health care scenario, this should be a relatively easy standard to apply, and in the huge majority of cases the standard MCA capacity test will be failed (rendering the proposed heightened standard in this book non-applicable anyway). In these (majority) cases, where there has been no capacitated choice to die, the priority is to prevent the death and provide appropriate treatment to the person whose life is at risk. If there is an underlying mental disorder, compulsory treatment for that disorder is permissible under the mental health laws. Compulsory detention is also permissible alongside the treatment and properly enforced should serve to prevent attempts to end life. Proposed reforms to the mental health laws seek to strengthen protection for the rights of the mental health patient. Where there is a foreseeable risk of a self-caused death by a patient, legal duties will arise on the mental health institution to take reasonable steps to prevent that death.

In assessing foreseeability, a range of factors will be relevant including patient history and diagnosis, previous suicide attempts or self-harm and suicidal thoughts or threats. The most significant factor, however, will be whether there are immediate signs of physical or mental distress. If so, and appropriate steps are not taken to prevent the death, there may well be legal liability under Article 2's protection for the right to life. Reasonable steps that might be expected in such a scenario include appropriate accommodation to minimise opportunities for suicide[7] and sufficient security to prevent departure from the hospital – even for voluntarily detained patients.[8]

Beyond the mental health context, it needs to be recognised that most attempts or threats to end one's own life will nonetheless be linked to a mental illness. It would therefore be legally permissible to intervene to prevent an attempt to end life on the assumption that it is not a capacitated exercise of autonomy, although there would be no legal liability for failing to do so outside of certain specific scenarios. It is a sensible precaution to intervene where reasonable to do so to prevent a death that is likely not to be a capacitated or autonomous choice, and one that reflects the high priority rightly given to the preservation of human life in our society, but this assumption can be displaced. In situations where it is clearly established that a choice to die is a capacitated one, no intervening actions should be taken to override that decision, short of the use of persuasion.

Those working within specific contexts such as prisons, hospitals or schools face more complex legal expectations. While the question of capacity should remain central (even under existing laws), the duties to take steps to prevent deaths are more refined. Within the detention context, legal duties to prevent suicide only arise where there is foreseeability of risk to life. To date, the law has placed great emphasis upon psychiatric diagnosis as a key factor in assessing this, but good practice would go further and look beyond psychiatric history and diagnosis in assessing whether there is an identifiable risk of suicide, and include consideration of the prison environment generally and its likely impact on vulnerable prisoners. If a risk to life is foreseeable, a duty to take reasonable steps to prevent a self-caused death arises and in previous cases has required a variety of measures from the need for appropriate hospital care, to supervision of medication, to avoiding the use of disciplinary punishments and isolation at this time of particular vulnerability.[9]

Such legally enforced duties to take reasonable steps to prevent suicide do not apply generally but only in the specific circumstances of mental health hospitals and places of detention including prisons and immigration centres. It is also possible that the duty exists in other circumstances where it is the authorities who have created the risk of suicide. This is hard to define and has not yet been the subject of much judicial consideration. It is a possibility that should be borne in mind, however, when public authorities such as the police or armed forces intervene in

[7] *Reynolds v United Kingdom* (App 2694/08, 13 March 2012).
[8] *Fernandes de Oliveira v Portugal* (App 78103/14, 31 January 2019) [GC].
[9] See ch 6.

ways that may cause risk to an individual's mental health and well-being. Perhaps taking an even broader view, policy decisions about housing, employment or social security may also benefit from the implementation of strategies to avoid causing risk to life including by self-inflicted death.

Another desirable and non-contentious means of seeking to prevent self-caused deaths that should be considered by the Government is the introduction of restrictions on the common means of causing death. For example, Herring discusses the 'ample evidence that restrictions on gun ownership, removal of hanging and strangulation points in psychiatric impact settings and prisons, and putting up barriers at high-risk locations, especially rail and underground networks, are highly effective methods of reducing suicide'.[10] There is certainly evidence that removing easy options to end life on a whim reduces suicide rates rather than merely postponing the ending of life until another means is found. This means that the deaths prevented are unlikely to be autonomous, capacitated choices to die because they are dissuaded by the lack of immediate and easy means to end life. For example, there were notable reductions in suicide rates in England after the removal of carbon monoxide from household gas and the introduction of catalytic converters to remove carbon monoxide from car exhaust fumes.[11] This should encourage the Government to take those small steps to increase safety within society and thereby prevent some non-capacitated attempts to end life.

Within the physical health context, the legal duty not to provide treatment without appropriate legal justification means that patients with capacity who refuse consent to life-sustaining treatment, should have those wishes respected and treatment withdrawn, regardless of the views of health care professionals. Failure to facilitate a request to withdraw treatment will result in legal liability, and potentially damages, for the hospital. The same rules should apply to a capacitated request to withhold life-sustaining treatment, although health care professionals will need to be confident that capacity existed at the time of such a request. For those engaged with children or young persons, it is highly unlikely that a choice to die will be a sufficiently capacitated one outside of a health care context (and even then, it remains unlikely). Therefore, reasonable steps should be taken to prevent a self-caused deaths and the involvement of those with parental responsibility at as early a stage as possible is to be recommended.

Criminal liability in relation to self-caused deaths is reserved for those encouraging or assisting suicide, and is not generally imposed for failing to prevent such a death. Although prosecution is now extremely unlikely for these offences, certain activities may still run the risk of prosecution. These would include encouraging or assisting the death of a person under 18 or lacking mental capacity, pressuring a

[10] Herring, *The Right to be Protected from Suicide* (2022) 185.

[11] ibid 1856. See also M Barbagli, *Farewell to the World: A History of Suicide* (Cambridge, Polity Press, 2015, English edition translated by L Byatt) 170: 'Even the strongest and apparently most irreversible urge to self-destruction … does not necessarily lead to suicide if the means of accomplishing it are not available or are too difficult or too repugnant to use'.

person to end their life, encouraging or assisting more than one person, or having a motive other than compassion for providing the encouragement or assistance. Even if not prosecuted for the offence, it is important that people are aware that their actions in assisting a self-caused death may lead to police investigations at a difficult time of bereavement. This in itself may have a deterrent effect upon such actions, and is a further reason why an urgent change to the law on this issue is recommended. Health care professionals will need to be particularly aware of the heightened risk of prosecution if they assist or encourage the death of a patient with whom they are in a relationship of care such that it may raise concern about the exercise of inappropriate influence over the person whose death is assisted.

To conclude, therefore, the law on suicide is regrettably unclear and complex. It does, however, recognise a number of different legal duties that should be taken into account when dealing with a person at risk of ending their own life. There is a duty, backed up by a criminal offence, not to encourage anyone to take their own life, nor to assist anyone in doing so; there is a duty to take reasonable steps to prevent a foreseeable self-caused death if working within detention or mental health contexts; and there is a duty to respect a choice to refuse life-sustaining medical treatment even when death will result. Beyond that the law does not impose duties to save the lives of others and, while it recognises every one's right to life, it protects a right to autonomy over choices about life and death. Such autonomy is not unrestricted and any doubts about the nature of a decision to attempt to end life would justify interventions to save life. A simple motto of 'if in doubt, do all you can to prevent' would be viable starting point.[12] Beneath that, however, in the small, but still important, arena of proven capacitated choices to die, there is room for autonomy to be respected and for persons to be supported in their informed decisions to take control over the timing of their death.

[12] In this book, I take a very different approach to that of Jonathan Herring in his recent book on the topic, but I certainly agree with his gentle plea that 'the central legal message we should be sending out to people wishing to commit suicide is "please don't"': Herring (n 6) 205.

BIBLIOGRAPHY

Allen, N, 'The Right to Life in a Suicidal State' (2013) 36 *International Journal of Law and Psychiatry* 350.

Alvarez, A, 'The Background' in M Pabst-Battin and DJ Mayo (eds), *Suicide: The Philosophical Issues* (London, Peter Owen, 1980).

Anderson, O, *Suicide in Victorian and Edwardian England* (Oxford, Clarendon Press, 1987).

Andriessen, K, 'On "Intention" in the Definition of Suicide' (2006) 36 *Suicide and Life-Threatening Behavior* 533.

Annas, G, 'When Suicide Prevention Becomes Brutality: The Case of Elizabeth Bouvia' (1984) *Hastings Center Report* 20.

Appleby, L et al, 'The National Confidential Inquiry into Suicide and Safety in Mental Health. Annual Report: England, Northern Ireland, Scotland and Wales' (Manchester, University of Manchester, 2021).

Aquinas, T, *Summa Theologica* (New York, Benziger Bros, 1947).

Augustine, *The City of God Against the Pagans* (Cambridge, Cambridge University Press, 1998, edited and translated by RW Dyson).

Bähr, A, 'Between "Self-Murder" and "Suicide": The Modern Etymology of Self-Killing' (2013) 46 *Journal of Social History* 620.

Barbagli, M, *Farewell to the World: A History of Suicide* (Cambridge, Polity Press, 2015, English edition translated by L Byatt).

Bartlett, P, '"The Necessity Must be Convincingly Shown to Exist": Standards for Compulsory Treatment for Mental Disorder under the MHA 1983' (2011) 19 *Medical Law Review* 514.

Battin, M, 'Suicide: A Fundamental Human Right?' in M Battin, *The Least Worst Death: Essays in Bioethics on the End of Life* (Oxford, Oxford University Press, 1994).

—— *The Least Worst Death: Essays in Bioethics on the End of Life* (Oxford, Oxford University Press, 1994).

—— *Ending Life: Ethics and the Way We Die* (Oxford, Oxford University Press, 2005).

Battin, M and Mayo, DJ (eds), *Suicide: The Philosophical Issues* (London, Peter Owen, 1980).

Biggs, H and Jones, C, 'Legally Vulnerable: What Is Vulnerability and Who Is Vulnerable?' in M Freeman, S Hawkes and B Bennett (eds), *Law and Global Health* (Oxford, Oxford University Press, 2014).

Binder, G and Chiesa, L, 'The Puzzle of Inciting Suicide' (2019) 56 *American Criminal Law Review* 65.

Blackstone, W, *Commentaries on the Laws of England* (Oxford, Clarendon Press, 1770).

Brancaccio, MT, Engstrom, EJ and Lederer, D, 'The Politics of Suicide: Historical Perspectives on Suicidology before Durkheim. An Introduction' (2013) 46 *Journal of Social History* 607.

Brandt, RB, 'The Rationality of Suicide' in M Pabst Battin and DJ Mayo (eds), *Suicide: The Philosophical Issues* (London, Peter Owen, 1980).

Bratman, M, 'Reflection, Planning and Temporally Extended Agency' (2000) 109 *Philosophical Review* 35.

Brazier, M and Bridge, C, 'Coercion or Caring: Analysing Adolescent Autonomy' (1996) 16 *Legal Studies* 84.

Callaghan, S, Ryan, C and Kerridge, I, 'Risk of Suicide is Insufficient Warrant for Coercive Treatment of Mental Illness' (2013) 36 *International Journal of Law and Psychiatry* 374.

Cartwright, N, '48 Years On: Is the Suicide Act Fit for Purpose?' (2009) 17 *Medical Law Review* 467.

Cave, E, 'Goodbye Gillick? Identifying and Resolving Problems with the Concept of Child Competence' (2013) *Legal Studies* 103.

Cave, E and Wallbank, J, 'Minors' Capacity to Refuse Treatment: A Reply to Gilmore and Herring' (2013) 21 *Medical Law Review* 423.

Chico, V and Hagger, L, 'The Mental Capacity Act 2005 and Mature Minors: A Missed Opportunity?' (2011) 33 *Journal of Social Welfare and Family Law* 157.

Cholbi, M, 'Self-manslaughter and the Forensic Classification of Self-inflicted Death' (2007) 33 *Journal of Medical Ethics* 155.

—— 'Suicide' in EN Zalta (ed), *The Stanford Encyclopedia of Philosophy* (Fall 2017 edition), available at plato.stanford.edu/archives/fall2017/entries/suicide.

Clarke, P, *Hope and Glory: Britain 1900–2000*, 2nd edn (London, Penguin, 2004).

Cloon, S, 'Competent Hunger Strikers: Applying the Lessons from Northern Ireland to the Force-Feeding in Guantanamo' (2017) 31 *Notre Dame Journal of Law, Ethics and Public Policy* 383.

Cluley, E, 'Preventing Prison Suicide: Staff Perspectives' (2017) 64 *Probation Journal* 158.

Coggon, J, 'Varied and Principled Understandings of Autonomy in English Law: Justifiable Inconsistency or Blinkered Moralism? (2007) 15 *Health Care Analysis* 235.

Coughlan, S, 'Would Universities Call Parents in a Mental Health Crisis?' BBC News, 18 April 2021, available at www.bbc.co.uk/news/education-56763189.

Cowley, C, 'Suicide is Neither Rational nor Irrational' (2006) 9 *Ethical Theory and Moral Practice* 495.

Craigie, J, 'Capacity, Value Neutrality and the Ability to Consider the Future' (2013) 9 *International Journal of Law in Context* 4.

Crown Prosecution Service, 'Suicide: Policy for Prosecutors in Respect of Cases of Encouraging or Assisting Suicide' (2010, updated 2014), available at www.cps.gov.uk/legal-guidance/suicide-policy-prosecutors-respect-cases-encouraging-or-assisting-suicide.

Davey, J and Coggon, J, 'Life Assurance and Consensual Death: Law Making for the Rationally Suicidal' (2006) *Cambridge Law Journal* 521.

Daw, R and Solomon, A, 'Assisted Suicide and Identifying the Public Interest in the Decision to Prosecute' [2010] *Criminal Law Review* 737.

Dawson, J, 'A Realistic Approach to Assessing Mental Health Laws' Compliance with UNCRPD' (2015) 40 *International Journal of Law and Psychiatry* 70.

Devine, P, 'On Choosing Death' in M Pabst Battin and DJ Mayo (eds), *Suicide: The Philosophical Issues* (London, Peter Owen, 1980).

Draghici, C, 'The Blanket Ban on Assisted Suicide: Between Moral Paternalism and Utilitarian Justice' (2015) 3 *European Human Rights Law Review* 286.

Durkheim, E, *Suicide: A Study in Sociology*, 2nd edn (London, Routledge, 2002).

Dworkin, G, *The Theory and Practice of Autonomy* (Cambridge, Cambridge University Press, 1988).

Eekelaar J, 'The Interests of the Child and the Child's Wishes: The Role of Dynamic Self-determinism' (1994) 8 *International Journal of Law and the Family* 42.

Feinberg, J, *Freedom and Fulfilment: Philosophical Essays* (Princeton, Princeton University Press, 1992).

Fortin, J, 'Accommodating Children's Rights in a Post Human Rights Act Era' (2006) 69 *Modern Law Review* 299.

Foster, S, 'Prisoners' Rights: Suicides in Detention' (2002) 24 *Journal of Social Welfare and Family Law* 185.

Gather, J and Vollmann, J, 'Physician-assisted Suicide of Patients with Dementia. A Medical Ethical Analysis with a Special Focus on Patient Autonomy' (2013) 36 *International Journal of Law and Psychiatry* 444.

Gilmore, S and Herring, J, '"No" is the Hardest Word: Consent and Children's Autonomy' (2011) 23 *Child and Family Law Quarterly* 3.

Graham, L, '*Jeanty v Belgium*: Saving Lives Provides (Another) Exception to Article 3 ECHR' (2021) 21 *Human Rights Law Review* 1.

Harris, J, 'Consent and End of Life Decisions' (2003) 29 *Journal of Medical Ethics* 10.

Harris, T, 'Changing Prisons, Saving Lives – Report of the Independent Review into Self-inflicted Deaths in Custody of 18–24 Year Olds' (London, Ministry of Justice, 2015), available at dera.ioe.ac.uk/23552/1/moj-harris-review-web-accessible.pdf.
Herring, J, *The Right to be Protected from Suicide* (Oxford, Hart Publishing, 2022).
Herring, J and Wall, J, 'Autonomy, Capacity and Vulnerable Adults: Filling the Gaps in the Mental Capacity Act' (2015) 35 *Legal Studies* 698.
—— 'The Nature and Significance of the Right to Bodily Integrity' (2017) 76 *Cambridge Law Journal* 566.
Hobson, C and Papadopoulou, N, 'Regulating Risk and Autonomy in Assisted Suicide: *Conway v Secretary of State for Justice*' (2021) 29 *Medical Law Review* 128.
Hoffman, DE and Webb, VJ, 'Suicide as Murder at Common Law' (1981) 19 *Criminology* 372.
Huxtable, R, '*Re B (Consent to Treatment: Capacity)*: A Right to Die or Is it Right to Die?' (2002) 14 *Child and Family Law Quarterly* 341.
—— *Euthanasia, Ethics and the Law: From Conflict to Compromise* (London, Routledge-Cavendish, 2007).
Jansson, A, 'From Suicide to Diagnostics: Medical Certificates, Melancholia, and "Suicidal Propensities" in Victorian Psychiatry' (2013) 46 *Journal of Social History* 716.
Jox, RJ, Black, I, Borasio, GD and Anneser, J, 'Voluntary Stopping of Eating and Drinking: Is Medical Support Ethically Justified?' (2017) 15 *BMC Medicine* 186.
Juhnke, GA, Granello, PF and Granello, DH, *Suicide, Self-Injury, and Violence in the Schools: Assessment, Prevention, and Intervention Strategies* (Hoboken, John Wiley & Sons, 2010).
Kennedy, I, 'Consent to Treatment: The Capable Person' in C Dyer (ed), *Doctors, Patients and the Law* (Oxford, Oxford University Press, 1992).
Khan, MM and Mian, AI, '"The One Truly Serious Philosophical Problem": Ethical Aspects of Suicide' (2010) 22 *International Review of Psychiatry* 288.
Laidlaw, J, Pugh, D, Riley, G and Hovey, N, 'The Use of Section 136 (Mental Health Act 1983) in Gloucestershire' (2010) 50 *Medicine, Science and the Law* 29.
Laragy, G, '"A Peculiar Species of Felony": Suicide, Medicine, and the Law in Victorian Britain and Ireland' (2013) 46 *Journal of Social History* 732.
Lewis, P, 'Informal Legal Change on Assisted Suicide: the Policy for Prosecutors' (2011) 31 *Legal Studies* 119.
Liebling, A, 'The Meaning of Ending Life in Prison' (2017) 23 *Journal of Correctional Health Care* 20.
Liebling, A and Ludlow, A, 'Suicide, Distress and the Quality of Prison Life' in Y Jewkes, B Crewe and J Bennett (eds), *Handbook on Prisons*, 2nd edn (London, Routledge, 2016).
Luzon, G, 'The Practice of Euthanasia and Assisted Suicide Meets the Concept of Legalization' (2019) 13 *Criminal Law and Philosophy* 329.
Lyons, B, 'Dying to be Responsible: Adolescence, Autonomy and Responsibility' (2010) 30 *Legal Studies* 257.
MacDonald, M and Murphy, TR, *Sleepless Souls: Suicide in Early Modern England* (Oxford, Clarendon Press, 1990).
Mackenzie, C and Stoljar, N (eds), *Relational Autonomy: Feminist Perspectives on Autonomy, Agency and the Social Self* (Oxford, Oxford University Press, 2000).
Martin, RM, 'Suicide and False Desires' in M Pabst Battin and DJ Mayo (eds), *Suicide: The Philosophical Issues* (London, Peter Owen, 1980).
Martin, S, 'Declaratory Misgivings: Assisted Suicide in a Post-*Nicklinson* Context' [2018] *Public Law* 209.
Matthews, M, 'Suicidal Competence and the Patient's Right to Refuse Lifesaving Treatment' (1987) 75 *California Law Review* 707.
Mayo, DJ, 'The Concept of Rational Suicide' (1986) 11 *Journal of Medicine and Philosophy* 143.
McGee, A, 'Does Withdrawing Life-Sustaining Treatment Cause Death Or Allow The Patient To Die?' (2014) 22 *Medical Law Review* 26.

McGee, A and Miller, FG, 'Advice and Care for Patients who Die by Voluntarily Stopping Eating and Drinking is Not Assisted Suicide' (2017)15 *BMC Medicine* 222.

Mendelson, D and Freckelton, I, 'The Interface of the Civil and Criminal Law of Suicide at Common Law (1194–1845)' (2013) 36 *International Journal of Law and Psychiatry* 343.

Mikell, EW, 'Is Suicide Murder? (1903) 3 *Columbia Law Review* 379.

Mill, JS, *On Liberty* in J Gray and GW Smith (eds), *JS Mill's On Liberty in Focus* (London, Routledge, 1991).

Miller, F, Truog, R and Brock, D, 'Moral Fictions and Medical Ethics' (2010) 24 *Bioethics* 453.

Minois, G, *History of Suicide: Voluntary Death in Western Culture* (Baltimore, John Hopkins, 1999, translated by LG Cochrane).

Mishara, BL and Weisstub, DN, 'The Legal Status of Suicide: A Global Review (2016) 44 *International Journal of Law and Psychiatry* 54.

Moore, S, *The Decriminalisation of Suicide* (PhD thesis, LSE, 2000), available at etheses.lse.ac.uk/1573/1/U136493.pdf.

Muehlenkamp, JJ, 'Distinguishing Between Suicidal and Nonsuicidal Self-Injury' in MK Nock, *The Oxford Handbook of Suicide and Self-Injury* (Oxford, Oxford University Press, 2014).

Mulligan, A, 'Self-determination, Capacity and the Right to Die by Hunger Strike: *Governor of X Prison v P McD*' (2015) 54 *Irish Jurist* 165.

Munro, V and Shah, S, '*R v Dhaliwal*: Reconstructing Manslaughter Cases in Domestic Violence Suicide' in C McGlynn, C Hunter and R Rackley (eds), *Feminist Judgments: From Theory to Practice* (Oxford, Hart Publishing, 2010).

Munro, VE and Aitken, R, 'Adding Insult to Injury? The Criminal Law's Response to Domestic Abuse-Related Suicide in England and Wales' (2018) 9 *Criminal Law Review* 732.

Nedelsky, J, 'Reconceiving Autonomy: Sources, Thoughts and Possibilities' (1989) 1 *Yale Journal of Law and Feminism* 7.

Nock, MK, *The Oxford Handbook of Suicide and Self-Injury* (Oxford, Oxford University Press, 2014).

O'Neill, O, *Autonomy and Trust in Bioethics* (Cambridge, Cambridge University Press, 2002).

Ormerod, D and Laird, K, *Smith, Hogan and Ormerod's Criminal Law*, 16th edn (Oxford, Oxford University Press, 2021).

O'Sullivan, C, 'Mens Rea, Motive and Assisted Suicide: Does the DPP's Policy go Too Far?' (2015) 35 *Legal Studies* 96.

Parker, C, '"We will have Blood on our Hands": The Judiciary Shines a Light on the Inadequacy of Adolescent Mental Health Care' (2018) 40 *Journal of Social Welfare and Family Law* 98.

Pickard, H, 'Choice, Deliberation, Violence: Mental Capacity and Criminal Responsibility in Personality Disorder (2015) 40 *International Journal of Law and Psychiatry* 15.

Pilpel, A and Amsel, L, 'What is Wrong with Rational Suicide' (2011) 39 *Philosphia* 111.

Posner, K et al, 'The Classification of Suicidal Behaviour' in MK Nock, *The Oxford Handbook of Suicide and Self-Injury* (Oxford, Oxford University Press, 2014).

Price, DPT, 'Assisted Suicide and Refusing Medical Treatment: Linguistics, Morals and Legal Contortions' (1997) 4 *Medical Law Review* 270.

Ravitsky, V, 'Timers on Ventilators' (2005) 330 *British Medical Journal* 415.

Rawlinson, K, Bowcott, O and Campbell, D, 'Judge Warns of "Blood on our Hands" if Suicidal Girl is Forced Out of Secure Care', *The Guardian*, 3 August 2017, available at www.theguardian.com/society/2017/aug/03/judge-warns-of-blood-on-our-hands-if-suicidal-girl-is-forced-out-of-secure-care.

Raynor, G and Savill, R, 'Bridgend Suicides: A Town Tainted by Death' *The Telegraph*, 23 February 2008, available at www.telegraph.co.uk/news/uknews/1579574/Bridgend-suicides-a-town-tainted-by-death.html.

Raz, J, *The Morality of Freedom* (Oxford, Clarendon Press, 1986).

Reed, P, 'Is "Aid in Dying" Suicide?' (2019) 40 *Theoretical Medicine and Bioethics* 123.

Richardson, G, 'Mental Capacity at the Margin: The Interface between Two Acts' (2010) 18 *Medical Law Review* 56.

—— 'Mental Disabilities and the Law: from Substitute to Supported Decision-making' (2012) 65 *Current Legal Problems* 333.
—— 'Mental Capacity in the Shadow of Suicide: What can the Law do? (2013) 9 *International Journal of Law in Context* 87.
Rivlin, A, Fazel, S, Marzano, L and Hawton, K, 'The Suicidal Process in Male Prisoners making Near-lethal Suicide Attempts' (2013) 19 *Psychology, Crime and Law* 305.
Rogan, M, 'Human Rights Approaches to Suicide in Prison: Implications for Policy, Practice and Research' (2018) 6 *Health and Justice* 15.
Savulescu, J, 'A Simple Solution to the Puzzles of End of Life? Voluntary Palliated Starvation' (2014) 40 *Journal of Medical Ethics* 110.
Schramme, T, 'Rational Suicide, Assisted Suicide, and Indirect Legal Paternalism' (2013) 36 *International Journal of Law and Psychiatry* 477.
Skowron, P, 'The Relationship between Autonomy and Adult Mental Capacity in the Law of England and Wales' (2019) 27 *Medical Law Review* 32.
Steinberg, L et al, 'Are Adolescents Less Mature than Adults? Minors' Access to Abortion, the Juvenile Death Penalty, and the Alleged APA "Flip-flop"' (2009) 64 *American Psychologist Journal* 583.
Stewart, C, Peisah, C and Draper, B, 'A Test for Mental Capacity to Request Assisted Suicide' (2011) 37 *Journal of Medical Ethics* 34.
Szasz, T, *Suicide Prohibition: The Shame of Medicine* (Syracuse, Syracuse University Press, 2011).
Tait, G and Carpenter, B, 'The Continuing Implications of the "Crime" of Suicide: A Brief History of the Present' (2016) *International Journal of Law in Context* 210.
The Commission on Assisted Dying, 'The Current Legal Status of Assisted Dying is Inadequate and Incoherent' (London, Demos, 2011).
Thoonen, E and Duijst, W, 'Suicide in Detention in the Light of the Human Rights Convention' (2014) 5 *New Journal of European Criminal Law* 121.
Titheradge, N, 'Police Uncover Teenage Girl 'Suicide' Instagram Group' BBC News, 3 April 2021, available at www.bbc.co.uk/news/uk-56617838.
Tucker, J, 'The Geometry of Suicide Law' (2015) 43 *International Journal of Law, Crime and Justice* 342.
Van Assche, K, Raus, K, Vanderhaegen, B and Sterckx, S, '"Capacity for Discernment" and Euthanasia on Minors in Belgium' (2019) 27 *Medical Law Review* 242.
Van Ginneken, EFJC, Sutherland, A and Molleman, T, 'An Ecological Analysis of Prison Overcrowding and Suicide Rates in England and Wales, 2000–2014' (2017) 50 *International Journal of Law and Psychiatry* 76.
Wheat, K, 'The Law's Treatment of the Suicidal' (2000) 8 *Medical Law Review* 182.
Wicks, E, *The Right to Life and Conflicting Interests* (Oxford, Oxford University Press, 2010).
—— 'The Supreme Court Judgment in *Nicklinson*: One Step Forward on Assisted Dying; Two Steps Back on Human Rights' (2015) 23 *Medical Law Review* 144.
—— *The State and the Body: Legal Regulation of Bodily Autonomy* (Oxford, Hart Publishing, 2016).
—— 'Assisted Dying Reframed in the Context of English Law's Approach to Suicide' (2020) 20 *Medical Law International* 287.
Williams, G, *The Sanctity of Life and the Criminal Law* (London, Faber and Faber, 1958).
Wilson, K, 'The Call for the Abolition of Mental Health Law: The Challenges of Suicide, Accidental Death and the Equal Enjoyment of the Right to Life' (2018) 18 *Human Rights Law Review* 651.
Windfuhr, K and Kapur, N, 'Suicide and Mental Illness: A Clinical Review of 15 Years Findings from a UK National Confidential Inquiry into Suicide' (2011) 100 *British Medical Bulletin* 101.
Wittwer, H, 'The Problem of the Possible Rational Suicide and the Ethics of Physician-assisted Suicide' (2013) 36 *International Journal of Law and Psychiatry* 419.
Wood, D, 'Suicide as Instrument and Expression' in M Pabst Battin and DJ Mayo (eds), *Suicide: The Philosophical Issues* (London, Peter Owen, 1980).
World Health Organization, 'Preventing Suicide: A Global Imperative' (Geneva, WHO, 2014).
—— 'Suicide Worldwide in 2019: Global Health Estimates' (Geneva, WHO, 2021).
Wright, CL, 'The English Canon Law Relating to Suicide Victims' (2017) *Ecclesiastical Law Journal* 193.

INDEX

www.ingramcontent.com/pod-product-compliance
Ingram Content Group UK Ltd.
Pitfield, Milton Keynes, MK11 3LW, UK
UKHW020811290926
15470UKWH00003B/1090

9 781509 932702